D1477761

Longing for Dawn

RABBI YAAKOV YISRAEL BAIFUS

פרקי אמונה ונחמה
THE LEKACH TOV SERIES

Longing

Translated by **Rabbi Nachman Bulman**

Assisted by Rabbi Shabsai Bulman
& Rabbi Yehuda Bulman

Edited by A. Rappaport

TASHBAR HARAV PUBLISHERS
Rechasim, Israel

for
Dawn

Inspiration and Consolation

RABBI YAAKOV YISRAEL BAIFUS

Originally published in 1993 in Hebrew
as *Yalkut Lekach Tov Pirkei Emunah
v'Nechamah*, by Tashbar Harav Publishers.

First published 1995

ISBN 0-87306-719-3

Book design / Typesetting: Akiva Atwood

FELDHEIM PUBLISHERS
POB 35002
Jerusalem, Israel

200 Airport Executive Park
Nanuet, NY 10954

Printed in Israel

10 9 8 7 6 5 4 3 2 1

Library of Congress Cataloging-in-Publication Data

Baifus, Ya'akov Yisra'el ha-Kohen
   [Yalkut Lekah Tov. English]
   Longing for Dawn: The Jewish guide to consolation / by Y. Y. Baifus.
     p.   cm.
   ISBN. 0-87306-719-3 (hc)
   1. Consolation (Judaism) 2. Faith (Judaism) 3. Judaism --Doctrines.   I. Title
BM729.C6B3513 1995
296.4'45—dc20   95-18057

I put my faith in Hashem, my soul hopes,
I await His word;
My soul yearns for my L-rd, more than
watchmen longing for dawn,
longing for dawn.

— Tehillim

בית המוסר

ע"ש ר' חיים מנחם להמן ע"ה
רח' הרב סורוצקין 39 ירושלים
מיסודו של תנועת שוחרי מוסר, ירושלים

בס"ד, עש"ק כי תשא תשנ"ג

ברחמים מרובים מנהיג הקב"ה את דורנו, והננו רואים נסים ממש איך שהוא
ית' שומר את הישוב בארצנו הקדושה ואף מוציא אסירים בכושרות ומעלה רבים
מנדחי ישראל לארץ ישראל. מאידך – מידת הדין מתוחה עלינו, וכמעט אין יום
שלא נשמע על אסונות ר"ל המשרים אבל וצער על רבים מאחינו בני ישראל. ולא כמו
גילויי מידת הרחמים כך הן פגיעות מידת הדין: נסים וחסדי ה' יתברך מחזקים
האמונה ומקרבים אפילו רחוקים לאבינו שבשמים. אסונות וסבל ר"ל משאירים
את הנפגעים המומים: מלבד כל הצער אינם יודעים איך להשלים עם הגזירה
שנגזרה. "אם חסד אשירה ואם משפט אשירה", לקבל גם את מידת משפטו ית'
בשמחה כדברי חז"ל בגמ' ברכות דף ס' ע"ב – כמה קשה היא עבודה זו!

לכן נכיר טובה לידידי הדגול הרה"ג ר' **יעקב ישראל הכהן בייפוס** שליט"א על
החיבור הנוכחי העוסק בענין קבלת יסורים, שיהיה להרבה מבעלי-יסורים לחיזוק
ולתועלת רבה. יחד עם זה ישנם כאן מכתבי תנחומים על אבל שצירף לילקוט הנפלא
"ילקח טוב" על פרשיות השבוע קונטרס "זה ינחמנו", ובו מכתבי תנחומים מגדולי
ישראל, אשר כל האבלים ימצאו בהם תנחומים נפלאים. כעת יוצא קונטרס זה
לדפוס בהרחבה כספר לעצמו, אשר שמו יקבנו **"פרקי אמונה ונחמה"**, וזה חסד
גדול לכל אלה הזקוקים לדברי תנחומים.

יתן השם יתברך שיתקיים מהרה דברו "בלע המות לנצח ומחה ה' אלקים דמעה
מעל כל פנים וחרפת עמו יסיר מעל כל הארץ כי ה' דבר".

שלמה וולבה

Letters of Approbation to the Hebrew Edition

ישיבת כנסת חזקיהו
כפר חסידים, ת.ד. 7

בס"ד, י"ט אדר תשנ"ג

לכ' ידידי ... הרה"ג ר' **יעקב ישראל הכהן בייפוס** שליט"א

אחדשה"ט וש"ת בידידות רבה

מה גדולה הזכות ומה רב חסדך שטרחת ועמלת לאסוף ולערוך ולחזק דברי חיזוק
ועידוד להחיות לב סובלים, וכן דברי תנחומין נפלאים אשר בכוחם להחיות נפשות
ממש ולהעלות ממעמקי היגון והיאוש אל מרומי התקוה והבטחון אשר זה כוחה
הנפלא של תורתנו הקדושה. וכבר אמרו : בלי אמונה — כדי לשמוח צריך לשכוח
את האמת. ועם אמונה — כדי לשמוח צריך לזכור את האמת. כשאדם זוכר וחי שכל
הדברים באים ממי שהוא תכלית הטוב והכל להביא אל פסגת הטוב וכי כל רעות
העולם הזה אינם אלא כטיפה מול הים הגדול של האושר הנצחי וכו' וכו', יש בכוחו
להיות מאושר גם במצבים קשים שבלי אמונה מתמוטטים.

אף על פי שתחילת כוונתך היתה לנחם אבלים ולעודד שבורי לב — יש בספר
תועלת חשובה לכל אדם בעניינים העומדים ברומו של עולם, כמו שכתבת בהקדמה.

יהי רצון שתזכה לחבר עוד חבורים מועילים ומעלין בקודש.

בברכת אוהב

דב יפה

Table of Contents

Faith begins where human reason ends.

Faith — Framework of Jewish Life

The World to Come

Resurrection of the Dead

Man's soul is Hashem's flame.

Go, My sons, console your brother . . . lighten his grief.

For my father and mother have forsaken me; G-d will gather me in.

Hashem has given, and Hashem has taken; may His Name be blessed.

Encouragement and Consolation

Letters of Consolation

May His great Name be glorified and sanctified.

Bringing Merit to the Deceased

Take this amulet...

Accepting Divine Judgment

Prefatory Remarks

To console those who mourn for loved ones is among the greatest of mitzvos, but is also among the most difficult to fulfill.

The grief of mourning reflects deep wounds in the bereaved. The mourner shrivels into himself. One who wishes to console may say the wrong words, or may use the wrong tone. His words may seem trivial and trite. The mourner may seem incapable of receiving solace.

One who attempts to console needs rare sensitivity, compassion, and above all, deep faith in Divine Justice and Mercy. He also needs to know how desperate the mourner is for solace. He needs to awaken faith and hope in broken hearts.

The son of a deceased *tzaddik* once said to a friend of his father's: "I hoped to dream of my father, but he has not appeared to me."

Said his father's friend: "But I have seen your father. I dreamt that I was in Gan Eden, and I asked to see my life's friend, the Rabbi of V_____. Angels accompanied me from Hall to Hall, but we did not find him. Till we came to a final Hall. There we saw him, bent over a fountain. I asked why he was there. The angels told me that on arrival he had been offered admission to a variety of Heavenly dwellings. He went further and further till he came to this fountain. When told that here Jewish tears were treasured till the Redemption, the Rabbi of V_____ said, "Here I remain."

In the end, only Hashem can console. At best we are messengers for Him, who try to bring His consolation to those whose *Tzelem Elokim* (the image of the Divine) is 'veiled' in grief.

We therefore say to those in mourning: May He Who encompasses the world, console you, _____. In the end, no one else can really console. And all specific expressions of condolence are branches of the central stem of Divine consolation.

From the teachings of our sages, a number of illustrations follow of human words of condolence which root in Divine condolence.

MOED KATAN 21b

> It happened that two of R. Akiva's sons died. All Israel gathered and greatly lamented [their death]. R. Akiva stood on a large bench and said: Our brothers the House of Israel, hear: Even if my two sons were grooms I would be consoled because of the honor you did me. Is it then for Akiva's sake that you came? Surely, there are many Akivas in the market place. But thus did you say (*Tehillim* 37:31): "The Torah of his G-d is in his heart." All the more is your reward multiplied. Go to your houses in peace.

At times consolation eases mourning, when the Torah in the mourner's heart is thereby honored.

MOED KATAN 28b

> When the sons of R. Yishmael died, four Elders entered to console him: R. Tarfon, R. Yosi the Gali-

lean, R. Elazar the son of Azaryah, and R. Akiva....
R. Yishmael [the grieving father] said: "My sins
are numerous, my mournings have frequented me
[two sons had died]. I have troubled my masters
once and a second time."

R. Tarfon, R. Yosi, R. Elazar the son of Azaryah, and R. Akiva then recounted in turn, that all
Israel had lamented the respective deaths of
Aharon's sons, of Yeraveam's son Aviyah, of King
Tzidkiyahu, and of Achav, the King of Israel,
though each of those had only committed a single
good deed. How much more did R. Yishmael's
sons deserve to be lamented, for they had learned
and taught and had observed mitzvos.

At times, lamentation for deceased who learned and
taught and lived Torah itself consoles, though the mourners
feel that their own shortcomings had caused their loss. But at
times, the loss of individuals who practiced lone good deeds
may also arouse the grief of all Israel.

The grief of many may help heal the sorrow of individual
mourning.

KESUBOS 8b

R. Chiya the son of Abba lost a child.... Resh Lakish went with his interpreter, Yehuda the son of
Nachmani, to offer condolence. Resh Lakish said
to his companion: "Speak words of solace over R.
Chiya's deceased child." He then spoke words of
severe reproof over the sins of the generation,
which appeared to be personally directed to R.
Chiya. R. Chanan the son of Rav then wondered:
How could words of stern rebuke console R.
Chiya? Why inflict greater pain on the grieving
father?

The Gemara then explains that Yehuda the son of Nachmani had conveyed to R. Chiya that his eminence in Heaven had caused his loss to atone for the sins of the entire generation.

At times a *tzaddik* is "seized" (in this instance, through the loss of a child) as atonement for many. Such knowledge of the meaning of his loss then has the strength to console him.

The Chidushei HaRim lost thirteen children in his life-time. Each of them died on Shabbos. When the last of his children died, his Rebbetzin said to him: What do you say now, Yitzchak Meir? He answered: My hope is that if a Jew anywhere suffers the loss of loved ones, he may hear that Yitzchak Meir of Warsaw lost all of his thirteen children, and did not murmur against his G-d. Perhaps that will help ease his grief.

AVOS D'R. NASAN (chap. 14)

> "When the son of R. Yochanan ben Zakai died, his disciples entered to console him...."
>
> R. Eliezer inferred that since Adam had accepted condolence for his son's death, so should R. Yochanan.
>
> R. Yehoshua derived the same from Iyov, who said: "Hashem gave, Hashem took; may Hashem's Name be praised."
>
> R. Yosi deduced it from Aharon's silence in the face of his sons' deaths.
>
> R. Shimon learned thus from David, who not only overcame his own grief, but even consoled Bas Sheva for the loss of their child.
>
> To each of the four, R. Yochanan demurred: To add to my own suffering, you have reminded me of the respective suffering of Adam and Iyov, and Aharon and David.
>
> Whereupon R. Elazar the son of Arach...said: The matter may be likened to a trust which the

King charged a person to watch over. Daily, [the custodian] wept and said: Woe to me, when will I emerge from this trust in peace?

You too, my Master, had a son who read Torah...[learned] Mishna, Halachos, and Aggados. He departed from this world without sin. It is for you to accept consolation now that you returned your trust whole.

Said he: R. Elazar, my son, you have consoled me after the manner of human consolation.

At times, only the knowledge that a father has not desecrated his Divinely given trust in raising his child — as attested to by the child's entire life — may console. For the parent then discovers that he was never an owner, but rather was granted a sacred trust, which he did not betray.

In the teachings of our Sages there are innumerable such instances, of which only a few have been mentioned here. But there is a common denominator in all of them: namely, that Providential suffering can be a healing, if perceived correctly. Such is the genuine purpose of consolation, to help ease the pangs of mourning, by awakening a sense of Divine Justice and Mercy in the bereaved.

In the work *Toras Avraham*, by the sainted R. Avraham Grodzinsky of Slobodka Yeshiva, there is a profound study of the meaning of suffering from which we may learn the following:

1. Initially, the purpose of prophecy was "to disclose the reality of the heart," so that a person might not delude himself into thinking that he was observing the Torah properly, if such were not the case. Likewise do we need prophecy, "to illuminate the eyes of the generation in matters that relate to the general [community]."

Now that prophecy is withheld from us, what takes its

place as a source of guidance — for both individual and community — when we are blind to our failings?

2. The experience of suffering can serve us in the place of prophecy — provided we have not allowed habit to dim our awareness of suffering.

3. Through a proper understanding of suffering, "the one who has sinned, becomes as a Prophet in seeing what is hidden in his own heart." Even though he could have turned to the Torah itself as "his prophet."

"The matter is endlessly wondrous. G-d's lovingkindness is unlimited even after sin, and man's greatness [is likewise boundless]." For even after sin, one can become as a prophet unto himself through suffering.

4. Beyond prophecy, suffering reveals to a person how his suffering is "measure for measure" in relation to his sin.

5. Prophecy reveals the hidden truth to the sinner. Suffering awakens fear of G-d and then love of G-d in the transgressor. Suffering can even awaken joy and the striving for perfection in one's attributes of character and soul.

The above words are a modest preface to *Longing for Dawn*, the English adaptation of *Lekach Tov: Emunah v'Nechamah*, by Rabbi Yaakov Yisroel Baifus, which is here presented to the wider Jewish public as an aid in the attainment of consolation in the face of mourning. It contains a wide array of letters and teachings by many of the greatest and holiest of our People. It is a testimony of endless sanctification of G-d's Name, and that the Divine Presence always dwells in the People of Israel.

May G-d grant His People the great and final consolation which He has promised them, and which alone has sustained them in life all these thousands of years. May He rejoice us equally to the affliction He has ordained for us.

Nachman Bulman

Preface

"Hashem saw all He had done, and behold, it was
very good." In R. Meir's Torah they found written:
"Behold, it was very good — behold, death is
good."

(*Bereishis Rabba* 9:5)

In these few words, our Sages express the Torah's view on
death.

Two conflicting forces affect a person in mourning: one,
the natural grief felt upon the death of a loved one; and two,
the certain knowledge that the departed has gone to an eternal dwelling place for his lasting good. The purpose of
nichum aveilim, visiting and comforting the mourner, is to
console him and lessen his grief by helping him adopt a
proper attitude towards death. The present book is designed
to help us achieve that stated goal.

The following essays contain reflections that, with the
help of Heaven, can help comfort the bereaved in their difficult hour, calming their hearts and enabling them to accept
the Will of Heaven.

Introduction

After the Exodus we were promised: "If you will listen to Hashem, your G-d...then I will not strike you with any of the illnesses I placed upon Egypt, for I am Hashem your Healer" (*Shemos* 15:26). If we understand the verse as saying that Hashem will no longer cause illness, then why should there still remain a need for healing?

R. Simcha Zissel Ziv זצ"ל, the Saba of Kelm, resolves the question in an essay which offers insight into the Torah's outlook on *yissurim* — misfortunes and suffering — and punishment. He explains that not every hardship or disaster which befalls a person is really the blow it may appear to be. Much depends on how one reacts.

R. Simcha Zissel explains that "any of the illnesses I placed upon Egypt" refers to the plagues of Egypt. The Egyptians remained unmoved by the plagues; they were not inspired to repent or to become better people — they remained as they were. Therefore, the plagues led to no improvement, nor finally, to healing. We Jews, on the other hand, were promised that we would be able to learn from our hardships and benefit from them. When we do so, the hardship itself becomes the remedy. This verse is telling us that Hashem promises not to strike us with a purposeless illness, a plague of the Egyptian type.

It is within our power to transform any hardship imposed by Hashem into a true remedy, "for I am Hashem your Healer" Who "prepares the cure from the blow itself." For example, we read in *Megillas Esther* that when the Jews of that era repented, it became obvious that what had at first seemed to be an utterly evil decree was, in fact, the seed of salvation.

Should we live by such words, our reward would be great and we would become spiritually elevated. In the words of the *Pesikta*: "Fortunate is the man touched by *yissurim*, who yet controlled his anger and did not complain over the Attribute of Justice. If Iyov had controlled his anger when *yissurim* befell him and had not complained over the Attribute of Justice, he would have deserved even greater and more honored status. R. Chanina bar Papa said: If Iyov had not complained, then even as we now say 'The G-d of Avraham, the G-d of Yitzchak and the G-d of Yaakov,' we would likewise say 'and the G-d of Iyov' " (*Pesikta* 48:3).

Acceptance of *yissurim* is the hardest, but most definitive test of a person's faithfulness in the service of Hashem, because it reveals how faithful a person is in *every* circumstance.

Aharon possessed such faith: When the Attribute of Justice struck him with the death of his two sons, he accepted the Heavenly ruling wholeheartedly, knowing that good had been done him. His reward was that the blessing, "May *HaMakom* [the Omnipresent] console you," was fulfilled for him, for Hashem Himself sent consolation to Aharon.

> Said the Holy One to Moshe: "Since the Attribute of Justice has struck Aharon with a blow and yet he still thanks Me for the kindness I have done him, go console him, as is written: 'Hashem said

to Moshe, "Speak to Aharon your brother...." ' "
The word *speak* refers to consolation, as in: "Speak
to the heart of Yerushalayim...."

(ibid., 48:2)

We can learn from this Midrash that with strength of faith
and a proper outlook on *yissurim* a person can elevate himself
and transform his suffering and mourning into healing and
salvation. Furthermore, he will be consoled personally by the
Master of Consolation to the very extent that he himself accepts the judgment properly.

Faith begins where human reason ends.

— R. Chaim Soloveitchik

Faith — Framework of Jewish Life

All humans share the need to make sense out of their lives, to create order from chaos. This order may take the form of a lifestyle, such as the Western work ethic, or a religious belief system.

As Jews, we believe that the Creator Himself provided the one and only framework for our lives: our holy Torah. The Torah is comprised in part of commandments in deed — the framework for our daily actions — and in part, of the principles of our faith — the framework for our thoughts, so that we may make sense of events that occur around us and to us.

When confronted with hardship, a Jew can relate to his situation and find solace in the central tenets of faith: faith in Divine Providence, faith in the World to Come, and faith in the Resurrection of the Dead. A person possessing strength of faith will be able to handle hardship more easily than someone with weak faith.

In fact, life would be meaningless without such faith. We would constantly question why good fortune smiles upon one person while misfortune strikes another. We would question if there is an accounting for our deeds: Will we be rewarded for our good deeds? And we might think that life in this world ultimately comes to a final end, without any hope of resurrection.

Upon losing a loved one, we would agonize: Where has he gone? What will become of him? Will we ever be reunited?

But with firmer faith, our doubts and questions fade and we need no longer wonder. We are then confident that there *is* meaning to life, and that in the end, hope is justified.

The purpose of this chapter, then, is to clarify these tenets of faith, so that we might strengthen ourselves in the face of hardship and loss.

৵ All Is Decreed from Above

Great, public miracles lead us to believe in the hidden ones which are the foundation of the entire Torah. A person has no share in the Torah given to us by Moshe Rabbeinu unless he believes that *all* our affairs and circumstances are miracles; that life's events, whether public or private, are never simply "nature" or "the way things go." If a person fulfills the mitzvos, his reward will be prosperity; but if he does not, his punishment will be destruction. All is decreed from Above (Ramban, *Shemos*, end of *Parashas Bo*).

Events do not occur at random; they are decreed from Above. R. Shlomo Wolbe שליט״א, leading *mussar* authority in our time, summarizes the fundamentals of Divine Providence in his classic work on faith *Alei Shur* (Vol. II, p. 300), as follows:

A.   The laws of nature are unchanging and have been set in their present form since Creation. For example, Hashem does not repeatedly establish the Law of Gravity.

B.   Unlike the *laws* of nature, life and existence are renewed constantly. Life continues only as long as Hashem wills it to continue.

C. Hashem's knowledge of existence is all-encompassing. Every movement, every flutter of even the smallest leaf, is known to Him, for His Presence fills the universe just as the *neshama*, soul, fills the body. As King David said: "You know when I sit [idly] and when I rise [to act]; You anticipate my thoughts from afar" (*Tehillim* 139:2). Hashem's knowledge is everlasting and will not cease for all eternity.

D. Hashem *directs* the world. He wants the world to endure, and devises plans to ensure that no individual shall be lost (see II *Shemuel* 14:14). The Ramban indicates that reward and punishment is the mechanism by which G-d governs the world; those who cleave to Hashem will be rewarded, but those who do not will be penalized.

E. Hashem's intent in governing His world is to lead it towards a Final Redemption. Supreme Wisdom synthesizes *all* the actions of each and every person in the service of bringing that Redemption closer. In a way that is beyond our comprehension, even the evil of the wicked is harnessed to bring the Redemption closer. (This topic is treated at length by the Ramchal in his *Da'as Tevunos.*)

The above list describes briefly the ways of Divine Providence. It is worthwhile for us to understand and become aware of the pervasive Providential character in all that happens — life and death, health and illness, fruitfulness and barrenness, success and failure.

Practically, however, we should be careful not to blur the distinction between Divine Providence and our own obligation to use logic and intellect to guide our behavior. For example, when deciding upon a marriage partner, a person should use both intellect and emotion to judge mutual suitability. In that situation, no Heavenly signal informing one whether or not Providence decreed the match should be expected. Hashem desired that Man make his own decisions in such matters and therefore endowed him with intellect.

The *Chovos HaLevavos* explains:

> It is correct that when acting we should follow the opinion of those who believe that all action is up to man [that is, that man has free will and that he will be rewarded and punished for his deeds]. Therefore, we should attempt to do everything which will be to our benefit both in this world and the next. However, we should place our trust in Hashem, joining those who believe that all events — gains as well as losses — are a result of Hashem's decree.... Hashem will have the final word against man [because of his misdeeds], but man will have no complaints against Him.

> ("Gate Three: Service of G-d," chap. 8)

So we see that although we have a duty to behave wisely, we must still realize that gain and loss, success and failure, are solely in the hands of Hashem.

In order to acquire perfect faith in Divine Providence, we must consistently react to events, whether apparently good or bad, with personal acknowledgment that they are Divinely decreed. We should recognize and admit that they come from Hashem, Who is good and does good, and that He is the True Judge. We should focus on that principle frequently and regularly review the quality of our faith in the matter.

The Rosh (Rabbeinu Asher) writes:

> Trust in G-d with your whole heart and believe in His specific Providence. Then, your heart will

keep faith in His perfect Unity, through believing
that His eyes view the whole earth and see all
Man's actions, and that they test the heart and
probe the emotions. Someone who does not believe in "I brought you out of Egypt" will also not
believe in "I am Hashem your G-d," and his faith
in G-d's Unity will be less than perfect. In fact,
Israel's status as chosen over the other nations of
the world is based on this very faith — it is the
foundation of the entire Torah.

(*Orchos Chaim* 26)

There is no doubt that strengthened faith in Divine Providence will alter a person's entire way of behaving. It is only
through concrete belief in Divine Providence that a person can
attain a level of behavior in which his sitting, his movements,
and all his affairs are conducted as if in the presence of a great
king. It is this belief that sets us apart from the other nations and
that serves as the foundation of the Torah. Therefore, it is essential for us to continue training ourselves until our faith in Divine
Providence becomes firmly implanted in our hearts.

🌢 A Foundation of Faith: Never Lose Hope

True belief in Hashem, as explained by R. Yechezkel
Levenstein ל״צז (*mashgiach* in Mir and later in Ponevezh Yeshiva) in *Ohr Yechezkel — Emuna*, demands that a person
should not lose hope even in what appears to be the most
hopeless of situations. We should not despair even in the face
of mortal illness, even when doctors give no chance for sur-
vival. Of this our Sages said (*Berachos* 10a): "Even if a sharp
sword lies on a person's neck he should not refrain from
prayer." At such times, the only proper change is in the *level*
of one's prayer. Our prayers should become even more fer-

vent, in order to arouse Heaven's mercy.

The basis for this hopefulness is our obligation to believe that nothing is beyond Hashem's ability. We are required to believe that the apparent causes of events are not ultimate reality and that there is no independent system of law or nature in the world, but that everything happens only through the Will of Hashem.

We learn this from Hashem's complaint against Sarah (*Bereishis* 18:13): "Why did Sarah laugh?" After being childless for ninety years, wasn't it natural that upon hearing a stranger, who seemed to be an ordinary Arab, promise her a son, she would scoff and ask, "Will I indeed give birth now that I am old?"

Yet Hashem said, "Is anything beyond the ability of Hashem?"

This is the essence of true belief: knowing that Hashem created the world and that He is constantly renewing the act of Creation. It is obvious, then, that the laws of nature can be changed at any time; if Hashem does *not* alter nature, it can only be because we are not worthy of such change.

This level of belief is not a matter of extreme piety — it is a basic belief. If a person lacks it, he will be called to judgment. In the words of the Mishna: "Know before Whom you are destined to give a final accounting, before the King of Kings, *HaKadosh Baruch Hu*." In the judgment of Heaven, one is accountable for any lack of belief in Hashem's unlimited ability, even in areas where human reason sees no hope. Why? Because as humans, we are to stand humbly before Hashem, Who is all-powerful. To Him, it makes no difference whether or not there are natural means of salvation — all is possible. Therefore, a person should trust in Hashem's capability in any situation.

In actuality, our level of belief is usually on a much lower level. Even when we see that there is some possibility of salvation and our hope is aroused, instead of attributing the matter to Hashem, we look for other causes.

Belief must be complete, unlimited, uncompromising. This concept is alluded to in the words of the prophet Habakkuk (2:4): וצדיק באמונתו יחיה — "The *tzaddik* will live by his belief." If a person doesn't believe that Hashem can change the order of Creation, then he is setting limits on Hashem's ability, and his belief is not true belief at all.

We must know that Hashem's ability is unlimited. In an instant, He can create new limbs for one whose arm or leg was amputated. If He does not do so, it is because we are unworthy of receiving open miracles.

If we take an even deeper look, we can see that not only is there no benefit to be gained from relying on natural means of help, but that damage is actually caused by this approach. Salvation comes at the time when all hope is lost, as we see in *Tehillim* 34:20: רבות רעות צדיק ומכולם יצילנו ה' — "Many evils befall a *tzaddik*, but he will be saved from them all by Hashem." As long as a person has hope in some natural means of deliverance, his true salvation will remain distant. Hashem conducts the world this way in order to test man. He brings the righteous person to a point where there is no hope through natural means, thereby testing the perfection of his belief. Salvation then comes only at the last possible moment, for it makes no difference to Hashem whether it is the last moment or not.

*   *   *

The Gemara tells us that, "Even if a sharp sword lies on a person's neck he should not refrain from prayer" (*Berachos* 10a). R. Yitzchak Zev Soloveitchik זצ"ל, son of R. Chaim, and Rav of Brisk, illustrated this point as follows:

Picture a person who is being tried for a serious crime for which the penalty is death. He and his relatives hire an expensive, expert attorney. This renowned lawyer invests a great deal of time in preparing a defense. Despite his efforts, though, the accused is found guilty and sentenced to death.

Hope is not yet lost. The defendant appeals the verdict in higher courts, hiring even greater lawyers to defend him. But all the appeals are rejected, and his death sentence stands.

Hope is still not lost — perhaps he can obtain a pardon from the king. His friends and relatives seek every avenue of access to the royal court. Letters are sent describing the plight of the poor man's family, the unfortunate widow and orphans who will be left behind, and the sick, elderly parents who rely on his help. High officials in the palace are contacted, and even they plead before the king for the life of this unfortunate man.

But all their pleas remain unanswered. There will be no pardon. The man is moved to the cell of those condemned to death. Yet somehow a feeling of hope remains — perhaps some miracle will occur. Still, as the time of punishment draws closer, even this hope fades.

The appointed hour arrives. The executioner enters the cell and unsheathes his sword, checking the sharpness of the blade. Still, deep in the heart of the condemned man there is a hope that perhaps...perhaps some miracle will occur.

As the sword is placed on his neck, he knows he is only a hairsbreadth away from his death. There is really no reason left for hope. All is lost.

The Brisker Rav concluded the story by saying: Without *emuna*, faith, all is lost. But at that very moment, just when the sharp sword is upon one's neck, a person should continue to pray. Even when all hope seems to be lost, one should still pray and hope and trust in Hashem, for there is yet hope.

❧ Belief in the Face of Doubt — the Essential Mitzva of *Emuna*

Belief that Hashem created Heaven and Earth is a very elemental, basic belief. A much deeper level of *emuna* is necessary to believe in Hashem even when observing events that defy human understanding and raise difficult questions about Hashem's conduct of the world. This is the true test of *emuna*. If we recognize the impossibility of understanding our Creator, yet continue to put our faith in Him — ignoring completely our personal doubts — we have achieved the highest level of *emuna*.

R. Yaakov Naiman זצ"ל, Rosh Yeshiva in Ohr Yisrael, Petach Tikva, in *Darchei Mussar*, finds this principle alluded to in the verse (*Devarim* 32:4): "[Hashem is] without injustice" — even where there seems to be, to human eyes, great injustice.

We all face this test of faith when we think about the murder of millions of our People in the Holocaust, among them, the saintly, the scholarly, the righteous, and all the whole-hearted men, women and innocent children. Entire cities were uprooted and large families cut down without leaving a trace. Nonetheless, we must have firm belief that Hashem is "without injustice" and that "whatever Hashem does is for the good." For there can be no doubt in the heart of the genuine believer that there is a just accounting Above for everything that happens.

R. Naiman illustrates this concept with a parable he heard from the Chazon Ish זצ"ל, who was one of the previous generation's Torah giants and rebuilder of the Torah world in Eretz Yisrael: When a tailor cuts expensive material into small pieces, we can be sure he intends to sew a fine garment. So too, although Man is not given the wisdom and perception to understand Hashem's ways — they are simply beyond human comprehension — we can be sure that whatever He does is for the good.

The essence of *emuna* is belief in Hashem even where human understanding is contradicted. Avraham's most difficult test came when he was told to sacrifice his beloved son Yitzchak, specifically because it went against Avraham's own knowledge and understanding. In that test, he was called upon to perform an act similar to the very same *avoda zara*, idol worship, he had always struggled to uproot. Not only that, but Hashem had promised him that his future generations would come through Yitzchak, and now he was being told to slaughter this only son. Nevertheless, even though the command opposed his personal understanding, Avraham did not ask any questions, since he had simple faith in Hashem.

In the words of R. Chaim Soloveitchik זצ"ל, Rav of Brisk and Rosh Yeshiva of Volozhin Yeshiva, "Faith begins where human reason ends."

✌ Belief in G-d Eases Suffering

In his preface to *Avi Ezri*, R. Eliezer Menachem Shach שליט"א, Rosh Yeshiva of Ponevezh Yeshiva in Bnei Brak, poses a seeming difficulty with the verse (*Devarim* 31:17): "[the Nation] will be beset by great evils and calamities, and it will say on that day, 'Behold, because my G-d does not dwell within me I was beset by these evils.' " R. Shach asks: Why does the verse start with both "evils and calamities" and end with just one of them, "evils"?

R. Shach begins his explanation by pointing out that calamities, *tzaros*, refers to the evil itself. The word *tzaros* however, is related to the root *tzar*—narrow, tight, which the Targum translates as "things that press." We can learn from this that suffering has two parts: In addition to the actual difficulty or pain itself, there is also a general feeling of being pressed, as if there were no room to move; a person's world appears dark and his spirit is broken. This feeling comes from a lack of belief and faith in Hashem. When a person doesn't feel Hashem's Presence within himself, he feels continually distressed and broken. In contrast, a person who believes in Hashem and His Divine Providence does not see evils as calamities — troubles and suffering do not depress or break him. As King David said, "Even when I walk in the valley of the shadow of Death, I fear no evil, for You are with me" (*Tehillim* 23:4).

So the "evils and calamities" mentioned in the beginning of the verse refer to a period in which people's lack of faith brings them to perceive their troubles as calamities, thus doubling their suffering. The continuation of the verse, "[the Nation]...will say on that day, [these evils befell me] because my G-d does not dwell within me," shows that they have come to realize that their problems stem from a lack of faith. From that moment on, their faith is strengthened and they are no longer broken in spirit, no longer in *tzaros*. Now we may understand the verse's ending: "I was beset by these evils," that is, by evils alone, a single aspect of suffering.

Mazal — Our Unique Role in Service of Hashem

I. Every individual's circumstances — whether he lives expansively or in constraint — are in accordance with his unique part in the perfection of Creation

> The angel appointed over pregnancies takes a drop to the Holy One and asks Him: "Master of the Universe, what will become of this drop? Will it become mighty or weak, wise or foolish, wealthy or poor?" The angel does not ask: "Will it

become wicked or righteous?" This is in accord with R. Chanina's statement: "All is in the hands of Heaven, except Fear of Heaven."

(*Nidda* 16b)

A person's unique service to Hashem is determined prior to his birth, just as are the traits and talents given to him to fulfill his mission. Indeed, all the events which arise throughout life are based on that personal mission. For example, poverty is decreed upon a person in order for him serve Hashem through the test of poverty.

This concept is expressed in the Gemara as: "Life, children, and sustenance do not depend on merit, but rather on *Mazal*" (*Moed Katan* 28a). The word *mazal* does not, as many people think, mean "luck" or "a random event"; instead, it refers to anything that "flows" to a person from Above (the root verb in Hebrew is *nozel*, to flow). This Gemara teaches us that life, children, and sustenance *flow* to us from Heaven and are actually predetermined. However, the same is not true of Fear of Heaven. "All is in the hands of Heaven, except Fear of Heaven" means that Fear of Heaven depends on our decisions: What will I do with the life and children that are given to me? Will I choose good, or, Heaven forbid, bad?

The story of R. Elazar ben Pedas can clarify the matter for us:

R. Elazar ben Pedas lived in extreme poverty. Once, after a blood-letting treatment, he had no food with which to revive himself. Desperately hungry, he ate a head of garlic and fainted. When the Torah scholars of the city came to visit him, they saw that he was both smiling and crying at the same time. After he had recovered, they asked him to explain the cause of his mixed emotions. He replied: "The Holy One was sitting with me and I asked Him, 'How long must I suffer?'

Hashem answered: 'Elazar, my son, if you wish
I'll destroy the world from the beginning and re-
build it again, and then perhaps your *mazal* will be
that you should be wealthy.' "

(*Ta'anis* 25a)

At this point, we are bothered by a simple question: Why
should the world have to be overturned in order to provide R.
Elazar ben Pedas with food? Surely Hashem, Who is all-powerful, has other means of providing for R. Elazar! If we
broaden our understanding of the way *Mazal* works in the
world, the answer will become apparent.

II. The operating mechanism of Mazal is beyond our comprehension

Concerning the topic of *Mazal*, the Ramchal writes:

The Creator divided the task of perfecting Creation among all the souls created for His service.
The division of tasks was made in accord with
what He knew to be appropriate for each person,
and in accord with the purpose for which that
individual was created. However, how this division takes place is beyond human comprehension.
Not even the Prophets were able to fathom its
workings, since this concept is categorized as one
not in the realm of human understanding. We can
only observe the outcome of this appropriation.
[For example, we can see that one person is poor
while another is rich, but we don't understand
why this person's portion is poverty and the
other's is wealth.] There may be one person who,
according to his root purpose, will receive an
abundance of Heavenly assistance...while yet another person, because of his root purpose, will

only receive a small portion...in order to perfect
Creation. This does not happen as a result of their
deeds, but rather because of their role in the perfection of Creation as dictated by Hashem.

(Da'as Tevunos, p. 312, Feldheim)

To summarize:

1. Hashem created each person according to his task in
   Creation.

2. Each individual complements all others in the overall
   perfection of Creation.

3. We do not know how the role of each person is
   determined, nor is it essential for us to know how our
   role is determined in order to serve Hashem.

But we *do* have to know that each and every individual is
needed in order to complete the whole. Each person operates
within the framework given to him to complete the task as-
signed to him. Whether born with a gifted intellect or a limited one, whether born rich or poor, each and every person
will have to work with what Divine Providence gave him.
When he does so, he fulfills Creation's purpose.

*III. Man's ultimate reward will be based both on his effort
and on his degree of achievement of his task*

The Ramchal continues:

G-d will pass judgment, granting positive reward
to those who were righteous despite the fact that
Divine Providence had determined that their lives
be filled with hardship and affliction. They deserve reward for the hardship they endured and
for the good deeds they performed.

Reward is based on Man's freedom of will. A person who

passes the difficult test of poverty will receive corresponding reward, as we have learned: "The reward is in proportion to the suffering."

R. Elazar ben Pedas' lot in life was to be poor. His task was to serve Hashem within such an environment and to pass the test of poverty. He was supposed to use poverty in his service of Hashem. Conversely, R. Yehuda HaNasi, who was extremely wealthy, was supposed to use his wealth in *his* service of Hashem. The duty placed on each individual is dependent on the overall plan of Creation, and this plan was set at the very beginning of Creation. If R. Elazar ben Pedas wanted the framework of his task — poverty — to be altered, then Creation itself would have to be altered as well. Hashem would have to take the riches of so-and-so and transfer them to R. Elazar; then the poverty of R. Elazar would have to be given to someone else. The tasks of all would have to be reassigned, and the world would have to be re-created with a new agenda; only then could individual tasks be redefined.

> (From a discourse given by R. Chaim Friedlander זצ"ל,
> *mashgiach* in Ponevezh Yeshiva)

༺ There Are No Coincidences

The following discussion is based on an essay entitled "Let Us Behold the Hand of Hashem" by R. Chaim Friedlander.

> I believe with complete faith that the Creator, blessed is His Name, created and directs all creatures and that He alone made, makes, and will make everything.
>
> (*The Thirteen Principles*, Rambam)

A. "Do I really believe?"

We can test ourselves to see if we fulfill the first of the Thirteen Principles of Faith properly. We all believe in Hashem's existence; we believe that Hashem created the world, and that He directs the world; and we believe that, in His kindness, He renews the world daily. But at this point we should ask ourselves the following question: Do we *always* believe that "He alone made, makes, and will make everything"? If we were truly convinced that everything that happens to us comes directly from Hashem, wouldn't we react to events differently? When something happens that goes against our wishes and plans, do we then too remember that "Hashem made, makes, and will make everything"?

B. We should examine our deeds when trials befall us

The Rambam, in Chapter One of *Hilchos Ta'anios*, speaks sharply against those who forget that everything is in Hashem's hands:

> It is a positive commandment of the Torah to cry out and sound trumpets when a community faces tribulation.... This is one of the ways of repentance: When painful times arrive, and people cry out and sound trumpets, then they acknowledge that it was their bad deeds which brought harm upon them. This type of repentance will cause their suffering to be removed. But if they don't cry out and don't sound trumpets, saying instead that it was "just the way the world works" when troubles occur; or if they say, "this trouble just happened," then they have chosen a cruel path. Of this the Torah writes: "And if you will act towards Me with *keri* [randomness] then I too will act towards you with angry *keri*." Meaning, if when I

cause you hardship to prod you to repent, you say, "It was an accident [*keri*]," then I too will add random fury to what you think is accidental.

Our conclusion: A person should examine his deeds and return to Hashem, Who will then have mercy on him.

C. Sin is the cause

One basis for the mitzva of not taking revenge is that a person should realize that all that befalls him, whether apparently good or bad, is from Hashem. Even when one man hits another, it is only the Will of Hashem acting. Therefore, if someone causes you anguish or pain, realize that your sins were the cause, and Hashem decreed it so. Do not dwell on thoughts of revenge, for sin is the cause [of your troubles], not any given individual (*Sefer HaChinuch*, mitzva 241).

D. Ultimately we understand that hardship is for our own good

Evil people are often not punished in this world. Instead, they are often rewarded here for their few good deeds. It says in *Devarim* (7:10): "He rewards His enemies to their face in order to destroy them." Rashi explains that "during the wicked man's lifetime he is rewarded, in order to annihilate him in the World to Come." Hardship helps a person, for it cleanses and purifies him, provided that he also repents and does *teshuva*. In the words of the Midrash:

"Praise Hashem for He is good, for His kindness is everlasting" (*Tehillim* 136:1). As R. Yehoshua ben Levi explained: "Praise the One Who deducts the debts of guilty people from their assets: the rich man through his ox, the poor man through his goat, the orphan through his eggs, and the widow through her hen" (*Yalkut Tehillim* 136).

Occasionally, hardship befalls a person in order to save

him from an even greater hardship.

R. Yosi HaGalili expounded: "What is the meaning of the verse, 'I thank You, Hashem, that You were angry with me; may Your anger turn away from me, and may You comfort me'? [Rashi explains: I thank You for being angry with me, since it was for my benefit.]

"This is like two people planning a business trip. When a thorn became lodged in the foot of one, preventing him from traveling, he began to curse and blaspheme. Later, though, he heard that the ship he had intended to board had sunk, killing his friend, while he was spared. Then he began to sing and praise Hashem. Hence: 'May Your anger turn away from me, and may You comfort me' " (Nidda 31a).

With this idea in mind, we can better understand the blessing, "He Who bestows good kindness." Is there a kindness that is not good?

Imagine that two people were scheduled for the same flight. One of them overslept and missed the flight; the other was injured in an accident, and he too missed the flight. The plane, they later found out, crashed. Kindness had clearly been bestowed upon both of them, but for one it was done in a "good" way, while for the other it was done in a "not-so-good" way. Ultimately, both men realized that evil does not emanate from Hashem, and that even injury can be good for man.

E. Whoever serves Hashem even when beset by suffering sanctifies the Name of Heaven

At times a person acts as a messenger of Heaven to help others. For example, the mission of someone destined to be poor might be to demonstrate to others that it is possible to serve Hashem despite such difficulties. Our Sages teach us that the reward given to people who study Torah despite poverty is greater than that given to those who study Torah in comfort.

Such a thought should help console people undergoing hardship — Heaven may be giving them the opportunity to sanctify Hashem's Name in this world.

F. Tribulation is a means to a goal

Let us return to the beginning of our theme. We who have faith in Hashem may not complain over His decisions. If events in this world do not seem to make sense, we should remind ourselves that this world is only a means to an end, a way to reach the World to Come.

The following parable illustrates the concept:

There once was a wealthy man who worked in dirty, rag-like clothing. When he was asked how he, a man of such wealth and status, could dress the way he did, he replied: "This is where I work and earn my money, so I wear work clothes — it's the only way I can work. If you'd like to see my elegant clothes, come visit me at home after work hours — that's where you'll see my affluence."

This world is the "factory" in which we work. All the trouble, suffering, and anguish we encounter are our "work clothing"; with their help, we can arrive in the World to Come.

G. Calamity is the seed of growth and development

A person should view his suffering as a seedling from which good will yet grow (Sha'ar Bas Rabbim, Haftara Lech Lecha). Our Sages tell us that "a person is obligated to recite a blessing over evil just as he would over good." Complaining against Hashem when hardship strikes is improper, for if a person does so, then Hashem may not complete His intention, leaving the affected person unfulfilled and unhealed.

Someone who complains against Hashem is like the foolish homeowner who became enraged as he watched the carpenter he had hired to build his kitchen begin to saw precious boards of wood into pieces. He demanded that the workman stop the destruction at once. But when the carpenter stopped his sawing, all that was left to the homeowner were the useless pieces of partially sawed wood.

H. Life is too short for us to comprehend

A well-known parable of the Chofetz Chaim explains clearly why we cannot understand Hashem's ways:

A traveler arrived in a small town and stayed for Shabbos. When the time came for the Torah reading on Shabbos morning, the guest noticed that the *gabbai* gave the *aliya* of Kohen to a man who sat in the front section of the *shul*, while Levi was given to someone who sat on the opposite side of the *shul*; the person honored with *shelishi* sat in yet another part of the *shul*, etc. There seemed to be no method to the *gabbai's* choices.

Afterwards, the traveler approached the *gabbai*: "Forgive me, sir, that I, a guest in your town, should have the chutzpa to suggest something to you. But you see, I simply can't hide my astonishment at your strange method of giving out the *aliyos*. Where I come from we have a system, but here there doesn't seem to be any order at all. It looks like your selections are made totally at random!"

"Not at all," answered the *gabbai*. "You are mistaken. We too have a system and a method. But since you've only been with us for one Shabbos, our choices seem strange to you. Had you been with us longer, you would have understood why this particular Kohen was called up. The same is true of the other *aliyos*. It really does all make sense."

We mortals are only "guests" in this world, yet we expect to understand the workings of a plan that was meant to last for thousands of years! We should follow Hashem with pure faith and trust that His decisions are perfect.

I. When we accept Hashem's decrees with love, we pass the test

R. Yechezkel Levenstein highlights the steadfast faith of the Jewish People before they were redeemed from Egypt: For three years the Egyptians cast all newborn Jewish boys into the Nile, yet not one Jew lost his faith. Amram, Moshe's father, remarried his wife, Yocheved, despite the edict, thereby demonstrating a firmness of faith which enabled loving acceptance of Hashem's painful decrees (*Ohr Yechezkel — Letters*, p. 109).

When his grandson passed away, R. Levenstein wrote:

> If only our faith were stronger, we would readily accept Divine Judgment. All of Heaven's ways are tests. Divine Providence acts entirely on the basis of the principle: "Thought precedes the deed." When we accept hardship lovingly, we pass the test for which we will merit all that is good from our Father in Heaven, just like Aharon, who remained silent [when his two sons died], thereby meriting the revelation of Hashem's Presence.
>
> (ibid., p. 114)

J. Hashem's kindness outweighs hardship

If we were to make an accurate listing of the anguish we experience and the pleasures we enjoy, we would quickly see that our "pleasure column" is much longer than our "anguish column." For every breath we take we need to thank our Creator!

Opening our eyes to the wonders of Creation will arouse our love of Hashem and bring us to greater awareness of all the kindness He bestows upon us. The universe is managed by Divine order: day and night, winter and summer, trees produce fruit and people are born, etc. All this provides irrefutable evidence that every detail of our lives is managed by Divine Wisdom.

As the Rambam writes:

> It is a mitzva to love and fear the great and awesome G-d.... What is the path to love Him and to fear Him? When a person contemplates Hashem's creations and His wondrous and mighty deeds, he will then understand that Hashem's wisdom is limitless. Then love, praise, and exaltation of Hashem will flow spontaneously, and he will be filled with a great desire to know His great Name. As King David said, "My soul thirsts for *Elokim*, the living G-d."
>
> (*Yesodei HaTorah*, chap. 2)

A continuation of this theme can be found in the words of the Chazon Ish:

> When a person's mind merits seeing the truth of Hashem's existence, boundless joy enters him; his soul is at peace, while emotion and intellect unite to help him see Hashem's beauty. All the pleasures of the flesh slip away from him. His sensitive soul becomes enveloped in holiness, almost as if it had separated itself from the coarse body. His soul soars to the highest Heavens. When a person ascends to these holy levels, a new world unfolds before him. He becomes like an angel for a few brief moments, enjoying the radiance of all that is holy. All the pleasures of this world are nothing, compared with the pleasure of man's cleaving to his Creator, blessed is He.
>
> (*Emuna u'Bitachon*, p. 11, no. 49)

K. Yaakov withstood the test of hardship and saw Hashem's wonders

In light of the above, we can understand why Yaakov's heart was filled with boundless love for Hashem when his twenty-two years of suffering ended. At the very moment when he was finally about to be reunited with his son Yosef after their prolonged separation, Yaakov lovingly unified Hashem in his heart, declaring: *"Shema Yisrael...."* Yaakov was able to do this because his life's ambition was to serve Hashem — human emotions were secondary for him.

Because he had been able to withstand the trial given him, he merited seeing Hashem's wonders. At precisely that moment, he felt compelled to thank Hashem.

L. When Redemption's light will shine, all will become clear

We are in a period of transition, waiting for our Redemption. Just as the soldier in combat does not understand the importance of his particular role in the battle, so too, we do not understand the process we are in.

The Chofetz Chaim describes what we can expect when *Mashiach* arrives: When Yosef's brothers arrived in Egypt, they encountered many strange events. First the ruler accused them of being spies, then some of them were imprisoned. In fact, there were so many out-of-the-ordinary occurrences that they finally wondered out loud, "What has Hashem done to us?"

We too are lost in a maze of doubts and questions concerning events in our lives. We too wonder: "What has Hashem done to us?"

Two words — "I'm Yosef" — spoken by Yosef to his brothers, resolved all their doubts, and answered all their questions. Confusion vanished — suddenly everything made sense.

We too will experience the same happiness and relief, when in the future the words "I am Hashem" will reverberate throughout the world. When *Mashiach* comes, all questions will be answered, all doubts will be resolved, and all riddles over the way Divine Providence works will disappear. Then we will all understand and believe with perfect faith that the Creator, blessed is His Name, created and directs all creatures, and that He alone made, makes, and will make everything.

Reaching this level of faith now, is not a simple task which can be accomplished overnight. It takes a lot of effort to reach the point where we can identify with this belief in a clear, definite, and practical manner. May Hashem help us to serve Him, may we do His Will wholeheartedly, and may we be amongst those who truthfully trust Him.

M. *It can take time to see the benefit contained in suffering*

A group of Jewish youths from Germany were forced to flee the Nazis and were sent to England. When World War II began, the English government deported the entire group, along with thousands of other German nationals, to Australia, on suspicion that they were spies. The voyage to Australia was a difficult one. Not only was the ship overcrowded, but the British had appointed hardened criminals as guards on the boat, in exchange for their release from prison. These criminals secretly searched all the suitcases of the other passengers, plundering valuables and throwing overboard whatever they didn't want.

One morning, the ship, which sailed under a British flag, was spotted on the high seas by a German submarine. The German commander ordered his men to fire torpedoes at the enemy ship. The first torpedo missed. But the second one was aimed perfectly and headed directly towards the ship's propeller. Suddenly, an enormous wave lifted the ship, and the torpedo sailed underneath, sparing all those on board. The feelings of the passengers can best be described as "rejoicing with trembling." They rejoiced over the miracle they had witnessed, but they trembled over what might happen next. Much to their great surprise, though, no more torpedoes were fired and the submarine disappeared.

Forty years later, a German newspaper published the memoirs of the commander of that very same German submarine. He wrote of the crew's surprise at the failure of the second torpedo to hit its mark, and cleared up the mystery of why the submarine didn't pursue its attack. It seems that during the shelling, the submarine crew noticed strange objects floating in the water, which appeared to be coming from the direction of the ship. An order was given to collect the objects for examination. The strange objects bobbing on the waves turned out to be the suitcases of the English ship's passengers. When the officers of the submarine opened the suitcases, they were shocked to see letters written in German. They realized that the ship they had been attacking was carrying German nationals and they called off the attack. (A true story.)

"You have turned my mourning into dancing" (*Tehillim* 30:12). When the words "I am Hashem" will be proclaimed throughout the world, all questions will be answered and all doubts will be resolved.

❧ Hashem Governs with Profound Counsel

A person should not complain against the Holy One, blessed be He, when he observes what happens to people, that one righteous person enjoys the good, while another righteous person suffers misfortune; that one evil person enjoys the good, while another evil person suffers misfortune. For if a person comes to complain against Him, he forfeits his life....

Our Sages have taught: 974 generations before the world was created, Hashem sat and searched, examined, purified, and tested all the words of the Torah 248 times, corresponding to the 248 limbs in man. Afterwards Hashem took those words of Torah and fixed them in His Torah, so that a single word may not be moved from its place, as it is written, "The words of Hashem are pure words, purified silver, purified sevenfold." Every single word in the Torah, if it were to be moved even slightly from its place, would lead the entire world to ruin.

(Tanna d'Vei Eliyahu Zuta, chap. 10)

The two statements above seem to be unrelated, says R. Simcha Kessler שליט״א, Rav of Kiryat Sefer. The first deals with the problem of the suffering of the righteous, while the second teaches how the Torah preceded the Creation of the world. Understanding the connection between them may help us develop a deeper faith.

What is the meaning of Hashem analyzing the words of Torah for so many generations and so many times over? Taking the 248 limbs of man as an example, we can see that each limb must match every other limb. The small heart of a baby cannot provide the blood circulation needed for an adult body. Similarly, all the other organs must match each other perfectly in size and function. It follows that each limb created must be tested to match every other limb of the body, that is, it must be tested 248 times. Since the 248 positive commandments correspond to the limbs of man, the various mitzvos must be in consonance with each other in the same way that the limbs of a body must match each other. Therefore, each mitzva was tested with every other mitzva 248 times.

Further, the 613 specific commandments are one part of the Torah, not its entirety: "Hashem peered into the Torah and created the world." Everything in the world and every event from the beginning of time is found in the Torah. All of these must fit with each other as parts of one unified Torah. Hashem, therefore, analyzed and considered the pattern of Creation for so many generations prior to creating the world.

This brings us to a wondrous conclusion: Every event that occurs to the community or to an individual is the product of careful analysis for hundreds of generations. Since every event is the result of meticulous analysis by the Creator Himself, there can be no doubt that everything done by Hashem in this world is done for the good.

This, then, is the point of the *Tanna d'Vei Eliyahu*: Knowing that all events are the product of such careful planning by Hashem Himself, we can be reassured of the absolute justice of the suffering of the righteous or the good fortune of the wicked.

Yet we should be aware that there is another factor which affects Hashem's conduct of the world — the actions of the Jewish People. The *Tanna d'Vei Eliyahu* explains that if a single word in the Torah is moved from its place, it affects the entire Creation. When a Jew moves part of the Torah from its place — by failing to fulfill that particular mitzva — he has adversely affected all of Creation. Imagine the great planning that created the Torah and the world based upon Torah! A thousand generations of analysis were devoted to bringing the world to its purpose. Only Man can affect that plan. His misdeeds will affect it negatively, or his proper actions will affect it positively and help bring Creation towards its ultimate purpose.

Then Yisrael said [speaking to his sons], "Why did

you do evil to me, to tell the man that you have another brother?" (*Bereishis* 43:6). R. Levi said in the name of R. Chama bar Chanina: "Yaakov never spoke in vain except here. The Holy One, blessed be He, said: 'I am occupied with making his son king of Egypt and he says: "Why did you do evil unto me?" ' Of this it was said (*Yeshayahu* 40:27), 'Why, Yaakov, do you say: "My way is hidden from Hashem"?' "

(*Midrash Rabba Bereishis* 91:10)

The Ramchal finds in these words an essential outlook demanded of Man:

At the very time when the world seems to have been abandoned by Him, He is devising good for His world; His wonders and thoughts are constantly directed towards the perfection of the universe and not to its undoing. But He conceals His counsel to such a great extent that the world seems to be abandoned, and men suffer punishment for their sins....

This, then, is the meaning of the above-mentioned midrash: All of the time that Yaakov was in despair over Yosef's separation from him, Hashem was "turning the wheels" to make Yosef king and to enable Yaakov to live in tranquillity. But because the matter was shrouded in deep secrecy, grief descended upon Yaakov. This teaches us a basic principle: With respect to any improvement which Hashem wishes to accord an individual or the world, the entire time the good is in the process of materializing it is generated only within the depths of hidden counsel, for which reason it is preceded by suffering. As our Sages

wrote: "Three wonderful gifts were given by
Hashem to Israel, and all were given only through
suffering."

(Da'as Tevunos, p. 143)

The complaint lodged against Yaakov teaches us what is
expected of man. We might wonder what was improper
about what Yaakov said. He was suffering not only the loss of
his beloved Yosef, but the absence of Levi and the threat of
danger to Binyamin. Could he really be expected to bear all
that? He did not even direct any complaints against Hashem;
he simply complained of the evil his sons were doing to him.

We can learn from this that perfect faith is demanded of
man — faith that does not entertain any sense of "You have
done evil to me." Even in Yaakov's trying situation, he should
have recognized that Hashem was acting on deeply concealed counsel directed only towards his ultimate benefit.
Every Jew, in whatever situation, is required to believe with
perfect faith that whatever Hashem does is for the good.

On this the Ramchal writes:

There is no act, small or large, whose inner intent
is not directed towards the complete rectification
of the world. This is as our Sages said (*Berachos*
60b): "All that is done by Heaven is done for the
good." In the future Hashem will make His ways
known, showing how even persecution and suffering were only preparation for blessing. For
Hashem wants only the rectification of His Creation. He does not reject evildoers; on the contrary,
He purifies them in a furnace to cleanse them of
any dross."

(Da'as Tevunos, p. 43)

*   *   *

The Maggid of Dubno, in *Ohel Yaakov*, similarly explains this theme. Yosef said to his brothers (*Bereishis* 50:20): "You thought bad about me; Hashem planned it for the good." The Midrash comments, "If Yosef, speaking gently to his brothers' hearts, was able to so console them, how much more so will *Klal Yisrael* be consoled when Hashem comes to console Yerushalayim, as it is written: נחמו נחמו עמי —'Console, console My nation.' "

The Maggid explains: Yosef consoled his brothers by showing how all the difficult events that befell him in Egypt were preparation for the good that resulted from them. In hindsight, it was clear that all the troubles were brought about in order to bring Yosef to the throne, thereby saving Yaakov and his family.

This is the kind of consolation we will receive in the future. It will then become clear to us in what way all the suffering and persecution we now undergo are a preparation for the great blessings and reward that await us in the End of Days. Just as there can be no harvest without prior plowing and planting, so too, the wondrous blessing at the End of Days cannot come about without all the accumulated suffering preceding it.

On the verse (*Yeshayahu* 35:10): "Those redeemed by Hashem will return — crowned with everlasting joy and happiness they will come to Zion," our Sages comment: "Do not read 'everlasting joy' but 'joy of all time.' " When we look back, we will see that what seemed to be a reason for sadness was in fact cause for great joy, since it was in preparation for future blessings.

The verse continues: "They will attain gladness and joy; sorrow and sighing will flee." The Maggid of Dubno explains this with a parable:

Someone posing as a doctor was brought to treat a seriously ill patient. Naturally, the "treatment" caused the illness to worsen. It soon became obvious that the so-called doctor had no knowledge of medicine, and he was thrown out in disgrace. Similarly, when Bilaam failed to curse *Klal Yisrael*, Balak said to him, "Away with you! Run away to your place."

With the perfect vision of hindsight, we too will see that there never existed a real reason for our sorrow. It will become obvious that the causes of all our sadness were actually the seeds of future good. Thus "sorrow and sighing will flee" — they will be exposed and banished as the impostors they really are, when Hashem brings His great consolation to Yerushalayim.

∂∞ The Suffering of the Righteous

> ...Know that what Iyov's friends told him — that sin causes suffering — is undeniably true and immutably accurate. This is the rule by which Hashem runs the world. Also, Iyov's question [צדיק ורע לו —Why do the righteous suffer?] is generally inappropriate, since we believe in the World of Souls and in just reward in the World to Come. It is known that most *tzaddikim* occasionally sin, and it is unlikely that they can avoid every minor or major sin, as it is written (*Koheles* 7:20): "For there is no righteous person on earth who does only good and never sins." Therefore, even the perfectly righteous person who commits some minor sin or unintentionally transgresses his Creator's command deserves penalty.
>
> Even if Hashem causes him to lose all the good that exists in this world and condemns him to Iyov-like suffering for his entire life, it is still better for him than for his soul to be punished with

the suffering of Gehinnom. It is still better for him to suffer in this world than for his sin to even slightly lower his soul's status in the World of Souls, or limit its closeness to the aura of the Above and the World to Come. The body is lowly, and the rewards of this material world — where the differences between good fortune and misfortune are minor and fleeting — are not significant. The soul and the goodness which fills it, the light of the countenance of the Living King, are great. This goodness is absolute and beyond compare.... Our Sages therefore say (*Kiddushin* 39b): "A person whose merits are greater than his misdeeds is treated harshly in this world. It appears that he is punished like someone who has burnt the entire Torah without leaving a single letter intact." Similarly (*Yerushalmi, Peah* 1:1), "Someone whose merits outweigh his sins is punished in this world for the slight transgressions he committed, in order to give him full reward in the World to Come."

Such is the rule, and justice demands that it be so. The punishment of a *tzaddik* should be reduced, so he is punished in a place that is less important, the body, and in a setting that is less important, this world. Later, he will be able to receive his reward in a place which is more important, the World to Come, and at a time which is more beneficial.

It is also unlikely that a person could be evil his entire lifetime and never do anything good for which he deserves reward. But even if Hashem would reward him with pleasures, status, and kingship like King Solomon's, all that can never equal even the smallest of the soul's rewards of pleasure in those worlds that are appropriate to the soul. Therefore, due to a person's many transgressions, the eternal, spiritual reward is withheld from him. Instead, he is rewarded with something small and insignificant, as Onkelos explains on the verse (*Devarim* 7:10): "He repays His enemies to their face to destroy them."

Our original question is now answered: Every evil person who thrives has done some good, for which he is rewarded in this insignificant, fleeting world; and every righteous person who suffers has committed some misdeeds, for which he is punished in this less important world.

But Iyov, who knew himself to be perfectly righteous, and of whom Hashem testified (*Iyov* 2:3), "You (Satan) have incited Me to consume him for no reason," and others like him, such as R. Akiva, are not included in this principle. Only the wicked, who deny Hashem, such as those who claim the preexistence of the material world, are given no credit for their deeds, even if they act nobly their whole lives. The question then remains: Why does Hashem bestow *any* good fortune upon them? The only answer is that mentioned above in *Iyov*.

(Ramban, Preface to *Iyov*)

❧ Our Understanding Is Limited

Throughout the centuries this matter of the suffering of the righteous and the easy life of the wicked has troubled many people. In every generation there have been those who have used the apparent injustice of things to justify their complete denial of faith. They ask, "Why is so-and-so successful? And why did those who appeared righteous perish?" This is the root cause of rebellion [against Hashem] amongst all those who rebelled in every nation.

(Ramban, Preface to *Iyov*)

This question of why the righteous suffer (צדיק ורע לו) is ancient, notes R. Yoel Shwartz שליט"א, contemporary Torah scholar and author (*The Shoah*, p. 38). It is asked in all times and all places. The entire *Book of Iyov*, as well as various other passages in Scriptures, is devoted to this question (see *Tehillim* 73; *Habakkuk* 1-2). The apparent conclusion of the *Book of Iyov* is that man cannot reach the deep level of comprehension necessary for understanding such a profound matter. Hashem appears from the storm and asks Iyov (*Iyov* 38:4), "Where were you when I founded the earth? Declare if you have understanding." Iyov responds (42:3): "Therefore I uttered that which I do not understand, that which is far beyond me, that which I do not know."

Superficially, this seems to be an admission that there is no answer, but Iyov's response actually reveals that the question [Hashem's] should not be asked, since, in essence, there can be no human answer to a Divine question. R. Nachman of Breslav writes (II *Likutei Maharan*, 62): "It is fitting that questions be put to Hashem in accordance with His greatness and exaltation. The very fact of His greatness and loftiness places Him far above our intelligence, so of course it is impossible for us to understand His ways. Hence, there must be questions. If His conduct conformed to our understanding, His thinking would be as limited as ours."

The Rambam writes in a similar vein:

The intent of the entire *Book of Iyov* is...to establish this principle of faith...that you not err and think that His knowledge could be like our knowledge, or that His intent, Providence, and conduct are like our intent, care, and conduct. When one knows this, every difficult occurrence becomes easier. Nothing that happens will cause him to question Hashem, wondering, "Does He know or not know? Does He watch everything closely or ignore matters?" Instead, a person will continue to increase his love of Hashem, as our Sages said: "Those who serve out of love and are happy in suffering." R. Yannai said, "It is not in our power to explain the tranquillity of the evildoer nor the suffering of the righteous" (*Avos* 4:14), on which Rabbeinu Yonah comments, "It is true that our wisdom cannot attain this understanding. We certainly know that an explanation exists, but we cannot reach it."

(*Moreh Nevuchim* 3:23)

In our era it is perhaps easier to accept this limitation of our understanding. Since it is now known that the physical world cannot be fully comprehended, we realize that if we do not understand the Creation, we cannot expect to understand the ways of the Creator.

In Scripture and in the words of our Sages we do find various explanations. Although we cannot understand the secrets of our Creator, we are still required to draw closer to His ways and try to understand them as much as possible. Although intellectually we can accept that the matter is beyond us, emotionally we demand some perspective from which to understand. In addition, striving to understand His ways is part of the commandments of "know G-d" and "love G-d" (Ramban, *Sha'ar HaGemul*).

The answers given by our Prophets and Sages make us realize that our questions stem from a very limited perception of events. Only the all-seeing eye of the Above can know the many factors involved in each judgment and thereby perceive the true nature of Good and Evil. Of this it is written (*Tehillim* 19:10): "The judgments of Hashem are true, altogether just." Only when all the facts are taken together is the judgment correct.

Moreover, our evaluation of what constitutes good fortune and what doesn't is often incorrect. The best example of this is death. We think of death as the worst thing that can happen to a person. Yet our Sages tell us (*Bereishis Rabba* 9): " 'Behold, it is very good' — this refers to death." As the *Matnos Kehuna* explains, death separates a person from this fleeting world and brings him to the everlasting world, a world in which he can no longer sin.

We cannot see death for what it really is — passage to another life which alone can be called "true life" — because we cannot properly comprehend spiritual concepts. We know that the soul is immortal and that this world is only a preparation for the next, yet we do not properly incorporate this concept into our thinking since we are emotionally involved in the trivia of this world. So too, what we perceive as evil decrees are not so at all. Our physical eyes are simply blinded by our mistaken perceptions.

Our Sages spoke at length in praise of suffering, especially about the fact that suffering expiates sin and saves a person from suffering in the next world. When Ivdan, one of the sages of the Talmud, was punished terribly for a minor transgression, R. Nachman ben Yitzchak responded, "Blessed is Hashem Who shamed Ivdan in this world, and did not shame him in the World to Come" (*Yevamos* 105b).

In asking why evil is decreed for the righteous, or good for the evildoer, we are assuming that we know what constitutes good and bad. We are mistaken. Even in this-worldly events we often discover that what seemed to be a blessing actually caused great harm, and that what seemed to be a tragedy really turned out for the best. This is even truer with regard to everlasting Good and Evil.

ಜ Faith During the Holocaust

In the ghettos of Nazi-occupied Europe, there was an underground group of yeshiva youth whose founder was a young man called Mattisyahu. Born into an assimilated Viennese family, Mattisyahu became a deeply committed Torah Jew, a *ba'al teshuva*, by age 15 — despite the fervent opposition of his father. He eventually left home and came to Poland, where he entered a yeshiva and quickly developed into a budding scholar.

By the time the Germans occupied Poland he had become the leader of a group of young men fervently devoted to Torah ideals. The Germans decreed that all Jewish men had to shave their beards and *peyos*. Jews had to work on Shabbos if they were to get ration cards to buy bread. Mattisyahu told his group that it was a *gezeras haShmad*, an attempt to get Jews to deny their religion.

"You can be sure," he said, "that they intend to kill all the Jews eventually. This is an attempt to take our souls before they take our bodies. We are not going to give in to their demands. We will go underground. We are going to keep our beards and *peyos*, observe Shabbos, and learn Torah until we die. We will dedicate ourselves to serving Hashem fully with the last days of our lives."

They went into hiding. The community secretly supported them with the little food they had, and came to view these young men as a source of pride. Other groups of young men in other ghettos modeled themselves after them. And these groups, wherever they cropped up, were invariably the last Jews to survive, going to their death with their holy books in their hands and with *"Shema Yisroel..."* on their lips.

A diary of one of the last survivors of Mattisyahu's groups was discovered. He describes how he is the last one left in his bunker. Dying of starvation and experiencing tortuous suffering, he writes how he knows that within a couple of hours the fires raging about him will end his life. He knows that according to Jewish law he is allowed to jump into the fire. Nevertheless, he debates with himself whether to jump into the fire and shorten his last few hours of pain or to stay alive until the fires burn him up. As he writes, he is reminded of a story about the plight of a Jew during the Spanish Inquisition.

The Marranos were Spanish Jews who converted to Christianity under threat of death but secretly maintained Jewish law and custom — despite the risk of getting burned at the stake if they were discovered. As the story goes, one aristocratic Marrano family was discovered. Forewarned by a friend that the authorities were coming to get them, they managed to flee, albeit empty-handed and barefooted. They wandered for weeks and weeks until they finally found their way to a refugee camp in Morocco. Conditions there were dire and impoverished — certainly a far cry from the aristocratic lifestyle they were used to — but at least they were with others like themselves.

Then plague struck the camp. Death hung everywhere. One morning, a child of this Marrano family did not wake up. Shortly thereafter, another child died. Soon, all the children died. The parents remained as strong as they could and accepted their fate. Then, finally, the wife died.

When that happened, the husband lifted his eyes to Heaven and said, "Hashem, I know that everything has been a challenge to see if I would stop believing in You and loving You, to see if I would break. What is left for You to try to break me with?

"When they forced us to feign Christianity, we remained dedicated to Your Torah in private. We lived under constant fear of being caught and that did not deter us. Then we had the choice to accept death or flee in order to continue living. We fled. And then you took away one child. We did not complain. And then You took our next child. And still we accepted Your decree. Eventually, You took all the children. And now You have taken away my wife. What else is there for You to break me with?

"As I see it," he exclaimed, "there are only two things left. One is my life and the other is my belief in You. If you want to take away my life, go ahead and take it. It is not mine to begin with; it is Yours. However, if you want to take away my belief in and love for You — that, even You, Alm-ghty, cannot take away. They belong to me — and to me alone."

Now, in a bunker in one of the burning Jewish ghettos of Nazi-occupied Europe, this starved, tortured young Jew recalled the story of the Marrano. He wrote: "When I reminded myself of this story, I reminded myself that these moments of 'confrontation' with Hashem are the most precious moments a person can possess because they allow one to prove absolute love of and devotion to Hashem." It was then that he decided not to jump into the flames prematurely. He turned to Hashem: "In these moments, where there is no hope, and no apparent reason or purpose to live, I know that everything You have done is a test to see if we still love You, to see if we still want Your Torah and mitzvos, if we still believe in You. You fought us. You fought me. But You did not break me. Soon I am going to be consumed by fire. But I will not rush to my death. These last few painful hours You have given me do indeed contain a purpose: to prove to You that even if the life You have given becomes a living hell, it is still the most precious possession because we can use it to tell You that You cannot stop us from loving You. You can test us with anything You like; I promise that I will fight You to the last moment."

Sometimes, it seems like Hashem is fighting us. We want to be good Jews and serve Him and keep His Torah, but everything seems to be working against us. However, we should never despair. Hashem may be engaging us — challenging us — but He does so in order for us to discover the lesson that no power can take away our ability to love Him.

(Reprinted with permission from *Darkness Before Dawn*,
by Rabbi Ezriel Tauber, Shalheves)

The World to Come

One of the most difficult tasks facing people in our era, says R. Shlomo Wolbe (*Alei Shur*, vol. II, p. 302), is developing a firm belief in the World to Come. The Midrash says that the verse "our souls yearned for Your Name and Your remembrance" (*Yeshayahu* 26:8) refers to the World to Come. It is not enough to believe in the World to Come — it must be truly desired. Our Sages describe even the smallest deeds as stepping-stones to this future world, saying: "Who will merit the World to Come? He who does not interrupt between the *Geula* blessing in the *Maariv* service and the *Shemoneh Esrei* prayer directly following." Also, "Whoever recites *Tehilla l'David* [*Ashrei*] three times daily is guaranteed a portion in the World to Come" (*Berachos* 4b). Hence, even with minimal effort, the World to Come is within our reach.

"There is none of Your likeness, *Hashem Elokeinu*, in this world, and there is nothing beside You in the World to Come!" This world is the world of so-called valuables; there are many things that a person might consider to be of supreme value, but only the intelligent person understands that the only true valuable, in the sense of being worthy of praise, is Hashem. In the World to Come, however, there is nothing at all besides Hashem that can be considered of value, since nothing else exists there besides Him. Man receives a share in the World to Come only to the extent to which he clung to Hashem in this world. Although the future is of certain value, we are far removed from feeling a strong desire for it.

The Ramchal writes in the first chapter of *Mesillas Yesharim*:

> Our Sages have taught us that Man was created to derive pleasure from Hashem, to enjoy the radiance of Hashem's Presence, for this is the only true pleasure, and the greatest delight that exists. The place of this delight is actually the World to Come, for it was created and prepared for that very purpose. This world is the path leading to our destination. Therefore our Sages say: "This world is like a hallway preceding the World to Come."

But in Chapter Nineteen the Ramchal writes:

> Although someone who purifies himself solely to merit dwelling in Hashem's Presence along with other upright and righteous people...and to receive his reward in the World to Come cannot be thought of as having an improper motivation, he cannot be considered as having the right motivation either. As long as a person's main concern is his own interests, he is, after all, striving for himself, and not for the sake of Heaven. Instead, the correct attitude towards which truly righteous people strive is to act only to increase Hashem's honor.

The question is obvious: If this latter attitude (that hopes of future reward in the World to Come should not be our sole motivation here in this world) is the proper one, then why did

the Ramchal begin his *sefer* with the axiom that the sole purpose in creating Man was for him to derive pleasure from
Hashem, and that the only place for this pleasure is the World
to Come? How do the two approaches fit together?

The answer is that the beginning of *Mesillas Yesharim* does
not discuss the question of what Man's attitude should be —
it discusses the purpose of Creation. Hashem's purpose in
creating Man was to bestow lovingkindness on him in the
World to Come, a fact we — as servants of Hashem — should
be aware of before we set out on our mission in life.

Why? What would Man lack if he devoted all his energies
solely to self-fulfillment? Eternity. It is crucial for us to know
this if we wish to transcend this temporal world. Imagine:
every thought, utterance, and deed is eternal! Everything remains — either for kindness or retribution — for the World to
Come. Man's portion in the World to Come is determined by
everything he did and said, or even only thought of, in this
world. In that other world, Man is stripped of the external
form given to him for use in this world, and his true, inner
self, whether good or bad, is exposed. A negative core is a
barrier between the person and Hashem; a good core allows
the Divine glow to rest upon him. We are eternal!

> The essence of Man is what we can only describe
> as "I". That "I" is the speaker and the thinker. The
> "I" is lustful, it exerts itself to achieve what it lusts
> for, and it is that which hides in the physical body.
> When the body's powers cease, an event known to
> us as "death," the "I" — now detached from the
> physical world — still lives, and still possesses its
> powers...with the capacity for pain and pleasure,
> good or bad — truly dreadful pain or wondrous
> pleasure.
>
> (*Ohr Yisrael*, chap. 6)

The "I" which feels and experiences pleasure and pain does not cease with death; the "I" is eternal. Likewise, its pleasure is eternal, and, Heaven forbid, its suffering is eternal. Fortunate is the person who weighs and evaluates his thoughts, utterances, and deeds by the standards of the World to Come. The eternity of those deeds will bring him the merit of having Hashem as his eternal heritage.

ৰ Death — A Necessary Passageway to Eternal Life

The Ramchal explains that death is an essential part of eternal life:

> Divine Judgment ordained that, beginning with Adam's sin, nothing, neither Man nor the world, can achieve perfection while still in the same forms which were damaged by sin and which were marked by increased evil. Instead, they must undergo a process of destruction: for Man, death; and for the other corrupted creatures, annihilation.
>
> The soul cannot fulfill its task of purifying the body without first leaving the body. The body then dies and ceases to exist until it is recomposed by the reentry of the soul, which then purifies the body. The same will happen to the world. Its present form will be destroyed, but it will be re-created in a form worthy of perfection.
>
> Therefore, it was decreed that Man die and then return to life. This is the concept of *Techiyas HaMeisim*, Resurrection of the Dead. The world too is destined to temporarily cease and then be renewed. This is the meaning of our Sages' teaching: "The world will exist six thousand years, and it will be desolate for one thousand. At the end of

one thousand years Hashem will renew His world" (*Sanhedrin* 97b).

True reward will be given after the Resurrection, in the renewed world. Man's body and his soul will then enjoy reward, for the body will have been purified by the soul, and will have been prepared by it to enjoy the intended good.

Individuals will, however, still face judgment when the Resurrection takes place. The level and status of each individual will be unequal. It will vary, depending on the amount of effort the person exerted in the world of action — our present world. This will also determine the amount of spiritual light the soul will radiate to the body, when both of them will be elevated and given honor, and both will be worthy of approaching the Master, blessed is He, to bask in His light, and enjoy His true good.

Since death has been decreed for Man, as mentioned above, the bond between body and soul must be temporarily severed until the time of re-unification. It is appropriate that during the period of separation there be a suitable place for each of the two parts. The body thus returns to its element and decomposes. Since it came from the earth, it must return there. This is what Hashem told Adam: "You are dust, and to dust you will return."

The worthy soul need only wait until the completion of whatever must be done to the body. After the body decomposes, remaining in the earth for an appropriate length of time, the body will finally be resurrected when the soul is to reenter it.

The soul, too, must have a resting place for the

interval between death and the Resurrection. It is for this purpose that the World of Souls was created. All the pure souls gather there after they leave the body, and remain there in a state of rest until all judgments passed against the body have been fulfilled.

During that period, the souls are in a state of delight, similar to the delight they will experience at the time of ultimate reward. The soul's position in the World of Souls will be precisely proportional to its accomplishments, just as it will be measured at the time of ultimate reward. True perfection, though, for those who merit it, cannot be attained by either the body or the soul alone — only by the two of them together when they are reunited after the Resurrection.

Besides being a resting place for the soul, the World of Souls benefits the soul — and ultimately the body as well — in another way. The soul can never separate itself completely from the evil, clinging material body; it is always darkened and dimmed by the body. Even though the soul becomes greater and more perfect through the good deeds a person does, this perfection can find no total expression. Its greater radiance cannot be revealed — all remains concealed within until the time arrives for its revelation.

This limitation is the body's fault, not the soul's. The body, since it is only physical matter, can only be purified to a certain degree; the soul loses too, for it is imprisoned and cannot radiate fully. Furthermore, the soul cannot accomplish its task of purifying the body completely.

But when the soul leaves the body and departs for the World of Souls, it expands and radiates in proportion to the individual's actions and achievements in this world. There, the soul regains the strength it lost while in the body, and is better prepared for what it will do after the Resurrection. Upon returning to the body at the proper time, it will be able to fulfill its function, namely, purification of the body.

(Derech Hashem, chap. 3: 9-11)

૨૦ The Bridge Called Life

There is a bridge leading from the womb to the grave. We call this bridge "Life." It begins at a point known as "birth" and ends at "death." The person who walks on this bridge imagines that this is the entirety of life; he has no recollection of his past and he has no idea of the nature of his long future. This person, therefore, has a hard time absorbing the fact that there is life before his birth and after his death. We can assume that if a fetus could think like an adult, it would undoubtedly conclude that the only real world is the narrow one it knows. Thinking that our world is the only world is no less ridiculous.

Let us expand the parable: Imagine unborn twins who had never seen the light of day. One believed the tradition that there is life after the womb. His brother, on the other hand, was an "enlightened" fellow who believed only what his intellect could grasp. The believer told his brother that after leaving the womb they would be born with new life into a spacious world, and that they'd walk upright on a gigantic planet filled with oceans, mountains, plants, and animals, that stars would fill the sky, etc. The unbelieving twin laughed and derided the naivete of his believing brother: "Only a fool would believe such nonsensical lies!

"In my opinion," continued the doubting twin, "the future

is perfectly clear. When we leave this world we will fall into an abyss from which we will never return. We'll be gone forever!"

In the midst of their conversation, their mother's birth pangs began, heralding the end of their stay in the womb. The "earth" beneath the believing brother slipped away and then he was gone. The remaining twin was shocked by the terrible "tragedy" which had befallen his brother. He began to cry. "Alas, my brother! Where have you gone? In your foolishness you believed that there would be a birth, so you didn't even try to hold on to keep from falling into the abyss."

Between his sobs and tears, the unborn twin heard the cries of his brother, who had by now entered this world. "Woe is me! Those must be the final cries of my lost brother!" But while he was mourning his departed brother, sounds of joy filled the delivery room: "Mazal tov! Mazal tov!"

Just as the nine months in the womb are only a transitional period leading to a spacious and breathtaking world, so too, the temporary life of this world is only a passageway to a brighter and more wondrous life in the World to Come. Just as we can understand the enormous difference between the narrow and cramped world of the womb and our own world, so too, we should believe that there is a vast difference between our world and the World to Come.

How great is the expanse of Earth and Heaven! In Heaven's first level alone there are millions upon millions of stars. Can any comparison be made between the tiny world of the womb and the enormity of the universe?

The non-believer in his narrow world of the womb cannot comprehend this. The person of our world, likewise, cannot comprehend anything concerning the life of the soul after it departs this world.

Anyone who thinks that his physical body is the only place life can exist, and who believes that when that body returns to dust, life ceases, is as unknowing and narrow-minded as the non-believing twin in the womb.

Just as the body's departure from the womb is its birth, the soul's departure from the body is *its* birth. Pregnancy is the preparation for worldly life, while life in this world is the preparation for Heavenly life.

Birth, life, and death are interwoven. Birth leads to this world, in which a person prepares himself for his ultimate destination, the World to Come. Death leads a person to the eternal world of true light, for his everlasting benefit. (Based on the first essay of *Gesher HaChaim*, Part III, R. Y.M. Tikuchinsky.)

Resurrection of the Dead

Shlomo Wolbe concludes his discussion of Resurrection of the Dead (*Alei Shur*, vol. II, p. 307) with these words:

Resurrection of the Dead is a very remote concept for us. We feel a sense of shock when we encounter death, because a living person adamantly refuses to believe that he will eventually die, i.e., that he will no longer be within his body, which is how we perceive "life." It takes a great deal of thought and spiritual development to internalize the idea that one's soul will continue to exist in a completely spiritual form with no connection to the physical. After that, a person must come to grips with the difficult awareness that his body will completely disintegrate, leaving not a trace of its previous physical existence. Once the absolute reality of Death is perceived, it is seen to be the complete opposite of physical life as we know it. It then seems to have an immutable finality.

This is where the words of the Prophets can be of comfort. They reveal the wondrous miracle of Hashem's Resurrection of the Dead:

> See now that it is surely I, and there is no god (or force) with Me. I kill and bring to life, I have

smitten and I cure, and nothing can save from My hand.

(*Devarim* 32:8)

Hashem kills and brings to life; He lowers to the abyss and raises up.

(I *Shemuel* 2:6)

Give life to Your dead (those who died for Your sake — Rashi), let my [people's] dead bodies arise; [say to them] "Awaken and sing joyfully, you who rest in the earth," for Your dew is the dew of lights (of Torah), may You throw the evil to the ground.

(*Yeshayahu* 26:19)

He said to me, "Will these bones live [again]?" I said, "Hashem, *Elokim*, You know." He said to me, "Prophesy on these bones and say to them, 'Dead bones, hear the word of Hashem! So says the Lord Hashem to these bones: "Behold, I am investing spirit into you and you will live!" ' "

(*Yechezkel* 37:3-5)

Many of those who sleep in the earth will awaken, some to everlasting life and some to shame and everlasting disgrace. The wise will shine with the brightness of the Heavens, and those who bring righteousness to the many, like stars forever.

(*Daniel* 12:2-3)

The second blessing of the *Shemoneh Esrei* refers to this concept: "Who is like You, Master of mighty deeds, and who is comparable to You, the King Who causes death and restores to life, Who causes salvation to sprout forth." On Shabbos we say in the blessing of *Yotzer Ohr*, Who created light: "No one is comparable to You, our Savior, at the Resurrection of the Dead."

Divine Providence is so vast that G-d knows the number of all those who died, from Adam until the present, and His returning them to life will be with the greatest precision and justice. As we say in the blessing recited at a cemetery: "Who created you with justice, Who fed and sustained you with justice, Who caused you to die with justice; Who in justice knows the sum total of all of you, and Who in justice is destined to restore you to life."

מלך ממית —"Hashem brings death." He takes the soul from a person when the time comes, and מחיה —"He will return the soul as it was in his lifetime." During the body's time in the grave, a person is prepared to return in a purified body to live forever, after having been purified of the contamination caused by his sins. Hashem promised this through the words of the Prophets, and He is נאמן להחיות מתים — "trusted to fulfill His word and return the dead to life."

Since it is difficult for us to envision such a great miracle, Hashem gave us the changing of the seasons as a vivid model. Trees which stand cold and barren during the winter, as if dead, suddenly burst into life when spring arrives. Dormant leaves unfold and flowers bloom. A believer who contemplates the beauty and miracle of this annual rebirth can emerge strengthened in faith in *Techiyas HaMeisim*.

In our prayers, we can best learn to internalize this essential belief when we recite *Elokai Neshama*, which we say in the morning blessings, and in *Atta Gibbor*, during the *Shemoneh Esrei*, which is even clearer and more explicit. We should recite this latter blessing slowly, thinking deeply about its meaning. After reciting it this way over a period of time, a person will be able to feel the results — his faith will be stronger. Then he should intensify his concentration in the same way when reciting *Elokai Neshama*.

🌿 It's a Promise

R. Y.M. Tikuchinsky זצ״ל, *menahel* of Etz Chaim Yeshiva in Yerushalayim, explains Resurrection of the Dead (*Gesher HaChaim*):

> It is the greatest of all the promises the Creator promised them for the time of salvation.
> (R. Sa'adya Gaon, *Emunos v'Deos* 3)

Man has two ultimate ends: One is his personal *ketz*, "end" or "goal," meaning the end of his days on Earth. The second is a communal *ketz*, referred to as *Ketz HaYamin*. The first *ketz* (*ketz hayamim*) comes to each person at his designated time, while the general *ketz* will come at one time, for all of those who merit being brought back to life. This second *ketz* is referred to in the final verse of *Daniel*: "You go to your end [*ketz*] and find rest, and (afterwards) arise to your lot at the End of Days."

Our Sages derived from many verses that the body too will come back to life. The *Zohar* teaches that at the Resurrection of the Dead each person will return with the same soul and the same body he had in his earlier life, but that the soul and the body will then be perfect and possess an understanding which will enable them to perceive everything they weren't able to comprehend when alive in this world. The shape and characteristics of the body will be the same as they were before death, including even the physical blemishes the person had, which will be instantly healed.

The Talmud (*Sanhedrin* 90b) adds that the dead will arise fully clothed: Queen Cleopatra said to R. Meir, "I know that the dead are destined to live again, but will they arise naked or clothed?"

He answered, "We can deduce [the answer to this question] with an a priori deduction from a kernel of wheat. If a kernel of wheat which is buried naked (i.e., planted), sprouts forth with a covering, then the righteous, who are buried in their clothing, will certainly arise fully clothed."

The Rambam (*Hilchos Teshuva*, chap. 9-10, and *Hilchos Melachim*, chap. 12) teaches us about the nature of life after the Resurrection. In his view, those who return to life will return again to the grave, but they will first have a long and peaceful existence, giving them the opportunity to achieve great spiritual heights. Apparently the Rambam equates the time of *Mashiach* with the time of the Resurrection. If so, we must assume that the purpose of the Resurrection of the Dead is to enable people to achieve spiritual levels which could not be achieved in an earlier, physical existence. In the future, when a person's body will be cleansed of its previous spiritual imperfections, he will be able to achieve the greatest heights.

Based on the Rambam's approach, we can suggest the following projection: After a person dies, he receives his punishment in the World to Come and his body decomposes, to be rebuilt again at the time of *Techiyas HaMeisim*. At that time, he will return to the state of Adam Before the Sin, and, while in his renewed body, he will feel a great yearning for Torah and mitzvos. Through this stage he will achieve his level of spiritual completion, and the soul will then depart and rise up to an independent life of endless pleasure.

The Ramban, however, in his *Sha'ar HaGemul*, disagrees. He maintains that the righteous who return to life will live forever. The body and soul will unite for eternal existence as they did for Moshe Rabbeinu and Eliyahu HaNavi. We find in *Tanna d'Vei Eliyahu* that "the righteous whom *HaKadosh Baruch Hu* will resurrect will not return to their graves" (*Sanhedrin* 92a).

In *Pirkei d'Rabbi Eliezer* (chap. 34) we find that there will be Resurrection of the Dead for the righteous among the nations also. The *Tiferes Yisrael* (*Sanhedrin*, chap. 10) seeks to reconcile this with the words of the Mishna: "All Israel has a share in the World to Come." If the nations will be resurrected too, then what is unique about Israel? The *Tiferes Yisrael* concludes that only the righteous of the nations will return, but the evildoers amongst them will go to oblivion after receiving their punishment. Among the Jews, however, even those who committed the most severe sins will not be completely destroyed. Their Upper Soul will remain, and, after receiving dire punishment, their souls will be cleansed and purified to bask in the "Light of Life" and to gaze at the sweetness of Hashem. The Rambam (*Hilchos Teshuva* 3:5) agrees with this.

Man's soul is Hashem's flame.

— Zohar

Understanding Suffering

We begin the study of *yissurim*, pain and suffering, with great trepidation. For the reader who has not experienced suffering, there is the risk of insensitive oversimplification. For the reader who has suffered in the past or is now suffering, we are perhaps too challenging, perhaps making the burden heavier rather than lighter; or, worse yet, implying an accusation against the sufferer who does not or can not reach the lofty and demanding teachings included in this chapter.

However, "these matters are part of our holy Torah and must be studied" — despite our limitations. All of us are obligated to strengthen our faith in preparation for life's ordeals, as we will see in the words of the *Sefer HaYashar*. For those who are currently undergoing trials and tribulations, we pray that they will find herein words of wisdom which will heal, encourage, and comfort.

The material in this chapter is arranged into five groups: passages on the reasons why Hashem brings suffering upon man; our obligation to accept and acknowledge the justice of Divine decree, and the benefits that come from such acceptance; words of inspiration and parables which draw these teachings closer to our hearts and minds; *mussar* (ethical) discourses by contemporary scholars; and reflections by, and for, people who have suffered great tragedies or anguish.

ᕃᕦ This World Is a Place of Hardship

אדם לעמל יולד —"Man was born to toil" (*Iyov* 5:7). Hashem created the world in order to bestow His goodness on man. Yet undeserved gifts embarrass the recipient. Hashem wanted to give man his share in the place of true reward, *Olam HaBa*, the World to Come, not as "bread of shame" (*nehama d'kisufa*), but as an earned and deserved reward. The World to Come can only be earned through the efforts a person makes and the difficulties he overcomes in this world.

Disconcerting events and difficulties that come upon a person, such as: radical changes for better or worse; feelings of being overwhelmed, or conversely, of being raised to prominence; gaining a fortune or losing great wealth; being taken captive; being struck by illness in the family; being exiled from one's country; being imprisoned; or having a friend die — these similar events upset a person's equilibrium and may distance him from serving Hashem.

It is precisely at such times, though, that a person's understanding and wisdom are tested and revealed. If he remains firm in his faith, such changes will not detract from his *avodas Hashem* (service of G-d). In the same way that the most violent storm winds cannot uproot a mountain, so too, no tragic event will be able to dislodge deeply rooted faith.

We should be particularly watchful during such periods, not to forget that our covenant with our Creator is conditional on our acceptance of His service. Everyone is thus obligated to acknowledge his contract and fulfill his commitment. A person needs to prepare himself in advance, so that he will be courageous in acceptance of whatever befalls him. Let him think of painful situations before they come, and anticipate them at all times, while telling himself that if these events do not come now, they will come tomorrow, or at some future time. If one keeps his sights set on the events that may befall him, he will be prepared to accept any eventuality, and will not be distracted from serving Hashem.

Such is the way of the *tzaddik*. He contemplates this world, recognizes it to be a place of hardship, and so always anticipates it. Therefore, difficulties will not frighten nor disturb him when they do come.

Such difficulties will, however, frighten someone who trusts in this world, someone who thinks that no hardship will ever befall him and that his tranquillity will continue always. When he is struck by the opposite of the tranquillity he expects, he will become frightened and lose his clarity of mind, his faith, and his ability to serve Hashem. A wise person must constantly guard his soul and not trust in the invariable goodness of this world. He should know that tribulations are to be expected. Knowing this, he will not fail, and his service to Hashem will endure.

(*Sefer HaYashar*, Gate VI)

Said Rava, and some say it was R. Chisda: "If one sees affliction coming upon him, let him examine his deeds, as it is said: 'Let us search our ways and probe them, and we shall return to Hashem.' If he searched and did not find, let him ascribe it to failure to learn Torah.... If he still did not find, then they are pangs of love, as it is said: 'Whomever Hashem loves He rebukes.' " Said Rava: "Whomever *HaKadosh Baruch Hu* desires, He crushes with affliction.... It is so even if he does not accept them with love.... We learn therefore: 'If you render your soul as guilty — just as guilt is conscious, likewise are afflictions to be conscious, and if he accepts them, what is his reward? He sees children, and lives long. Not only this, but his learning stays with him.... For, as R. Shimon ben Levi said: "Afflictions erase all of a person's transgressions." ' "

Said R. Shimon bar Yochai: "The Holy One, blessed be He, gave three good gifts to Israel but all of them are given only through suffering: Torah, the Land of Israel, and the World to Come."

(*Berachos* 5a)

We find it difficult to accept suffering because we don't appreciate the wonderful rewards of the World to Come, nor do we recognize the seriousness of sin and the great loss it brings. Our Sages in their wisdom saw clearly the rewards and punishments of *Olam HaEmes*, the World of Truth, and often brought *yissurim* upon themselves willingly, because they appreciated their purifying effect.

We, by contrast, assume that we automatically deserve "the good life." At times of misfortune, monetary loss, or illness, we look for someone else to blame — it is always our neighbor's fault, our doctor's improper care, or society's negligence. One result of this attitude is that we have become an increasingly contentious society. Blaming everyone except ourselves, we seek compensation and redress for our misfortunes from anyone and everyone — our fellow citizens, professionals who care for us, society at large, and especially, government. This attitude spills over to our relationship with Hashem. We feel so deserving of constant blessings and good fortune that when Divine Wisdom decrees otherwise, we are full of complaints and bitterness.

R. Hai Gaon quotes an ancient parable which wonderfully illustrates our problem:

A fox was attacked by a hungry lion. Said the fox, "How can *I* satisfy your hunger? I'll show you a big, heavy man. You'll be able to devour him and be satisfied."

The man stood on the far side of a camouflaged pit. When the lion looked at the man he said, "I'm afraid of his prayers — they'll catch me."

Replied the fox, "You and your son have nothing to fear. At the worst, Divine Justice might only catch up with your grandchild. In the meantime, you may as well satisfy your hunger."

The lion was tempted and approached the man, only to fall into the concealed pit. The fox stood at the edge, peering down at the trapped lion. The lion looked up and complained bitterly, "Didn't you say that only my grandson would be punished?"

"Yes," replied the fox, "but you are being punished for the deeds of *your* grandfather!"

Then the lion complained, "Why should it be that if the fathers eat sour grapes, their sons' teeth are set on edge?"

To which the fox retorted, "Why didn't you ask that before?"

It is amazing how little has changed over the centuries. We can easily empathize with the lion's problem. When things are going well, we rarely wonder if we deserve such blessings and good fortune. But when things are not as we would wish them to be, we are deeply troubled — where is the justice?

The struggle was never easy. But in our period of *Ikveisa d'Meshicha*, the footsteps of *Mashiach*, the Divine Presence and His ways are especially hidden, while we experience the particularly difficult trials our Sages foresaw for our era. We seek insight and understanding, a framework in which to relate to Divine Justice, a way to comprehend that which is elusive and beyond our grasp.

Let us travel in the footsteps of our Sages, listening to their words of wisdom as presented to us in the teachings of our Rabbis, from the *Rishonim* to present-day teachers, so that we can better grasp and accept Hashem's ways.

?• Why Does Hashem Bring Suffering?

Is it proper for us even to ponder the question? Should we perhaps accept the Divine decree with blind faith?

The Chazon Ish commented about faith after the Holocaust: "For one who is a believer, there are no questions; for one who is not, there are no answers."

Even after all of our contemplation we will never truly understand the harsh suffering that can befall man. We will be forced again and again to return to simple Faith. Hashem, in His wisdom, knows what is truly good for us. Is there anything to gain from trying to find the reasons for *yissurim*?

We are taught that when suffering comes upon a person, he should examine his behavior, searching for some deed for which his punishment is appropriate. Although our Sages in their wisdom could often find the particular cause of human suffering, we rarely can. Yet it is still a worthwhile obligation for us to study the manner and purpose of every Divine punishment in order to know how to react, how to grow, and how to accept our suffering wholeheartedly. If we understand the purpose of suffering, we are more able to reach the intended goal and maximize the benefit that can be drawn from it.

In the following section we will focus primarily on the original words of the *Chachmei HaDoros*, the great Jewish thinkers throughout history, as they express the reasons they found for the suffering in this world.

As we saw in the above passage from the Gemara, the most common purpose of suffering is atonement for sin. So our first reaction to suffering should be to examine our behavior.

An additional thought, suggested by the Rambam, is that much of man's suffering is self-caused. For instance, many diseases are caused by overindulgence or by self-induced stress. Family difficulties, business losses, and emotional difficulties often stem from a person's own carelessness. Often we question Divine Justice when we ourselves have in fact created our own problems.

Yissurim may also be a "wake-up call" to a person to prompt him to change direction and get back on course. Even though he may not deserve punishment now for previous misdeeds, he still needs a warning to straighten out his path in life.

Another consideration is that adversity brings out the best in a person. We will listen to R. Yerucham Levovitz זצ"ל, famous *mussar* personality and *menahel ruchani* of the Mir Yeshiva, explain why *yissurim* are a prerequisite to receiving Hashem's three great gifts to Israel.

Suffering humbles man, and humility is necessary in order to truly worship Hashem and become nearer to Him.

In the teachings of the Ramchal, we will see that the righteous suffer to expiate the sins of their generation. Thus suffering can be the result of sins not necessarily one's own. He teaches further that suffering sometimes has a hidden place in the Divine scheme of the world.

The Gemara talks of *yissurim shel ahava*, suffering which comes to the greatest of the *tzaddikim* only to demonstrate Hashem's love. We will listen to the dispute between Rashi and the Ramban as to the cause and purpose of such *yissurim*.

Related to all this is the concept of *nisayon*, a test: Hashem tests man's faith by bringing suffering upon him. The person can then be elevated, strengthened in his faith, and worthier of a greater reward.

Lastly, there is the matter of *gilgulim*, the reincarnation of a soul from a previous era into a body in this era. The Chofetz Chaim commented that since the masters of Kabbala have revealed the secret of the existence of *gilgulim*, there are no more doubts on the matter. Man in his suffering may well be rectifying his deeds from a previous life. His soul, before returning to this world, may have even begged to be given certain difficulties so as not to be tempted as it had been in its previous life.

To summarize, we have found ten reasons for *yissurim*:

1. *Yissurim* for personal atonement.

2. *Yissurim* which a person brings upon himself.

3. *Yissurim* as a warning to get back on course.

4. *Yissurim* which cause a person to fully develop his potential.

5. *Yissurim* which develop humility in a person.

6. *Yissurim* which atone for the generation.

7. *Yissurim* which have a hidden role in *Tikkun Olam*, Rectification of the World.

8. *Yissurim shel ahava*, testing a *tzaddik*'s faith in order to increase his reward.

9. *Gilgulim*, suffering in this lifetime to atone for one's deeds in a previous lifetime.

10. *Yissurim* which remove temptation, perhaps even requested by one's soul before its descent into this world in order to be spared from repeating sins of an earlier *gilgul*.

ن‍ Suffering Is for a Person's Benefit

Rabbeinu Yonah explains how we can benefit from suffering:

> Know and understand that the sting of Hashem's rebuke is for a person's benefit. If a person sinned before Him and did evil in His eyes, Hashem rebukes him for two purposes.
>
> The first is to atone for his sins and erase his iniquities, as it says, "See my toil and affliction and remove all my sins" (*Tehillim* 25:18). When Hashem brings ill-health upon him, the sickness of his soul will be healed, for sin is the sickness of the soul, as it is written, "Heal my soul, for I have sinned against You" (*Tehillim* 41:5); and, "Let not the inhabitant say I have become ill, for the people who live in the Land of Israel are acquitted of sin."
>
> The second purpose of Hashem's rebuke is to remind a person to turn back from his evil ways, as it is written, "Only fear Me and accept rebuke" (*Zefania* 3:7). If a person does not accept rebuke, is not humbled by Divine criticism, and does not circumcise the foreskin of his heart, woe to him, woe to his soul! For he has borne suffering, receiving the consequences of his sin, but his sin has not been expiated. Instead, the punishment he de-

serves has been multiplied.

But if a person accepts Hashem's rebuke, begins afresh and improves his ways, then he may rejoice in his troubles, for they have brought him great benefit. He should give thanks to Hashem for his troubles, just as he does for his successes, as it is written, "I lift up the cup of salvation and call out the Name of Hashem" (*Tehillim* 116:13); and, "I encounter trouble and anguish and call out the Name of Hashem" (*Tehillim* 116:3-4). As long as a person feels false tranquillity, none of his sins are atoned for; but through affliction, he becomes beloved by Hashem, as it is written, "Whoever Hashem loves, He rebukes, and like a father does a son, He loves him" (*Mishlei* 3:12; *Sifrei, Devarim* 6:5). The meaning of this verse is that just as a father loves his son and feels pleasure when the child accepts his admonition, so too, Hashem loves the person who accepts his suffering as the loving rebuke it is.

This verse can also be explained as follows: A father will admonish his favorite son, but not the sons he has despaired of, sons for whom he has lost hope that chastisement may help. Of people who do not realize the benefits of admonition it is written, "I have redeemed them and they spoke falsehood of Me" (*Hoshea* 7:1); and, "I have brought upon them suffering and strengthened their arms, yet they think evil of Me" (*Hoshea* 7:15); also, "I have made Efraim accustomed to being carried in My arms, yet they do not realize that it is I Who cured them" (*Hoshea* 11:3).

(*Sha'arei Teshuva* Gate Two, sec. 3-4)

*   *   *

R. Avraham Grodzinsky הי״ד זצ״ל, *menahel ruchani* of Slobodka Yeshiva in Lithuania, wrote: "It is self-understood that if a person understands the purpose of *yissurim* and he examines his ways and repents, then his atonement is incomparable. And with the smallest *yissurim* he can be cured of the greatest sins" (*Toras Avraham*, p. 20).

ಆ Suffering to Arouse Repentance

The Ramchal writes:

> Suffering may befall an individual in order to prompt him to examine his behavior and motivate him to repent. This is particularly true in the case of a righteous person who may have committed some few sins, or in the case of a person whose sins are balanced by good deeds.
>
> Such suffering, however, is not the same as that discussed earlier, which was an atonement for sin. What we are speaking of now are sufferings meant to motivate a person and awaken his heart to repent.
>
> Punishment was only created to exist in the absence of repentance. What G-d truly desires is that man not sin in the first place, and if he does sin, that he should repent. If a person does not repent, though, he can still be purified through these punishments and thus not be annihilated completely.
>
> Suffering, therefore, initially comes to an individual to motivate him to repent. If this is not effective, then he must also undergo further suffering to purify him of his sins.
>
> (*Derech Hashem*, Part II, sec. 15)

The *Menoras HaMaor* teaches us an additional benefit from *yissurim*: "At times Hashem brings *yissurim* to the righteous person for his benefit, in order to increase his righteousness."

This is further explained by the *Derashos HaRan* as quoted by the Shela HaKadosh:

> In times of tranquillity, a person doesn't evaluate his affairs with complete truthfulness because of the power of fantasy which is part of human nature. This confuses a person, constantly drawing his thoughts towards worldly pleasures. But when he is beset by difficulties, his fantasies cannot entice him in this way. He therefore comes to clearly recognize the truth and he seeks Hashem, not just to escape his difficulty, but with all his heart and soul, for this is the natural inclination of the intellect when it is not distracted.

In other words, man's physical urges usually rule over his thoughts. But in times of difficulty, his desires are weakened and his thinking becomes straightforward, since that is its true nature (because "Hashem created Man straightforward" [*Koheles* 7:29], but physical desires usually influence a person's thinking).

Our Sages tell us that, "Whoever pleases Hashem is burdened with suffering by Him." The *Noam Megadim* explains that a *tzaddik* whose behavior is just, is worthy of being a dwelling place for the Divine Presence, as it is written, ושכנתי בתוכם —"I will dwell among them." There are, however, various factors which make this impossible, among them an imperfect sense of humility and lack of subservience to Hashem. In order to perfect the humility of such a *tzaddik*, Hashem humbles him through suffering. He can then become a dwelling place in this world for the Divine Presence.

Hashem also brings suffering to one who is not a *tzaddik*

for a similar reason. *Yissurim* create humility in a person, and humility draws him closer to Hashem. It is no wonder then that Hashem burdens His People with the yoke of exile (*galus*) and the struggle for a livelihood, since independence and wealth bring people to haughtiness, which distances them from subservience to Hashem.

❧ *Yissurim* Which Atone for the Generation

"From the suffering of his soul, he will see and be sated..." (*Yeshayahu* 53:11). Based on this verse, our Sages commented that the outstanding Torah scholar of the generation bears the sins of his generation through private suffering of which only Hashem is aware. About this the verse concludes: "he will bear their sins."

The Ramchal explains this concept:

> When Supreme Wisdom considered everything needed to rectify human failing and lead Man to perfection, It saw that said goal would be furthered if some could benefit others and help them attain their place in the perfected human community.
>
> The rule that the community of the Future World be restricted only to those who attained perfection in their own right is therefore not absolute. For it was also decreed that an individual can reach a level where he can partake of perfection and be included in this community as the result of his association with a more worthy individual.
>
> As a result of this principle, suffering and pain may be imposed on a *tzaddik* as an atonement for his entire generation. This *tzaddik* must then accept such suffering with love, for the benefit of his

generation, just as he accepts the suffering imposed upon him for his own sake. In doing so, he benefits his generation by atoning for it, and at the same time, is himself elevated to a very great degree, since such a *tzaddik* is endowed with leadership in the community of the World to Come.

(Derech Hashem, Part II, chap. 3)

❧ *Yissurim* for *Tikkun HaOlam*

The Ramchal now explains a similar type of *yissurim*:

All this involves a *tzaddik* who is stricken because his generation is about to be annihilated and would be destroyed if not for his suffering. In atoning for them through his suffering, this *tzaddik* saves them in this world and greatly benefits them in the World to Come.

Within this same category, however, there is a class that is even higher than this. There is suffering that comes to a *tzaddik* who is even greater and more highly perfected than the ones discussed above. This suffering comes to provide the help necessary to bring about the chain of events leading to mankind's ultimate perfection.

According to the original plan, the sequence of worldly events required that man undergo at least some suffering before both he and the world could attain perfection. This was required by the very fact that one of the basic concepts of man's predicament was that G-d should hold back His Light and hide His Presence. This became all the more necessary as a result of the corruption and spiritual damage caused by man's many sins, which held back the good even more and caused

G-d's Presence to become all the more hidden. The world and everything in it are therefore in a degraded, evil state, and require that G-d's unfathomable wisdom bring about numerous chains of events to achieve their rectification.

Among the most important elements of this sequence is the requirement that man be penalized for his wickedness until the requirements of the Attribute of Justice are met. G-d arranged matters, however, so that select, perfect individuals could rectify things for others. The Attribute of Justice then acts upon them, rather than upon the world in general.

However, individuals such as these are themselves perfect, and hence deserving of good. The only reason they suffer is because of others. Thus, the Attribute of Justice must be as satisfied with minimal suffering on their part as with the maximal suffering of those who actually transgressed.

Furthermore, the merit and power of these *tzaddikim* are also increased because of such suffering, giving them an even greater ability to correct the damage caused by others. They can therefore not only rectify their own generation, but can also correct all the spiritual damage done from the beginning of things, from the time of those who first sinned.

It is obvious that individuals such as these will ultimately be the foremost leaders in the Perfected Community and the ones who are closest to G-d.

(ibid.)

The Gemara tells us that if a person examines his deeds and finds no sin which could be the cause of his *yissurim*, he can assume that they are *yissurim shel ahava*. Rashi explains:

"Hashem causes one suffering in this world, without any sin [on his part], in order to increase his reward in the World to Come beyond the merit of his own good deeds." Thus, according to Rashi, a person who has not sinned can in fact experience *yissurim*.

The *Beis Elokim* ("Gate of Repentance," chap. 9) illuminates Rashi's thought: Rashi (*Berachos* 5a) explains that Hashem brings *yissurim shel ahava* to a *tzaddik* not solely because of sin, but in order to increase his reward in the World to Come beyond the merit of his actions. This is difficult to understand. How can the suffering that Hashem brings upon a blameless individual be an expression of His love? If Hashem loves the *tzaddik* and he is completely righteous, would it not be better to reward him?

The matter can be explained like this: The purpose of the creation of Man in this world is that he should perfect himself by doing the Will of Hashem — through the study of Torah and the fulfillment of its commandments — so that he can attain life in the World to Come by choosing the Good. This was the purpose of the giving of the Torah — that Israel might perfect itself through study and fulfillment of the Torah. But there exist those among the righteous who yearn to do the Will of Hashem beyond what they are commanded. They see Torah and mitzvos as little compared to their love of Hashem and their intense desire to fulfill His Will. Accustomed to being totally engaged in service of Hashem, they no longer feel any difficulty or struggle in Torah. Their innermost longing is to serve Hashem, and no amount of effort is too great for them.

Hashem then sees that they cannot find ways to fulfill their great desire to elevate themselves to greater perfection through fulfillment of mitzvos, because so many of the commandments do not apply in differing times and circumstances. So, since Hashem does not withhold the Good from those who seek it, He brings suffering to such *tzaddikim*. They realize it is coming from Him solely for their benefit, so that their service of Hashem may require greater exertion; that way, they will be able to fulfill their desire to serve Hashem ever more fully. They will then perfect themselves in this world to the utmost of their ability, thereby earning a higher status in the World to Come, beyond what they could have achieved had Hashem not brought *yissurim* upon them.

The Ramban (*Sha'ar HaGemul*) quotes a number of sources to disprove Rashi's opinion. The Gemara relates that one day four hundred barrels of R. Huna's wine turned to vinegar. His friends suggested that he examine his deeds. He replied, "Am I suspect in your eyes of any wrongdoing?" They replied, "Is Hashem suspect of giving punishment without reason?"

Similarly, we find that when R. Eliezer underwent suffering, his student R. Akiva comforted him, saying that his suffering would atone for his sins. Although R. Eliezer seemed to be without sin, R. Akiva nevertheless quoted the teaching that "there is no righteous person on earth who does only good and does not sin at all."

In neither of these cases was the possibility considered that there could be suffering without any sin whatsoever, contrary to Rashi's opinion.

The Ramban defines the meaning of the term *yissurim shel ahava* as follows:

If a person is a complete *tzaddik*, having never transgressed any prohibitions nor having failed to perform any positive commandment, his suffering is surely *yissurim shel ahava*, intended to assure perfect reward for him in the World to Come.

But if *yissurim shel ahava* are designed to atone for sin, why should such a person suffer? Because these *yissurim* come to atone for acts of *shogeg*, sins committed unintentionally. Suppose a person ate *chelev* (prohibited fats) unintentionally. He is considered to have sinned. His sin is his lack of watchfulness over transgressing Hashem's words. For one should never act without first ascertaining the permissibility of what he is about to do in view of Hashem's decrees. This is why the Torah considered inadvertent transgression a sin. Furthermore, whatever is prohibited soils and defiles the soul.

Nonetheless, although a *shogeg* who unthinkingly transgresses doesn't deserve the full punishment of Gehinnom, he does need to be cleansed and purified of his unintentional sin so that he may be worthy of his proper place, based upon his good deeds, in the World to Come. Therefore, Hashem was merciful with His people, enabling them to offer *korbanos* (sacrifices) in the *Beis HaMikdash*, to atone for unintentional sins. When the *Beis HaMikdash* does not exist, Divinely ordained suffering cleanses from unintentional sins, so that the righteous can be utterly pure in the World to Come. Just as *korbanos* are expressions of Hashem's love and mercy, so too, are these *yissurim* expressions of Hashem's love and mercy for Man.

&❧ Suffering for Physical or Spiritual Benefit

At times, Hashem ordains lesser *yissurim* to save a person from the harsher *yissurim* which might otherwise befall him.

R. Yosi HaGalili expounded (*Nidda* 31a): What is meant by the verse "I thank You, Hashem, because although You were angry with me, You turn away Your anger and comfort me" (*Yeshayahu* 12:1)? The verse refers to two travelers. A thorn stuck in the foot of one of them and he began to curse and blaspheme because he could not continue his journey. Later, he heard that his companion's ship had sunk at sea. He then gave thanks and praise. Thus, "You turn away Your anger and comfort me."

As R. Elazar explained: What is meant by, "He Who does wondrous things alone, blessed be His glorious Name forever" (*Tehillim* 136:4)? That even a person who is granted a miracle is often unaware of his miracle.

About this the Ramchal writes:

> In truth, Hashem never despises His creation nor does He desert the world. When Hashem seems to have deserted the world, He is actually doing the opposite; He is renewing goodness in the world. His wondrous thoughts are then directed only to the betterment of the world and not to its ruination. However, He deeply hides His counsel; at such times the world appears abandoned by Hashem and people suffer punishment for their sins.
>
> (*Da'as Tevunos* 14:6, p. 18)

Similarly, we find in *Midrash Rabba* (*Bereishis* 91:10): Yisrael said [to his sons], "Why did you do evil to me?" (*Bereishis* 43:6). R. Levi said in the name of R. Chama bar Chanina, "Yaakov never spoke in vain except here. *HaKadosh Baruch Hu* said, 'I am busy enthroning his son over Egypt and he says, "Why did you do evil to me"!' About this it is written, "my path is hidden from Hashem" (*Yeshayahu* 40:27).

All the time Yaakov suffered over his son Yosef's absence, Hashem was forging the chain of events that brought Yosef to the throne, so that Yaakov could live in tranquillity. But because it was deeply hidden counsel, Yaakov was beset by pain and grief. This teaches us the lesson that any elevation and improvement, to an individual or to mankind, is preceded by a period of preparation for that elevation, which is marked by hidden counsel. Pain will precede the great event in making.

❧ "Man's Soul Is Hashem's Flame"

The *Mishpat Tzedek* explains:

> Know that if a person accepts *yissurim* with love, then such suffering cleanses, purifies, and sanctifies him in great degree. The *Zohar* explains that the soul is compared to an oil lamp: "Man's soul is Hashem's flame." When an oil lamp does not burn as it should, it is moved about and shaken until the fire catches properly. Similarly, when sin darkens the soul's light, Hashem brings suffering upon a person to stir him. When he finally accepts his sufferings as they were intended, his soul lights up and shines even more brightly.

Yissurim often come to test whether or not a person will question Hashem's conduct. Although Hashem discerns our innermost thoughts and knows in advance if we will pass the test, He still tests us, in order to bring the matter from potential to actual, and in order for others to recognize and learn from an individual's greatness.

Hashem tests only those He knows will pass the test, as it is written, "Hashem tests the righteous." Our Sages compare this to a potter who strikes his pots to test their strength. He only tests the strength of those pots which appear to be strong, never testing those he fears will break from the blow.

The *Likutei Yekarim* offers a beautiful parable: When a father wishes to encourage his child to walk, he distances himself from the child a step or two. Then, when the child totters those few steps to reach his father, the father withdraws a few more steps. By going further away each time, he encourages his son to walk.

Hashem wants us to develop ourselves in His service and not to remain stationary, as it is written, "Praiseworthy is every

G-d-fearing person who *goes* in His ways." The goal of man's *avodas Hashem* is not for him to remain at a given level, but that instead, through Torah study, observance of mitzvos, and perfection of character, he should rise to ever-higher levels of closeness to Hashem. To help man achieve this, Hashem occasionally distances His Divine Providence from people, and punishes them with the hiding of His Countenance. This brings them to examine their deeds and improve their ways.

The further Hashem distances Himself — like a father encouraging his child to walk — the more people will develop the humility which can bring them closer to Him.

‫‎ Trials and Suffering Uplift Man

There is double meaning to the word *nisayon*, trial, according to the Chofetz Chaim (*Chofetz Chaim on the Torah*, *Devarim* 8:16). In addition to the simple meaning — that Hashem tests man — the *Zohar* explains that the word also connotes exaltation, as in "Raise up a banner (*nes*) unto the nations" (*Yeshayahu* 62:10).

The two meanings complement each other, since a person who withstands a test develops his potential and is thus raised up. This sheds light on the verse: "In order to afflict you and in order to test you (*nasosecha*) for your ultimate good" (*Devarim* 8:16). The affliction is a test intended to see if the Jewish people are whole in their service of Hashem, so that they can be uplifted and exalted over the nations.

Hashem acts on this principle in every generation and with each person. When He wants to raise up a person to a higher spiritual level, He first tests him: "*HaKadosh Baruch Hu* does not raise a person to greatness without first testing him" (*Midrash Rabba Bereishis*). We find in the Gemara (*Bava Basra* 10b) that R. Yosef, the son of R. Yehoshua, heard in Heaven that no person can stand in the presence of the Martyrs of Lod, who sanctified Hashem's Name with their deaths. Their test raised them to unreachable heights.

This is true not only when a person gives up his life, but also for any pain or suffering which he undergoes for the sake of Hashem. His position in the World to Come is thereby greatly elevated, as we learned (*Berachos* 5a): "*HaKadosh Baruch Hu* gave three good gifts to Israel, and all of them were only given through *yissurim* — Torah, the Land of Israel, and the World to Come."

It is worthwhile to realize, concluded the Chofetz Chaim, that the days a person serves Hashem in pain and hardship are credited to him forever and that his name will be remembered for the good because of them; it is considered as if he did *chesed*, kindness, unto Hashem. This is reflected in the verse, "I remembered the kindness of your youth, the love at your wedding, when you followed Me in the desert, in an uncultivated land" (*Yirmiyahu* 2:2).

❧ Hashem's Judgments Are True When Taken All Together

Sometimes a person complains about his misfortunes, especially when poverty or ill health befalls him. He wonders: Where is the justice in Hashem's acts? Why do I suffer misfortune even though I try to do the Will of the Alm-ghty, while the wicked live in comfort?

The Chofetz Chaim (*Chofetz Chaim on the Torah, Devarim* 32:4) derived the answer to the question from the verse in *Tehillim* (19:10): משפטי ה' אמת צדקו יחדו —"The judgments of Hashem are true, *together* they are just." The Chofetz Chaim explains as follows: As is well known, Yom Kippur cannot atone for sins between man and his fellowman unless he has placated the aggrieved party. If a person insulted or berated his fellowman or if he struck someone and did not ask for forgiveness, he can have no atonement. Thus, his soul could be forced to return to this world in a *gilgul*, another incarnation, in order to correct his misdeed.

When a person stands before the Heavenly Court and hears the decree that he must return to this world, he cries bitterly over the sin that caused him such a punishment. In his despair, he mourns the fact that he was given wealth and good fortune in his earlier life, claiming that it was those very circumstances which bred the arrogance to insult or strike his fellowman. He begs in vain that he not be forced to return to the lower world.

When he realizes that Divine Wisdom has decreed that he must return to this world, he beseeches the Alm-ghty that at least he should be created in his new *gilgul* as a lowly pauper, or with some physical deformity or illness. He hopes these conditions will guarantee that he won't act with the arrogance of his earlier life. The Heavenly Prosecutor argues that if his soul is not given wealth and stature again, he will not be able to properly repair his earlier misdeeds, because of his changed circumstances. It is only after much prayer and pleading, accompanied by the intercession of his defending angels, that the soul's request is granted and the person is born as a pauper, handicapped, or a *ba'al yissurim*, someone constantly afflicted with suffering.

This is a fitting answer to people's complaints about the misfortune and suffering which fill their lives. It is possible that this very person who now decries his hard lot begged his Creator to give him suffering to humble his heart, so that he should not again mistreat his fellowman. Perhaps he had to plead fervently before the Heavenly Court that he be created with a physical deformity so that he would not come to strike another person.

This is the meaning of "The judgments of Hashem are true; *together* they are just." When are the judgments of Hashem just? When they are taken *together*. When all the circumstances of a person in this world are taken together with what happened to him before he was born, then it becomes clear that the judgment is true and that his poverty and suffering are actually to his benefit.

True Justice

R. Akiva says, "Do not do unto Me as others do in their lands: When goodness comes upon them, they bless their gods...and when misfortune comes upon them, they curse their gods. But you, when I grant you goodness, give praise, and when suffering befalls you, give praise. As King David said: 'I raise up the cup of salvation and proclaim the Name of Hashem; I encounter misfortune and sorrow and I proclaim the Name of Hashem.' As Iyov (*Iyov* 1:21) said: 'Hashem gave, Hashem took, may the Name of Hashem be blessed for now and forever.' When Iyov's wife said to him [sarcastically] (*Iyov* 2:9): 'Bless Hashem and die,' he answered her, 'The generation of the Flood, who were vulgar in good times, received their punishment against their will. Shouldn't we, who behaved properly in good times, behave properly in times of punishment?'

"Furthermore, one should be even happier with *yissurim* than with good fortune, for if one has good fortune his entire life, his sins are never forgiven. What causes his sins to be forgiven? We must say: only *yissurim*."

(Mechilta Shemos 20:20)

૨ે Acceptance of Divine Judgment

In enumerating the positive commandments which can be fulfilled daily using thought and emotion alone, with no physical action required, the *Sefer Chareidim* counts the following mitzva: To accept the justice of Divine Judgment in every event involving oneself, one's children, or one's property, as is written: "Know in your heart that just as a man punishes his son, so too Hashem your G-d will bring suffering on you" (*Devarim* 8:5). A person should incorporate this into his being, and bow his head and be silent, as it says: "And Aharon was silent." He should not regard himself as righteous before G-d [and hence not deserving of punishment]. Nor should he say it is a chance occurrence, for then Hashem will act towards him with the 'fury-of-chance.' Instead, let him examine his deeds and repent.

This is a fundamental aspect of the mitzva "Love Hashem your G-d *b'chol meodecha*," which the Sages interpret as *b'chol mida u'mida*—"with each and every measure He brings upon you" (*Berachos* 54a), whether for good or for suffering. It is written, "For kindness and for judgment I give song," meaning that if Hashem acts with kindness, I will sing, and if He acts with strict judgment, I will *also* sing (ibid., 60b).

Our Sages said: About those who are shamed but do not respond in kind, those who hear themselves vilified and remain silent, and those who act out of love of Hashem and rejoice in their suffering, it is written: "Those who love Him are like the sun's emergence at its strength" (*Yoma* 23a). For behold, He loves us, as it is written: " 'I loved you,' says Hashem." The tribulations He brings upon us are precious to us because they are all for our benefit. It is written: "The wounds inflicted by a friend are trustworthy" (*Mishlei* 27:6). Also: "Your rod and Your staff will console me" (*Tehillim* 23:4).

⁓ Hashem Helps Us Endure Suffering

The Skulener Rebbe, R. Eliezer Zisya Portugal (1896-1982), was known throughout the world for his boundless *ahavas Yisrael* (love of his fellow Jews). He and his wife personally adopted close to 400 children after World War II and took care of their needs, both physical and spiritual. The following story was heard from the Rebbe:

As a young man in Rumania, the Rebbe encouraged both young and old alike to come closer to belief in Hashem. He encouraged young men not to enter the Rumanian armed forces, for to do so would irrevocably tear them away from the paths of Yiddishkeit. Instead, he exhorted them to attend a yeshiva where they would be involved with Torah studies, a move which would assure them of remaining true to the traditions and heritage of their forefathers.

One day someone reported to the Rumanian authorities that a certain R. Portugal was instructing youths on how to avoid being drafted by the army. When the authorities checked into the matter, they found that the allegations were indeed true. In a fury, they arrested the Rebbe and had him imprisoned. The police put him into solitary confinement, took away his yarmulke and glasses, and left him alone in a dark, dirty cell. The Rebbe was a frail, sickly man, and now in the cold and damp dungeon — where the only place he could sit or rest was on the chilly, moist earth — he though that his end was near.

From the cell he had very little contact with the outside

world, nor had he any idea how long he would be there. The authorities had threatened that they would leave him there forever. He wanted to *daven*, but he had no head covering, so he took the jacket that he was wearing, pulled it up over his head, and began to sing aloud the prayers that he knew by heart.

It is known that the Rebbe's *Shacharis* could at times take up to four hours, and his recitation of *Shema* during a weekday *Maariv* could take up to twenty-five minutes; thus, on a regular basis he was always meticulous with every word of the prayers, and in this extraordinary situation he was even more so.

There in prison, with no other matter to claim his time or attention, he would recite the *Shacharis* service. Every word was uttered with heartfelt emotion, every phrase pronounced with piercing passion. The Rebbe came to the prayer of *Baruch She'amar*. This particular prayer begins with a series of phrases in which we bless various aspects of Hashem.

The Rebbe concentrated on each phrase as he never had before: "Blessed is He Who spoke, and the world came into being; Blessed is He Who speaks and does; Blessed is He Who decrees and fulfills (*gozer u'mekayem*)." As the Rebbe uttered this last phrase, a question occurred to him. Why was this particular phrase mentioned here? It seemed out of context with this whole prayer. For the term *gozer*, decrees, usually signifies an edict of a harsh nature, and not desirable to man. Moreover, we say that He not only makes decrees, but He even fulfills them! The Rebbe was puzzled, because all the other phrases in this prayer seem to describe positive aspects that man would rejoice over....

Suddenly the Rebbe became annoyed with himself. The question about the phrase belonging in this text was so obvious, why hadn't he thought about it before? For years and years he had been praying this prayer daily, and not once did the thought occur to him that *gozer u'mekayem* seemed out of place. Why hadn't he thought about it before?

He became despondent, for he felt that perhaps until now he had not been praying with the proper focus on the words of the prayers that he was saying every day. He said to himself, "I am not moving from this place until I figure out why that phrase is there."

He kept repeating the phrase, trying to force an answer into his head. And then, after a very long while, it came to him! He became ecstatic! He was simply overjoyed, because now he felt that he understood why *gozer u'mekayem* actually did belong in this prayer.

The word *kayem*, aside from meaning fulfill, also means to exist and endure, prevail and persevere. And that is what is meant here, thought the Rebbe. Sometimes Hashem must decree something against man. He must make him suffer, for whatever reason Hashem deems it necessary. But at the same time, Hashem gives man the power and strength to endure and prevail, to enable him to come through this decree and withstand it. And that is what is meant in the expression *gozer u'mekayem*.

The Rebbe realized that he himself, at that moment, was the victim of a decree. But he was positive from that moment on that he would also be *mekayem*, one who has endured the decree. He no longer was depressed. He was positive that it was only a matter of time until he would be saved, and indeed, within a few short days, at the intervention of people on the outside, the Rebbe was released by the Rumanian authorities.

The Rebbe was so touched by this episode that every year on the yahrzeit of his release from that prison he would recount this incident and explain to all his listeners the new and encouraging meaning he found in the words *gozer u'mekayem*. He would thus impart to all who listened never to be broken by events, for Hashem, even in His decrees, gives strength to His people. (Reprinted with permission from *Around the Maggid's Table* by Rabbi Paysach J. Krohn, Artscroll/Mesorah Publications.)

❧ Accepting the Decree Shields from Suffering

If the sinner is beset with hardships and trouble, and he justifies the punishment accorded him and accepts the chastisement with good will, this acceptance will serve to protect him from the many afflictions which, by right, he deserves. As is written: "I will give thanks unto You, O L-rd, for although You were angry with me, Your anger is turned away and You comfort me" (*Yeshayahu* 12:1). This means: I thank You for Your chastisement and accept it with love, and because I thank You for Your anger against me, Your wrath is diverted and You comfort me.

Similarly, in connection with gratitude for favor bestowed, it is said, "I will thank You forever because of what You have done and in the presence of Your pious ones I will hope in Your Name, for [it is] good" (*Tehillim* 52:11). That is, I will thank You for the kindness You have done for me, and because of this, I will hope for the continuance of Your kindness. As it is said, "I will lift up the cup of salvation and call upon the Name of the L-rd" (ibid. 116:13). "I found trouble and sorrow, but I called upon the Name of the L-rd" (ibid. 116:3-4).

Our Sages have said in reference to the verse "A Psalm of David, when he fled" (ibid. 3:1), "Justice enacted is joy to the righteous" (*Mishlei* 21:15).

It is a trait of the righteous to discharge their debt and sing to the Holy One, blessed be He. This is analogous to the situation of a tenant farmer who, when in debt to his landlord, collected the grain for threshing and put it into a pile which the landlord appropriated. When the farmer returned home empty-handed, but happy, he was asked, "You left your threshing-floor empty-handed, yet you still rejoice?" He answered, "True I leave empty-handed, but the bill has been paid — my debt has been discharged" (*Midrash Tehillim* 79:2).

A man must reflect and realize that the hardships he encounters and the afflictions he suffers are unequal to the severity of his transgressions and the multitude of his sins, but that the Blessed One, in His pity, chastises him as a father does his son. It is written: "Contemplate the following thought: Just as a father chastises his son, so too, the L-rd your G-d chastises you" (*Devarim* 8:5). "Your heart knows the deeds you have done and the afflictions I have brought upon you, and knows that I have not afflicted you in proportion to your deeds" (*Yalkut Shemos, Yisro* 303). "Know therefore that Hashem exacts less of you than your iniquity deserves" (*Iyov* 11:6); and, "You, our G-d, have punished us less than our transgressions deserve" (*Ezra* 9:13).

(*Sha'arei Teshuva*, Gate Four, sec. 12-13)

There are two dimensions to all of G-d's dealings with us: the revealed, and the concealed. The revealed dimension is reward and punishment; the concealed is the deep design always inherent in all of His deeds which guide Creation to universal perfection. There is no deed, great or small, whose ultimate end is not universal perfection, as stated by our

Sages (*Berachos* 60b): "All that is done by Heaven is for the good," and by the prophet (*Yeshayahu* 12:1): "Your wrath will turn back and You will console me." In the future, *HaKadosh Baruch Hu* will reveal His ways to all of Israel, showing how even chastisement and tribulation were precursors of good, and preparation for blessing. For He desires only the perfection of His creation, and does not totally repel the wicked. On the contrary, He refines them in the crucible of perfection to cleanse them of any impurity. It is this intent which characterizes every act of His towards us, whether for good or ill.

One should know, though, that all of G-d's deeds are awesome, infinitely broad and deep, as Scripture states (*Tehillim* 92:6): "How great are Your deeds, O L-rd." The very smallest of His deeds contains such endless wisdom that it can never be fully comprehended, as it is written (ibid.): "Your thoughts are exceedingly profound." G-d's acts, then, are ultimately incomprehensible to us. Only their surface layer is perceived, while their true core remains hidden. That inner core is thoroughly good, and contains no evil. Now it is impossible to understand this concept, but in the future we will at least realize that everything emanates from Hashem's profound plan for our ultimate benefit (*Da'as Tevunos*, p. 81, Feldheim).

❧ The Ways of Hashem Are Tests for Man

The Master of the Universe prepared profound designs for the perfection of the world...and He set forth two paths: the path of reward and punishment, and the path of *mazal*, independent of Man's free choice or merit. The choice is His. At times He applies one system and at times the other, whichever is better for His world. When He uses the system of reward and punishment, everything that happens is based on patterns of reward and punishment. When He uses the system of *mazal*, everything that occurs will be based on the system of *mazal*.

This will create greater merit for the righteous. If G-d would bring suffering only to the righteous, it would be a test, but not such a difficult one, for their suffering would be proof of their righteousness. Anyone with any sense would choose such suffering. But Hashem wanted the test to be even greater, so that people would not be able to understand how He is acting with each of us. This is why it appears that "All things come alike to all; the same fate awaits the righteous and the wicked..." (*Koheles* 9:2).

This matter is explained in the Midrash: "King Solomon gazed throughout time for generations to come and saw that what would happen to evildoers would also happen to the righteous..." (*Yalkut Shimoni, Koheles* 989). This is done in order to give even greater reward to the righteous whose faith remains strong, as is written: "The righteous person will live because of his faith" (*Habakkuk* 2:4).

It is therefore impossible for anyone to be certain about anything G-d does with him, since at times He acts through reward and punishment and at times through *mazal*, as has been explained. There is no one who can judge an experience and determine whether what is happening to him is directed through the system of reward and punishment or through *mazal*. Every event can be viewed either way, which can lead to emotional and mental turmoil. A person who is faithful to Hashem has no choice but to implant his belief so firmly that it cannot be budged. He must know that every one of Hashem's actions, no matter in what situation, is absolutely fair, trustworthy, and just. He should never react like the evil people who say, "Hashem's way doesn't make sense." Instead, he should be on guard to serve his Creator wholeheartedly, no matter what He measures out to him. Only then will he be called genuinely wholehearted.

G-d's Judgments Are Unfathomable

"Your righteousness is like the mighty mountains, Your judgments are like the great abyss. You, Hashem, save Man and beast" (*Tehillim* 36:7).

When R. Dovid Auerbach, ל״צז, Rosh Yeshiva of Sha'arei Shamayim Yeshiva, sat *shiva* for his son who was tragically killed by a bomb blast in Yerushalayim, he explained the verse this way:

It is possible and desirable to contemplate and analyze Hashem's acts of kindness in order to reach deeper levels of appreciation and in order to praise Him more fully. So, "Your righteousness" is like the awesome mountains people gaze at and contemplate, appreciating their majestic beauty, while "Your judgments" are like an abyss — if a person stands at the edge and stares down, he can become dizzy and fall into the depths.

Torah law limits mourning to "three days for crying, seven days for eulogy, thirty days for not washing clothes or cutting hair." Excessive focus on Hashem's wrath can cause a person to lose his spiritual bearings, since he will be unable to comprehend. Instead, a person should try to fulfill the conclusion of the verse: "You, Hashem, save Man and beast" (*Tehillim* 36:7), about which our Sages commented, "This refers to people who are wise in understanding but make themselves simple like a dumb beast" (*Chullin* 5b). A person must return to the simple faith of knowing that all that happens is Divinely ordained, fairly and justly.

Hashem Is Compassionate

In a letter of consolation written to a mourner, R. Simcha Zissel Ziv, the Saba of Kelm, discusses the brevity of suffering proportional to eternity. He prefaced his words with allusions to a number of personal hardships which made it difficult for him to write. At those times of personal difficulty, he found encouragement in the verse in *Eicha* (3:22) which says: "The kindness of Hashem has not ceased, for His compassion has not failed."

We read in *Yeshayahu* (54:7): "For a small moment I have left you, but I will gather you in with great compassion. With an outpouring of wrath I hid My Countenance from you for a moment, but with everlasting kindness I will have mercy upon you."

All of the exiles, enslavement, and persecutions of thousands of years are seen as nothing more than a fleeting moment in which Hashem did not hate us, but merely turned away from us. Hashem hid His Presence from us like a friend who momentarily hides his face, though he does not for a moment cease his watchful caring.

Hashem says that He is with us in suffering, although He does not then reveal His Presence. Even though He hides, He still remains with us and shares in our suffering.

In contrast, "I will gather you in with great compassion." We are promised in the prophetic vision that the mercy and blessing which will accompany the Redemption will be so great that all of the millennia of suffering will seem insignificant by comparison. This is the meaning of the prayer: "Bless us with a revealed and shining Countenance," not just with the "Presence" which guards over us.

If centuries of suffering, which seem so awful and so endless to us, are described as fleeting, how terrible then must be the suffering which befalls those who descend to Gehinnom! The Ramban teaches us that all of Iyov's suffering adds up to less than one moment in Gehinnom.

From this perspective, how accepting a person should be with the *yissurim* of this world, as compared with the much more horrible suffering of the World to Come!

One should certainly intend that his suffering not be like "the illnesses I placed upon Egypt" (*Shemos* 15:26). The Egyptians did not grasp the fact that their illnesses turned into even greater punishment when they ignored the Divine rebuke. One should follow our Sages' advice (*Berachos* 5a): "If a person sees that *yissurim* befall him, he should carefully examine his deeds."

"When Hashem presses man to his limits, He is only saying, 'Return, you sons of man' " (*Tehillim* 90:3).

Let us see to it that our sicknesses and tribulations do not become like the plagues of Egypt, which brought even greater suffering. Let them instead fulfill their purpose, to arouse us to return to Hashem, "For I am Hashem your Healer" (*Shemos* 15:26).

The Torah Teaches True Compassion

The following halachic question recently arose: A woman expecting her first child became deathly ill. The baby could only be saved through an operation which might shorten the mother's life. Unquestionably, the mother, who had already lost consciousness, would have preferred to shorten her own life by some hours or days in order to give birth to her only offspring.

This painfully difficult halachic-ethical question was brought before leading halachic authorities, whose ruling was unequivocal: Even if the mother had expressly agreed to the operation, it would still not be permissible to save one life by shortening that of another. Those who had asked the question found it difficult to accept and understand the decision. Wouldn't it be better to leave behind a living remembrance of the mother if it were only at the cost of a few moments of her life?

R. Yitzchak Zilberstein שליט״א, a leading authority on

medical halacha, refers to this ruling in an essay on halachic ethics which sheds light on the matter:

R. Chaim Vital, a disciple of the Ari HaKodesh, writes (*Sha'ar HaGilgulim*) that if a person could open the Gates of Heaven and perceive the deepest secrets, he would see the benefit that comes to him from his difficulties. When it was revealed to Iyov that he was a reincarnation of Avraham's father, Terach, he immediately became silent, since he saw that his mission was to repair the spiritual damage of Terach's idol worship.

The Midrash tells us that when the Jews in Egypt could not produce their daily quota of bricks, it was decreed that their small children be built into the walls to make up for the missing bricks. Who could bear the heartbreak of such a horrible and cruel decree? And yet, "what is hidden from us is revealed to Hashem."

The Midrash goes on to tell how Moshe Rabbeinu prayed and pleaded with Hashem to rescind this evil decree. In response, Hashem instructed him to save one of the children and see what would come of his future life. Moshe immediately saved a child who had already been mortared into a building. Years passed, and the child, named Micha, grew to adulthood. At the time of the Exodus, Moshe Rabbeinu went to fulfill Yosef's brothers' oath to bring his bones out of Egypt. Since he didn't know the location of Yosef's coffin, Moshe threw a gold plate inscribed with the words *alei shor*, into the Nile. When Yosef's coffin rose up together with the gold plate, Micha picked out the plate and took it with him.

What did Micha do with this gold plate? When Moshe was late in descending from Mount Sinai, the people came to Aharon, demanding that he make them a graven image. In order to delay the people, Aharon told them to collect a large amount of gold. As soon as they threw the gold into the fire to forge it, Micha threw in that gold plate, thus creating the Golden Calf.

We have here an incredible chain of events. How awesome were the results of the mercy that saved Micha when he was a baby! At Mount Sinai, the Jewish people reached the level of Adam in Gan Eden, and were free from the Angel of Death. When they worshipped the Golden Calf and caused Moshe Rabbeinu to break the Tablets of the Law, Death returned to the world. Countless other evil decrees befell us as a result, and we are taught that this sin is the partial cause of every calamity to befall the Jewish people throughout its history. To this very day, we suffer the results of the sin of the Golden Calf and the misplaced compassion that made it possible.

This provides an insight into the hidden mysteries of the world. No evil decree in the world contradicts G-d's feelings of mercy and compassion. No one is more merciful than Hashem. Our limited insight and awareness make this truth impossible for us to comprehend. But if we could discover the root cause of evil decrees, we would see clearly that all of Creation is enveloped in Hashem's kindness: "The world is built on lovingkindness" (*Tehillim* 89:3).

Since this world of kindness was created for the sake of the Torah (Rashi, *Bereishis* 1:1), the halacha does not alter the world for its purposes, but instead, it defines the essential nature of the world. "*HaKadosh Baruch Hu* peered into the Torah and created the world." In the case of the unborn fetus the halacha that we must not cause the death of one life to save another applies. It is a Heavenly decree that the soul of this baby should not enter the world and that its purpose in Creation was fulfilled in its mother's womb. This soul was sent down for only a brief period. Once it has fulfilled its designated task, it returns to its Maker. There is no reason for misplaced compassion or pangs of conscience.

"For What Should the Living Grieve?"

When a man whose son had died refrained from crying, people asked the Radvaz if it was proper or improper for him to act that way. He wrote in response, "This is an evil trait which shows hard-heartedness, bad character, and cruelty...."

Instead, he should have grieved and lamented. He should feel remorse for his behavior, as it is written, "For what should the living grieve? A man for his sins" (*Eicha* 3:39). Crying, mourning, and shedding tears for one's relatives, and certainly for worthy people, is the way of the pious, the Prophets, and the righteous. This indicates purity of soul and humility before the Creator. Furthermore, one should grieve over his sins and mourn the actions which caused him punishment.

In *Sefer HaYashar*, Rabbeinu Tam writes similarly that if a person is unaffected by the death of a fellow Jew, there is something wrong with his soul. And if, on the contrary, he is concerned and worried, this is a clear sign that he has a good soul.

There are those who are unconcerned when they are punished from Above. They claim that people should accept everything joyfully, so they exhibit only joy and happiness. But this is a complete lie, since it is a great obligation to react earnestly at such times. The main purpose of Hashem's punishments is to humble a person's heart, so that in humility he might worry over his sins, and examine his deeds. As our Sages teach us, "If a person sees *yissurim* befalling him, he should examine his deeds" (*Berachos* 5a).

I Thank You for My Suffering

It is told about R. Zerach Braverman, זצ"ל, Yerushalmi *tzaddik* and student of Maharil Diskin (*av beis din* of Brisk), that he suffered terrible *yissurim* in his final years. In those days, he was heard to say, "Master of the Universe, I thank You for my suffering, for without *yissurim* it is impossible to face judgment at the Heavenly Court."

Those present asked him, "Didn't the Sages of the Talmud say, 'Neither *yissurim* nor their reward'?" To which he replied, "They could afford such a luxury, but I cannot."

Parables

R Chaim Volozhin was a student of the Vilna Gaon and founded Volozhin Yeshiva. In *Ruach Chaim*, his classic commentary on *Pirkei Avos*, R. Chaim says that the phrase "Hashem is my shepherd" is an exemplary expression of true and perfect faith. A person with faith in Hashem is like a sheep in the flock of a caring shepherd. Sheep are blissfully calm, sensing that their shepherd is fully concerned with their safety and well-being. So too, if a person has faith, he casts his burdens on Hashem, Who will surely provide for all of his needs. As King David said, "Hashem is my shepherd." He is to me as a shepherd who grazes his flock, therefore, "I will lack nothing."

Sheep cannot understand their shepherd. Sometimes they think it is smarter to look for better pasture somewhere else, yet their shepherd keeps them where they are. Other times, the sheep may feel their present place is fine, but their shepherd forces them to move on to a place he knows is better for the flock. Although the shepherd's only concern is the welfare of his flock, the sheep in their ignorance do not see the wisdom of his actions.

Similarly, a person often thinks he would be better off in a different place or in a different set of circumstances, but he is forced by Divine Providence to remain where he is. Other times, although he thinks his present place or situation is ideal, he is forced to move. King David continues: "He lays me down in lush pasture, He leads me beside still waters." The place where Hashem causes me to remain is truly "lush pasture" — the best place for me. When He forces me to move, it is to a place that is truly "still waters" — the place where I can find inner peace and tranquillity.

At times a person is struck with suffering that seems purposeless, with no ultimate benefit. The verse continues: "Even when I walk in the valley of the shadow of Death" — even when I am beset by terrible suffering — "I will not fear evil" — even what seems to be absolutely evil. Though a person may need suffering to purify him, in order to remove the barrier between himself and Hashem, he will not fear troubles or misfortune, because "You are with me," i.e., the trials and misfortune make it possible for You to be with me.

The Divine traits of Mercy and Judgment both bring consolation. They are compared to sticks: Mercy's pleasant staff of support, and Judgment's difficult rod of punishment are both for the good — they both bring me consolation so that I can accept everything that Hashem brings upon me, with love.

ও We Never Walk Alone

There was once a man who was continually stricken with illness and troubles. Whenever he was struck by misfortune and felt alone and forsaken, he would lift his eyes to the One Above and ask: קלי למה עזבתני —"My G-d, why have You abandoned me?"

One night he dreamed that he was walking on a very long path. When he looked back, he saw two sets of footprints, but in some places, where the path narrowed, only one set could be seen.

As he contemplated the way behind him, he realized that this path was actually the path of his own life. Starting with his birth, he passed through his childhood, youth and middle age, finally reaching his old age. Upon this path he had traveled through life with Hashem accompanying him and lighting up his way. He saw the various periods of his life on this road, the good times where the path became wide, and the trying times where it narrowed. It seemed as if Hashem had been beside him only in the good times, but that in his difficult periods, he had been forced to make his way alone. At this, he cried out bitterly, "Oh, my G-d, why did You abandon me? Why did You leave me to travel alone at my most difficult times? Those were the times when I most needed Your support!"

Suddenly he heard a voice gently say, "My beloved son, you are mistaken. Yes, in difficult times the path becomes quite narrow and you seem to be walking alone, but actually, the opposite is true. At those times there is no need for a broad path, for then I do not walk beside you — I carry you. Please realize that at those times when you feel most forsaken, I am really closer to you than at any other time."

The man woke up from his dream a changed person. He learned to rely on Faith to help him shoulder his troubles, repeating always, "Even when I walk in the valley of the shadow of Death, I fear no evil, for You are with me."

◈ "I Call upon Hashem"

In *Yeshayahu* (1:5) it is written: "For that which you have been stricken, you still continue to revolt; every head is sick and every heart is faint." We can explain this as follows:

When Hashem inflicts punishment on the world, people will continue to sin if they view the punishment as a random event rather than a purposeful punishment. This is the meaning of the prophet Yeshayahu's statement: "You still continue to revolt." Because people see others suffering hardships similar to their own, they delude themselves into thinking that their own behavior has nothing to do with their punishment. But the truth is that Hashem gives similar punishment to everyone who has committed a similar transgression.

In this vein, we can explain the verse: "When I encounter troubles and sadness, I call on Hashem," recognizing that my misfortune comes from Him and is not a chance occurrence. (*Mishpat Tzedek*)

ᏸ Sand Castles

The verse says: "A widow and a stranger they kill, and orphans they murder, yet they say, 'Hashem does not see and the G-d of Yaakov does not perceive' " (*Tehillim* 94:7-8).

The *Kli Yakar* explains that people come to deny Divine Providence when they see that although the wicked oppress the righteous and the meek, Hashem does not avenge their misdeeds. The answer to this seeming paradox can be illustrated with a parable:

A child built a sand castle and his playmate came and destroyed it. The child was furious and heartbroken over the destruction of his project, and went crying and screaming to his father. His father realized the true value of the sand castle and was not very upset. When the child saw his father's calmness, he cried even louder, this time because he felt that his father was forsaking him. The child's mistake was in his perception of the sand castle as having true value.

This mundane world is our sand castle, where what seems

to be good may not ultimately be good, and where apparent evil may also not really be so. When the oppressed cry out to Hashem over the injustices they suffer, Hashem does not always respond. The verse therefore continues: "Understand, you fools among the people. When will you acquire wisdom? Does not He Who implants the ear hear? Does not He Who fashions the eye see?" In truth, "Hashem knows the thoughts of man, that they are emptiness."

Certainly there is Divine Providence, but Man lacks the proper perspective with which to evaluate events. All too often what seems, by earthly wisdom, to be a great misfortune is seen from Heaven's view as nothing but the destruction of a sand castle. Since we lack proper insight, we cannot understand why Hashem at times seems indifferent to injustice. This is why we are unable to accurately recognize the nature of Divine Providence in every aspect of life.

❧ Suffering Is a Kindness from Above

"Just as one utters blessing over the bad, so should he utter blessing over the good" (*Berachos* 54a).

How can a person honestly give praise and thanks for his hardships? Isn't it human nature to resent the hand that strikes one?

The *Be'er Mayim Chaim* (*Chukas*) describes four types of suffering, all of them beneficial. The least harsh type of suffering is comparable to the treatment of a skilled doctor who uses painful methods to cure a deathly ill patient. A thinking person will feel deep appreciation for his doctor's care. Although there was searing pain, the patient can only express deep thanks for the saving of his life.

Healing the illness of the soul is often similarly painful. Although Hashem is the source of all kindness and created the world solely in order to bestow goodness on His creations, He is also the ultimate Healer of all souls. When man's coarse physical nature overpowers his spiritual soul, by pursuing physical desires, his ability to receive Hashem's abundant spiritual light and blessings is diminished. In order to help him, Hashem in His great kindness brings bodily suffering to cleanse and elevate the person's physical nature. This way, man's evil nature can be subdued, letting his good nature — his intellect and the powers of his *yetzer hatov* (his good inclination) — rule over him. Once this has been accomplished, the person's capability to receive Hashem's holy light will be increased.

In fact, the kindness Hashem shows us when He accords us *yissurim* is greater than when He bestows good fortune. When a person is in travail, the *Shechina* (the Divine Presence) suffers with him, as it says: "In all their suffering, He suffers." Since Hashem afflicts a person with misfortune even though He Himself, as it were, also shares the suffering, it is clear that He does so only for the person's benefit. In His benevolence, He is even willing to bear anguish and bring suffering upon Man, for Man's ultimate good.

In contrast, this aspect of Hashem's kindness is not found when He bestows good fortune upon a person, because then there is no element of Divine pain or anguish. This is the meaning of the comment on the verse: "And Hashem saw all He had done and behold it was *tov meod*, very good." *Tov* refers to the trait of beneficence, while *meod*, means "extremely so," and refers to the trait of bringing suffering. Hashem's kindness is even greater when He brings suffering upon people, since it includes this element of Divine suffering. Also, when a person suffers, he feels a heightened awareness that Hashem is only chastising him as a cure, so that he may again be worthy of mercy and kindness.

One who understands and believes deeply that suffering

is intended only to heal Man will forever grow in his love of Hashem and in longing for "the G-d Who is Good and does good to the evildoer and the righteous." When King David perceived fully that all worldly trials are mercy and lovingkindness, he said: "I said that the world is built on *chesed* (lovingkindness)." For even the traits of judgment and retribution were created for the sake of kindness and beneficence.

❧ Suffering in This World Saves Us from Suffering in the World to Come

A person should not complain about his troubles in this world. In this connection the Chofetz Chaim (*Shem Olam*, chap. 3) quotes a midrash: Since Yitzchak knew the magnitude of judgment in the World to Come, he asked for *yissurim* in this world, to alleviate the severity of future judgment. Hashem answered, "[I swear] by your life that you have requested a good thing, and I will start with you," as it says, "When Yitzchak grew old, his eyes became dimmed."

The Chofetz Chaim writes in the name of the Vilna Gaon:

Were it not for *yissurim*, we could not stand in the World to Come. This may be explained as follows: When a person dies, his soul ascends and stands before a scale that weighs his deeds to ascertain whether his merits outweigh his misdeeds or, Heaven forbid, the opposite. As the soul stands there, a *bas kol* (a Heavenly voice) calls for all of his merits to be weighed. The voice is heard throughout Heaven, and all the angels created of his good deeds gather to the right side of the scale. The Heavenly voice then calls all the iniquities of the deceased to come forth. In response, troops of angels of destruction in black gather to the left. It becomes clear that the latter angels tip the scales towards condemnation; not only because they are more numerous, but rather because the person's merits are often weak, since his mitzvos were lacking in sincerity and joy, while his sins were committed with desire and excitement.

The soul is shattered when faced with such irrefutable evidence, evidence that marks him as a *rasha* (a sinner), whose place is in Gehinnom. As he stands in agony, another Heavenly voice calls forth: "Where is all the suffering this person underwent in his lifetime?" Immediately, all the pain and misfortune of a lifetime gather to be weighed together with the merits. The scale then tips to the good. As a result of his suffering, many of his sins were counterbalanced, and he is found deserving of entry into Gan Eden. Now, the person under judgment looks back at all his suffering and thanks Hashem for all that befell him.

❧ Suffering Is Our Teacher

The Vilna Gaon used to deliver a *mussar* discourse to his disciples late Shabbos afternoon. Once he mentioned that although people think that the description of Gehinnom found in the *Reishis Chochma* is exaggerated, they are completely mistaken.

One of the Gaon's students took his teacher's words very much to heart. He became depressed and even dangerously ill. When he had recovered, he went to the Gaon and described his illness, saying that if he had not recovered, his teacher would have been responsible.

When the Gaon heard this, he stood up to his full height and said, "I repeat — what is written there is *exactly* so. I do regret, however, not mentioning one point which, had you heard it, you would not have taken ill. What would I have said? That if a person realized the power this-worldly *yissurim* have to diminish punishment in the future world, he would not hesitate to take upon himself the suffering of Iyov for his entire lifetime."

We may learn from this comment how positively a person should react towards the suffering and troubles that befall him. The word *yissurim* is related to the word *mussar*, so we can say that a person who is beset by *yissurim* is being given *mussar* (rebuke) from Heaven to mend his ways. Suffering redeems a person from his genuine, ultimate problems. (Recorded by the son-in-law of the Chofetz Chaim.)

❧ Think of the Reward

"Recall the days of the world" (*Devarim* 32:7). [Moshe] said to them, "Whenever Hashem brings suffering upon you, recall how much benefit and consolation He is destined to give you in the World to Come."

(*Yalkut Shimoni* on that verse)

The Maggid of Vilna explained this midrash with a parable:

A Jew rented a house from a nobleman for three hundred rubles per year, which he paid on a certain date every year. The nobleman once traveled abroad, leaving an unscrupulous official in charge of the estate. This official was an anti-Semite who leaped at the opportunity to cause trouble for Jews. He immediately raised the rent to five hundred rubles. When the date of payment arrived, the official appeared at the Jew's home early in the morning and demanded full payment. The tenant had only four hundred and eighty rubles, so he requested a few days' delay to get the remaining twenty rubles. However, the wicked official refused to wait even a single day. When night fell and the twenty rubles had not yet been paid, the vicious man decided to whip the Jew with twenty blows, one for each ruble.

He did the same thing to a number of other Jews, finding various ways to cheat and steal from them. In time, he became wealthy and bought himself a large estate.

When the nobleman returned home, the Jew who had been beaten went to tell him about the lashes he had been given by the official. The nobleman was on good terms with his Jewish tenants and became furious at the corrupt official. He decreed that the Jew would receive one hundred rubles compensation for every blow he had received — a total of two thousand rubles. Since the official's property was worth four thousand rubles, the Jew was given half his estate as payment for the abuse he had suffered.

When the Jew returned home from his audience with the nobleman, his wife saw that he was upset. When she asked how the nobleman had treated him, he showed her the deed for half of the official's property.

"This is wonderful!" she exclaimed. "Why do you look so upset? You should be overjoyed with the valuable gift we received!"

"The pain of the blows I received is long since gone," he answered. "Now I wish the official had given me *forty* lashes, instead of only twenty — that way I would now own his *entire* estate."

We too will feel that way about all our suffering in this fleeting world. When a person is struck by misfortune, his suffering feels unbearable. But when he goes to the future world, where the payment is in eternal currency and where he receives great reward for every hour of suffering in this world, he will think to himself, "How I wish I had suffered many more *yis-*

surim in the lower world! Then I would now be receiving so much more genuine reward here in the Eternal World."

❧ Hashem Cares for Us Like a Father

Occasionally we feel that Hashem's treatment of the right-eous is unjust, Heaven forbid. When we see a G-d-fearing, righteous person suffering poverty, begging for food or clothing, we often wonder, "Is the hand of Hashem too weak to provide for this person's needs? Why does he have to ask for charity?"

The Chofetz Chaim offers us a story to calm our anxiety:

The only son of a wealthy person became extremely ill. The local doctors could find no cure for his sickness. His father spent a fortune to bring specialists from afar to cure his one and only beloved son. Finally, one of the doctors succeeded in restoring the child's health. Before he left, this expert doctor warned the father that the child must not eat any fatty meats, since doing so could bring back his sickness.

Some time later, the boy's father had to travel away on business. Before he left, he gave explicit instructions that his son not be given any of the forbidden fatty meats. But one day while the family was eating dinner, the boy grabbed a piece of the delicious-smelling meat from the table, stuck it in his mouth, and ran out.

His illness quickly returned and by the time his father came home, the boy was hovering between life and death. The father immediately summoned the specialist from abroad in the hope that he could again save the boy's life. The doctor once again worked day and night and finally restored the child's health. Then and there, father swore that he himself would guard the child and never leave him in the care of others. And so he did.

Months later this wealthy man made a feast for his friends and relatives. The tables were piled high with all sorts of delicacies. When the guests sat down to the feast, the boy came in to join them. When the father saw his beloved son go near the food, he ran over and chased him out. The guests looked at each other in amazement over the father's "cruelty" in not allowing the boy to partake of the feast. No one but the father knew that his supposed "cruelty" was really for the boy's own good.

Hashem is like the father in the story. At times He distances righteous people from the illusory wealth and good fortune of this world, and others seeing this are confused. But we are different. Even if we do not understand His actions, we still believe wholeheartedly that all of Hashem's dealings with the righteous are for their benefit. We know Him as "the Rock, His actions are perfect," for all His ways are just; He is a trustworthy G-d, without injustice; He is righteous and fair. The Holy One, blessed be He, knows that 'poverty is becoming to Israel' and we should not complain about His actions" (*Chofetz Chaim on the Torah*, Devarim 32:4).

❧ The Blow Itself Is the Consolation

R. Isser Zalman Meltzer ל״צז, the exceptionally brilliant and respected Rosh Yeshiva of Slobodka and later of Etz Chaim Yeshiva, used a parable to explain the verse (*Tehillim* 23:4): "When I walk in the valley of the shadow of Death, I will not fear evil, for You are with me. Your rod and Your staff, they will console me."

A father and son traveled through a dense forest. When they entered the forest, the father explained to his son the dangers of being lost in a forest and warned him to remain by his side at all times. At first, the child was very careful never to let go of his father's hand. But after a while, something caught his attention and he wandered off to the side of the path. His father continued on his way, and when his son next looked for him, the father was nowhere to be found.

The child became frightened and cried. He began searching for his father in the dense forest. Night fell, bringing with it terrifying darkness. The air was filled with the eerie screeches of birds and the frightening sounds of wild animals. The boy was petrified.

Suddenly he felt a sharp pain on his cheek. Before his cry left his throat, he realized that the sting came from a slap from his father. Instead of crying out in pain, the child shouted with joy. "Father!"

When a person sins, his situation is similar to the child's. He has distanced himself from his Father in Heaven and feels frightened. So too, when he feels the sting of suffering, he should realize that it comes from his Father in Heaven Who has come close to punish him for having strayed far away. As the beloved son of a concerned and watchful Father, he will feel happiness at the blow.

❧ Seven Herbs for Health

This section of the will of R. Avraham, the father of the Shela HaKadosh offers invaluable advice:

Your souls should always be humble and you should utter blessing for all that comes upon you. Do not "kick" in response to *yissurim*. Instead, accept them, and admit the truth of Divine Judgment, as our Sages say, "The very way a person blesses the good, so too, should he bless the bad." He should feel the same joy about the bad decree as he did for the good. King David said: "Whether I am treated with kindness or with strict justice, I will sing His praise" (*Tehillim* 101:1).

Our Sages interpreted the words in the Shema: *b'chol meodecha*, "with all your might," as: *b'chol mida u'mida* — with whatever measure He treats you," give Him appreciation.

It is a positive commandment to acknowledge the right-eousness of Divine Justice, as it is written, "You should know in your heart that just as a person punishes his son [to educate him] so too, Hashem punishes you." Further, if after a person has repented, his situation in life is not as good as it was before, it is a mitzva for him to realize that the decline in his fortune has happened for his benefit. The *Chovos HaLevavos* writes: "Someone saw that his friend's foot was wounded and he commented, 'I pity you for the wound on your foot,' to which his friend responded, 'I am grateful to my Creator that He did not wound my eye.' Someone else said, 'If I were sick, I would not try to become healthy, and if I were in the sun, I would not try to get into the shade; instead, my desire is to be where Hashem wills me to be.' Loving Hashem's judgments and giving thanks for all that befalls us, as did Nachum Ish Gamzu, is a pillar of Faith."

Note the fact that Avraham was judged to have passed his ten tests by virtue of his cheerful and good-natured accep-tance of them — all the praise he received was for this accep-tance. For this Hashem called him אהובי —"my beloved," and נאמן —"faithful," as we say: ומצאת את לבבו נאמן לפניך —"You found his heart faithful before You."

A wise man has said, "It is improper for a person to be bothered by what he has lost, but he must guard what he still has." In *Sar Shalom* it is written: "It is unworthy for a person to worry or be overly crushed by misfortune. For the misfor-tune that befalls a *tzaddik* in this world is for his benefit, in order for him to merit the World to Come. If he accepts his misfortunes with love, they may disappear after he has re-ceived only a small part of them. But if he doesn't accept *yissurim* with love, then his suffering will become even worse, and all his pain and worry will neither help him nor save him from further misfortune. If a person 'kicks back' and rejects his *yissurim*, they will multiply and remain with him even longer. Therefore, a person should habituate himself to saying, 'Everything Hashem does He does for the good.' "

A story is told of a wise doctor who fell into disfavor with a king. He was jailed in a narrow cell, locked in chains with an iron yoke around his neck and dressed in uncomfortably coarse wool clothing. His daily food was bread made of barley, a bit of salt, and a pitcher of water. The jailers were instructed to eavesdrop on him, but he remained absolutely silent. His friends and relatives were allowed to visit him in the hope that he would let down his guard and complain about his treatment. In their conversation, they commented on the horrible conditions he suffered in jail, his hunger, thirst, and great physical discomfort. But what amazed them was his physical appearance. How did he look so fresh and radiant?

"I have taken seven herbs," he told them, "and mixed them into an elixir from which I take a small drink every day, and my strength is revived."

His friends pressed him to divulge the secret formula of the elixir so that they too might use it in time of need.

"The first herb," he answered, "is Faith in G-d, Who can save me from the worst pains and difficulties. He can save me from my present situation and from the hands of the king, for 'as streams of water is the heart of a king in the hands of G-d; He turns it wherever He wishes.'

"The second herb is Hope and Yearning. These are good traits for one who is surrounded by misfortune, so that he not be overcome by his difficulties.

"The third herb is the knowledge that my sins are the cause of my suffering, as it is written: 'For your sins separated you from your G-d,' and our Sages say: 'There are no *yissurim* without sin.' I have brought this upon myself. How can I complain?

"The fourth herb: If there is no hope, what then can I do? If it has been decreed that I should die before my time, so be it.

"The fifth herb: my awareness that Hashem's punishment is for my benefit, in order to cleanse my sins in this world so that I may merit the World to Come, as is written: 'Fortunate is the man who You, Hashem, chastise.' I am therefore happy in my suffering, and with this happiness, I bring benefit to myself and the entire world; as we have learned (*Ta'anis* 8a): 'R. Yehoshua ben Levi said, "One who rejoices in the *yissurim* that befall him brings salvation to the world." '

"The sixth herb: I am happy with my lot and give thanks and praise to Hashem, for my troubles could be much worse. Although I am now suffering in iron chains, it could be worse. My jailers could punish me with flogging or some other torture. I am given barley bread as my only food, but I could be given nothing at all to eat. I am given just a small amount of water, but that too could be withheld. I am given stiff, coarse woolen clothes to wear, but I could have been left here completely unclothed.

"Furthermore, there are *yissurim* that grow steadily worse, as we find: 'In the morning you will say, "would that it were last night," and in the evening you will say "would that it were morning." ' The curses of *Tochacha* in this portion of the Torah describe suffering that becomes ever worse, so that people yearn for the suffering of yesterday which was less than that of the present. Thus, I am happy that my situation here remains the same and does not deteriorate and destroy me.

"The seventh herb is my knowledge that ישועת ה' כהרף עין — 'Hashem's salvation comes in the blink of an eye.' He is gracious and merciful, patient in judgment, abundant in kindness and truth, and reverses His evil decree. He can deliver me from my suffering and cure my ills."

R. Avraham concludes this section of his will with the

charge: "Every G-d-fearing person should accept Hashem's punishment cheerfully, for it redeems his soul and enables it to enter the World to Come. Let him have faith in his Creator, Who surely chooses the best for Man. And let him cast his burdens upon Hashem and have faith in Him at all times."

❧ His Creation Is Flawless

In the *piyut* of the ten martyrs put to death by the Romans, recited during the cantor's repetition of *Mussaf* on Yom Kippur, we say, "The Heavenly angels cried out bitterly, 'Is this Torah and is this its reward?' A voice from Heaven responded, 'If I hear another sound, I will turn the world into water, to void and emptiness.... This is a decree from before Me; accept it, you who delight in the Torah.' "

How can we understand this verse? The explanation has been given in a parable: A rich nobleman wanted to wear a special cloak for a banquet he was giving for his friends and neighbors. He bought an expensive bolt of cloth and gave it to the Jewish tailor who lived on his estate to make him a garment. The tailor put in his best effort and succeeded in creating an unusually beautiful cloak. When the nobleman wore the cloak to his banquet, everyone present commented on its beauty and fine tailoring.

A guest jealous of the honor given to the Jewish tailor went over to his host and pointed out that the cloak was smaller than the original bolt of cloth — the tailor must have kept the extra cloth for himself. The nobleman called the tailor and demanded the left-over material. The tailor answered that there had been nothing left over, and proceeded to explain patiently how the extra cloth had been used in the lining and various folds of the cloak. The nobleman was unconvinced and continued to demand the rest of the material.

Finally, the tailor asked to be given the cloak in order to prove his innocence. The nobleman took off the cloak and gave it to the tailor, who began to undo the stitches. The nobleman was outraged and shouted, "Why are you destroying my cloak?!"

The tailor answered, "I see that you do not understand and you still suspect me, so I decided to take apart the garment in order to show you exactly how all the material was used."

In the same way, Hashem said to the angels, "If you do not understand my decrees and you ask, 'Is this the reward for Torah?' I will return the world to its original state. Then you will see the chain of events since Creation and you will understand how everything is considered and flawlessly ordered."

✦ The *Ger Tzedek*

Count Potozki, who converted to Judaism and became the famous *ger tzedek* in the Vilna Gaon's time, was forced to flee from the wrath of church officials in Vilna. After spending some years in Holland, he returned to Ilya, a small town near Vilna. In appearance and dress he was by now like any other of the Jewish citizens of the area and he hoped to spend a quiet life engaged in Torah study.

But his anonymity was short-lived. A youthful informer discovered his previous identity and informed church officials of his return to the area.

He was immediately arrested and jailed in Vilna's central prison, where he was given the choice of returning to Christianity, or being burnt at the stake. Although the Vilna Gaon sent word to the *ger* that he could intercede in Heaven to save him, the *ger tzedek* responded that he preferred to die *al kiddush Hashem* (in Sanctification of the Divine Name).

The Christians, infuriated by his stubborn loyalty to the

Jewish religion, taunted and tormented him. Even as they were preparing to kill him, they mocked him, saying, "In this world, we are taking revenge against you; do not think that in the World Above you will be able to take revenge against us."

The righteous *ger* responded to their taunts with a story: "When I was a child I used to play with the peasants' children on my father's estate. Once I made a small army of clay soldiers and set them up in the garden. My playmates, those peasant children, came, and with their coarse boots, trampled the toy soldiers to dust. With tears in my eyes, I ran to my father and told him of my 'terrible tragedy' and asked him to punish the children severely. Instead, my father rebuked me, saying that since I was more intelligent than the other children, I should realize how unimportant those little toys were. At the time, I thought to myself that although I was powerless to take revenge immediately, I would be able to do so when I grew up.

"Do you think," he continued, "that when I grew up I even considered avenging myself? After all, what did those foolish children really do? They only broke pieces of clay and trampled mud — nothing more! Do you think, then, that when I will arrive in the World of Truth my mind will be occupied with thoughts of revenge against you? In your foolishness, you are burning my flesh and bones, which are in fact only dust of the earth!"

What the *ger tzedek* had to say about the lowly informer is even more striking: "If I will have any merit in the World to Come, I will not rest until I succeed in bringing the informer to the life of the World to Come, for he caused me the great fortune of being burnt alive *al kiddush Hashem!*" (Based on *V'Ohavav k'Tzeis HaShemesh b'Gevuraso*).

❧ No Matter How Hard It Is

When the Chofetz Chaim read *Shir HaShirim*, he would ponder the verse, "The guards who go about the city found me, they struck me and wounded me, they took off my precious scarf, those guardians of the wall. I put an oath upon you, the daughters of Jerusalem, if you find my Beloved, what will you tell Him? That I am sick with love." The Jew constantly suffers blows; even the so-called guardians of peace strike and wound him. He is besmirched, insulted, and cursed at every turn. Nonetheless, he does not budge from his love of Hashem. The Jew is bound with love to Hashem and he offers blessing for the evil as he does for the good.

In this verse, King Solomon spoke on behalf of the Jewish People: The guards who go about the city found me; they struck and wounded me, and stole my precious jewelry...nonetheless, when you find my Beloved, tell Him that I am lovesick. Just as before, now too I love Him with all my heart and all my soul. I am sick with love for my Creator and that love has not been diminished even a hairsbreadth. (*Ma'asei LaMelech*, by R. Shemuel Graineman זצ״ל, editor of *The Chofetz Chaim on the Torah*.)

The Value of Suffering

Rabbeinu Yonah teaches us the importance of accepting
Hashem's admonition and realizing that it is a sign of
His love and caring for us:

It is for he who trusts in G-d to hope, in the
gloom of his anguish, that the darkness be the
cause of light, as it is written, "Rejoice not against
me, O mine enemy; though I am fallen I shall
arise; though I sit in darkness, the L-rd is a light
unto me" (*Micha* 7:8). Our Sages of blessed memory have said, "If I had not fallen, I would not
have risen; if I had not sat in darkness, it would
not have been light unto me" (*Midrash Tehillim* 22).

Every man in his day of trouble should set his
heart to understand, and to undergo affliction in
repentance and prayer, just as the congregation is
obligated to fast and undergo affliction in time of
trouble, as decreed by our Sages of blessed memory. This constitutes a desired fast and a day of
acceptance. When the Blessed One's chastisement
comes upon a man who is pure and just, it is as a
trial for the magnification of his reward in the
World to Come, as it is said: "that He might afflict

you and test you, to do you good at your latter
end" (*Devarim* 8:16). Our Sages of blessed memory
have said: "Examining one's deeds in time of evil,
looking and searching and not finding oneself
guilty of any sin, indicates 'afflictions of love' "
(*Berachos* 5a).

(*Sha'arei Teshuva*, Feldheim, p. 79)

In his commentary on *Mishlei*, Rabbeinu Yonah explains
in detail the meaning of the verses (3:11-12): "My son, do not
detest Hashem's *mussar* and do not despise His admonition,
For he whom Hashem loves, He chastises as a father [chas-
tises] his beloved son."

מוסר ה' בני אל תמאס — "My son, do not detest
Hashem's *mussar* (instructive punishment)." This
is of great importance in reaching the higher levels of *bitachon* (faith). If the charitable and mitzva-
observant person sees that he is not succeeding
financially or that he is receiving Hashem's punishment, he should strengthen his faith and not
abhor Hashem's instructive punishment. He
should know that it is of greater benefit for him
than if he were to be repaid with success, wealth,
and tranquillity, since Hashem wished to make
him meritorious, cleanse him of any guilt or sin,
and increase his reward. As for tranquillity in this
world — what is it worth? A man's days are like a
passing shadow and his end is as if he had never
existed. Were he to live even a thousand years, one
hour of spiritual bliss in the World to Come is still
greater than all of life in this world. Man does not
know what is good for him, but Hashem knows
what will rectify and benefit man and what is best
for him, whether tranquillity or punishment.

ואל תקוץ בתוכחתו —"and do not despise His admonition."
After saying אל תמאס —"do not detest," Rabbeinu Yonah adds
אל תקוץ —"do not be short of patience and do not feel pained
by His admonition; rather accept it with love." As our Sages
said (*Shabbos* 88b): "About those who act out of love [of
Hashem] and who are happy in suffering *yissurim*, it is written, 'those who love Him [will shine] like the sun when it
goes forth in its strength.' " This is a form of *mesiras nefesh* —
giving oneself totally to the service of Hashem.

כי את אשר יאהב ה' יוכיח —"For he whom Hashem loves, He
chastises," so that no stain of sin should remain to diminish
his love of Hashem; so as to intensify his humility; to ensure
that tranquillity should not lessen his Fear of Heaven; and to
increase his future reward. There is nothing of benefit to man
in the lower world which can compare with this.

וכאב את בן ירצה —"As a father [chastises] his beloved son."
A father will be most diligent in correcting, educating, and
perfecting the character of his most beloved son so that he
will develop a beautiful and unblemished character. So too,
Hashem chastises those He loves more than others. Similarly,
we find: ה' צדיק יבחן —"Hashem tests the righteous" (*Tehillim*
11:5). Alternatively, the verse can be interpreted to mean that
"As a father to a son, He will favor him." The word ירצה —
yirtze here is understood not as an adjective meaning "a beloved son," but as a verb, meaning "favor." After Hashem
punishes a person, He will then favor him more, just as a
father's mercy for his son will increase after he has punished
him.

ᥱ *Yissurim* Are Beloved

The essence of this world, says R. Yerucham Levovitz, the
mashgiach of Mir, is that "Man is born to toil" (*Iyov* 5:7). It is

Hashem's Will that Man receive his place in the World to Come as reward for his effort, and not as *nehama d'kisufa*, "bread of shame," an undeserved gift that one is embarrassed to receive. Accordingly, Hashem initially created the world with the Attribute of Strict Justice, so that man could earn his reward justly. Strenuous effort, then, is an absolute requirement in the service of Hashem, and that is why one can only receive his share in the World to Come by suffering the difficulties of *yissurim*. "R. Shimon bar Yochai says: 'The Holy One, blessed be He, gave three special gifts to Israel and each of them is given only through *yissurim*. They are: Torah, the Land of Israel, and the World to Come.... The World to Come, as it is written: "instructive reproof is the path to everlasting life" ' " (*Mishlei* 6:23).

Hashem is especially strict in His judgment of *tzaddikim*. Because He loves them, He brings upon them severe penalty, so that their share in the World to Come will be complete and unblemished.

We can learn the greatness of *yissurim* from the following passage in *Berachos* (5a):

> There is a dispute between R. Yaakov bar Idi and R. Acha bar Chanina. One says: *Yissurim shel ahava* — suffering that Hashem brings upon a person out of love, in order to increase his share in the World to Come (Rashi) — are those *yissurim* that do not cause *bitul* Torah (diminution of Torah study); the other says: *Yissurim shel ahava* are those *yissurim* that do not cause a diminution of prayer. R. Chiya bar Abba said in the name of R. Yochanan: Both can be *yissurim shel ahava*, as it says, "Whomever Hashem loves, He rebukes."

Hashem brings suffering upon a person out of love for him, even at the expense of Torah study and prayer. This teaches us that the value of *yissurim* surpasses even Torah study and prayer.

In light of this, we can understand why our Sages so appreciated and loved *yissurim*, even calling them "my brothers and my beloved friends" (*Bava Metzia* 84b). They saw here a clear matter of profit, for the Mishna teaches: "An hour of spiritual bliss in the World to Come is greater than all the life of this world" (*Pirkei Avos* 4:22). All the pleasures of all of humanity throughout the entire history of the world do not equal a single hour for a single soul in the World to Come; and that boundless pleasure can only be achieved by the trials and tribulations of this world. Is it any wonder that our Sages so valued *yissurim* and willingly accepted them? (Based on *Da'as Chochma u'Mussar*.)

❧ Worldly Suffering Is an Easy Substitute

Since we do not recognize the seriousness of sin and its terrible effects, we do not appreciate the great benefit suffering in this world — a light substitute for the penalties of Gehinnom — brings. It is said in the name of the Ramban that one moment of suffering in Gehinnom is worse than seventy years of Iyov-like suffering in this world. Our Sages, because they *did* recognize the serious effects of sin, accepted suffering happily. When R. Akiva saw his teacher, R. Eliezer, struck by *yissurim*, he said: "Now that I see my rebbe in pain, I am happy [for him]" (*Sanhedrin* 101a). When R. Eliezer ben R. Shimon accepted upon himself *yissurim*, he spoke to them (the *yissurim*), saying: "Come in, my brothers and friends" (*Bava Metzia* 84b). In *Yevamos* (105b), we are told about Ivdan, the student of R. Yehuda HaNasi, who suffered terribly: he was struck with leprosy, two of his sons drowned, and two daughters-in-law renounced their (childhood) marriages.

When R. Nachman bar Yitzchak heard this he said, "Blessed is Hashem Who shamed Ivdan in this world, and did not shame him in the World to Come."

How awesome this comment is. Our Sages gave praise to Hashem for such harsh punishment only because they understood with their great wisdom that all this worldly suffering is an easy substitute for the heavy punishment of the World to Come. They reached this conclusion because they saw clearly the awesome damage caused by sin, and were aware that suffering atones. They therefore accepted *yissurim* willingly, with joy.

ટ્ર "Hashem Does Not Need Our Advice"

The following excerpts are from a letter written by R. Dan Segal שליט״א, *mashgiach* in Yeshivat Tifrach, to a close student and his wife, who had asked him to write words of encouragement in the wake of great misfortunes that befell them:

The *Mesillas Yesharim* writes that the main task of man in this world is to withstand *nisyonos*, the spiritual obstacles and tests that Hashem brings upon a person. Furthermore, the main tests are in the area of *emuna*. In the words of the *Chovos HaLevavos*: "The main activity of the *yetzer hara* (evil inclination) is in causing you to doubt what you believe to be true."

The trials of the Patriarchs and of King David were in fact virtually all in the area of *emuna*. Avraham was forced to descend to Egypt in poverty and disgrace, after he had been promised every manner of success in the land of Canaan. He was told to sacrifice his only son Yitzchak after being taught that Hashem abhors human sacrifice and after being promised that Yitzchak would be the inheritor of his legacy and life's work. Despite everything that befell him, Avraham remained steadfast in his belief and faith in Hashem's truth and justice.

So too, King David, who was oppressed by his brothers and then by Shaul. He fought many wars, his kingdom was beset by revolutions and uprisings, led by even his own sons, and yet he could say of himself, "I have stilled and quieted my soul like an infant at his mother's side" (*Tehillim* 131:2).

The Chofetz Chaim once commented, "We are allowed to pray, but we do not have to give advice to Hashem." After all of our prayers and hopes, what we are really asking is that Hashem do what is right in His eyes, because only He knows what is truly best for us.

Furthermore, noted the Chofetz Chaim, now that the masters of Kabbala have revealed the secret of *gilgulim* — that souls are reincarnated in later generations — all of our questions of faith are no longer difficult, for it is quite possible that what happens to a person now comes to correct something from a previous lifetime. Occasionally we see a baby who dies immediately after birth. It should be clear to us that he needed only to go through the process of birth and death before he could reach the place of true reward in the World to Come.

The famous Chassidic Rebbe, R. Chaim of Sanz (author of *Divrei Chaim*), lost his seven-year-old son. On the way home after the funeral, R. Chaim commented that his situation was like that of a person who was walking to shul when suddenly he felt a strong blow on his back. When he turned around to see the source of the blow and saw that it was none other than his best friend who had given him a friendly clap on the shoulder, he felt relieved. "I have just received a strong blow," continued R. Chaim, "but as I look around I see that the blow is from the One Who is my closest and most faithful friend. If so, let us say *Hodu*—'Give praise to Hashem!' "

On another occasion, when someone pressed him with questions about his troubles, he replied, "How long will you try to make the *Ribbono shel Olam* appear improper in my eyes?!"

This is the great level of *Klal Yisrael* who accept willingly whatever Hashem brings upon them, knowing that all that He does is for the best. Therefore, knowing that there are no natural events or coincidences that are outside of Hashem's ordained Will, you should strengthen yourselves and not allow your faith to waver for a single minute. Furthermore, the *Nefesh HaChaim* writes that a person merits salvation from his troubles to the degree that he strengthens his faith that everything is decreed from Above.

But if in fact everything is for the good, what room is there for prayer? Shouldn't we want to receive whatever Hashem brings upon us, trusting His wisdom and not asking for what seems to us to be good? We can compare this to a child who is punished for misbehaving. True, the punishment is in his best interests, but it would be better for him to behave properly without being forced to. When we are faced with Hashem's punishments we should realize that those penalties force us to improve our ways and draw closer to Him. Through prayer, we voluntarily strengthen our faith and draw closer to Him; we ask for His help, so that we may be worthy of receiving good without difficulties.

Try to make the most of this time of difficulty, for the reward you can achieve at this time is unimaginable. It is said that the daughter of the Vilna Gaon passed away just before her wedding day. The Gaon's mother came to him in a dream and said, "If you could only imagine what you merited for the way you accepted the punishment, you would have danced at her funeral more than at her wedding."

I will just add that when I begin to think, "Why did Hashem do such and such?" I am immediately overcome by shame and embarrassment. Hashem is called *Av HaRachamim* — the Father of all feelings of compassion that exist in this world. If I, who do so little for my fellowman, am still overcome by feelings of compassion at someone else's misfortune, how much more so does Hashem have compassion for him. If He nonetheless brings suffering upon him, that suffering must be genuinely good and compassionate.

R. Levi Yitzchak of Berdichev was known as the great advocate of the Jewish people, for he constantly pleaded with Hashem to lessen their burdens. Yet he declared: "If I were the Creator, I would run the world exactly as He does. It is not as we think — that if it were up to us we would save everyone from their difficulties and create a better and happier world." R. Levi Yitzchak knew the truth — that after all is said and done, what is good in Hashem's eyes is in fact true mercy, compassion, and goodness. And as the Chofetz Chaim said, "Hashem does not need our advice."

May you be blessed with a *refua sheleima*, may you see Hashem's salvation openly, and may you always grow stronger in perfect Faith. והבוטח בה' חסד יסובבנו — "He who trusts in Hashem will be surrounded by lovingkindness" (*Tehillim* 32:10).

౭‌ The Heavenly Smile

The Torah recounts that Yosef was taken down to Egypt by merchants whose camels carried various types of perfumes. Rashi comments (*Bereishis* 37:25), "Why does the verse mention the contents of their loads? To teach us the reward of the righteous. Arab merchants usually carry kerosene and tar, which have foul odors, but for this one [Yosef] there happened to be perfumes so that he should not be harmed by foul odors." We cannot help wondering — after all the pain and humiliation that Yosef endured, did he care at all about the odors accompanying him on his painful journey?

R. Mordechai Pogramanski זצ"ל, Lithuanian Torah giant

of exceptional genius and piety, explained this with a parable:
Imagine a sick child being wheeled into an operating room.
His parents must remain outside while he enters alone, to be
greeted by strangers dressed in white. Overcome by fear and
loneliness, he bursts into tears.

Suddenly he looks up and notices a small window in the
corner of the room. He can see his mother watching him from
a distance, her smiling face reassuring him. He feels secure,
stops crying, and even manages a smile.

What has really changed? Has the operating room with its
harsh lights and cold steel become less frightening? The only
difference is in the child's awareness that his loving mother is
with him, watching over him.

When Yosef smelled the sweet fragrance of the spices, he
was aware that Hashem was guarding over him, making sure
that his suffering would be only the exact amount needed.
The Heavenly smile, as it were, that accompanied Yosef to
Egypt, showed him that Hashem had joined him in his difficulty, and made his pain more bearable.

When a person is beset by the greatest of *yissurim*, he can
look up and find that Hashem is with him, giving him pain,
and at the same time giving him the ability to bear that pain
and accept it. "Your rod and Your supporting staff are my
consolation."

&❧ Pain and Suffering Can Multiply Our Reward

R. Chaim Friedlander, *mashgiach* in Yeshivas Ponevezh,
passed away in 5746/1986 after suffering from a prolonged,
painful illness. About nine months before his passing, he
wrote the following letter from his sick bed to a close friend in
a similar situation. In this letter he underscored and emphasized our obligation to serve Hashem even when challenged

by the severest limitations; how great is the reward for one who does so; how one can thus accomplish so much in a short time; and most important, the need for *chizuk* — strengthening one's faith in time of suffering.

Every situation in which a person finds himself was given to him from Above to use in *avodas Hashem* (service of G-d). Even sickness, suffering, and physical weakness are given to man so that he can serve the Creator from these difficulties and limitations.

The smallest improvement in prayer and strengthening of faith in such circumstances is regarded in Heaven as a great and mighty deed. For a mitzva done once with pain is equal to one done a hundred times without pain. My rebbe, Rav Dessler זצ"ל, *menahel ruchani* of Ponevezh Yeshiva, quoted his father (*Michtav MeEliyahu*, vol. 3, p. 14) in commenting that this rule applies to even the smallest difficulty. The Gemara (*Arachin* 16a) says, "What is the smallest level of *yissurim*? Even if one reaches into his pocket to take three coins and his hand picks up only two." Having to reach again into a pocket is also regarded as *yissurim*. If one's difficulty is a bit more than that, his reward is again multiplied one hundred times, that is, one hundred times one hundred or ten thousand, and if his pain is a bit more than that, his reward increases another hundredfold (altogether by a million) and so forth.

So if, when in the midst of pain and suffering, one struggles to serve Hashem, his reward is beyond description. The smallest amount of prayer, Torah study, and increased faith under such circumstances is highly valued in Heaven; it becomes possible for a person to accomplish in a short time what would normally require many years of effort.

Most important, we must strengthen our belief and faith that everything is from Above, that "one does not move his finger in this world unless it has been decreed upon him from Above" (*Chullin* 7b). And since every bit of suffering and pain is from Heaven, this too is surely for the good, for "all that Hashem does is for the good." Although right now we do not understand how it is for the good, in the future it will become revealed, and we will utter the blessing of *hatov v'hameitiv* for evil decrees as well (see *Pesachim* 50a).

The reward for faith is very great. In the merit of faith, *HaKadosh Baruch Hu* will remove the "cloak of hiding" and the suffering that He inflicts in order to test a person's faith. As Rabbeinu Yonah writes on *Mishlei* 3:26, "He who trusts in Hashem will be saved from misfortune in reward for his faith, although it was otherwise fitting that misfortune should befall him." He writes further, "And if he is overwhelmed and humbled by difficulties, he should trust in Hashem's mercy, for He will be merciful to him because of his suffering and humility, *and because his hope was upon Hashem*." Thus, sickness and suffering provide the time and the challenge to strengthen oneself in faith.

ɞ Don't Pay Too Much Attention to Difficulties

The Steipler Gaon, R. Yisrael Yaakov Kanievsky זצ"ל (1899-1985), was outstanding among all the great scholars of our generation for his great diligence in Torah study and for his prolific writing — his many *seforim* are a staple in every yeshiva.

On one occasion, he encouraged and consoled someone burdened with many problems with the following words of wisdom:

"Do not pay too much attention to the difficulties of this world. If I had been preoccupied with the difficulties that come upon a person in this world, I would have remained an *am ha'aretz* (a complete ignoramus). Do you know what kind of suffering I had in this world? For years I lived in great poverty. On Shabbos we ate plain bread, not to speak of the clothing we wore.... And how much did I suffer in raising my children? Do you think you are struggling and burdened? The difficulties I had in raising my children could have been divided among a hundred people!"

The Steipler enumerated some of the problems he had faced in this area and continued: "Hashem helped me find a son-in-law. One day he left me and I, poor and without means, was left to care for eight orphans. There were so many health problems and other matters.... If I had involved myself with all these, I would not have learned a single page! But Hashem was kind to me — perhaps because I studied *mussar* (ethics and character refinement) and perhaps because of the little Torah that I studied in my youth — and I did not concern myself with all of those difficulties.

"I understood everything with the words of the *Seforno* on the verse, 'Even when I walk in the valley of the shadow of Death, I do not fear evil; Your rod and Your staff, they console me.'

"King David said, 'I know that it is You Who hits me. Therefore, Your rod which hit me in the past and Your staff — the support which You gave me after every previous difficulty — they console me. I draw strength from the awareness that no calamity is forever, and that there is always salvation from it. I then hope that You will continue as in the past and again support me with Your deliverance.' "

The Steipler concluded his advice by emphasizing that "the only solution is not to be concerned with the world."

His visitor left feeling like a new person.

ટ Stop and Think

R. Ezriel Tauber שליט"א offers valuable tools for dealing with pain and suffering:

A natural reaction to the pain of suffering is to ask: "Why?" If you find no answers, it is likely that the very question "Why?" causes pain. And when it does, you tend to seek "tranquilizers" to kill the pain (just as it is natural to seek a drug when physical pain strikes).

Some turn to alcohol and become alcoholics. Others turn to work and become workaholics. Still others find other addictions and distractions. Whatever the tranquilizer of choice, a pain-killer is not a cure. When we are stricken with something unexpected, the first step toward true recovery is to realize that the affliction was meant to make us stop and think.

Stop and think.

Hashem is capable of anything. If we are talking about a Being Who created both the atom and the distant stars, Who animates the particles which circle the atom and gives motion to the distant stars, Who gave us intelligence and knows our deepest thoughts, then we are talking about a Being Who can do anything. Anything less is not Hashem.

Therefore, Hashem is certainly capable of taking away suffering — or preventing it in the first place. Why then does He allow us to suffer?

For our sake.

When Hashem told Avraham to sacrifice Yitzchak, it was a test which would have crushed all but the greatest human being. However, the Creator does not give someone a test he cannot handle. He knew Avraham was up to the test.

If Hashem knew that Avraham would pass the test, then why did He test him?

For Avraham's sake — to let Avraham, as well as the whole world, know the righteousness in his soul. As the Ramban remarks: "The benefit of a test is for the one who is tested" (*Bereishis* 21:1).

Hashem only tests the righteous. Evil people do not get tested. Suffering brings out the deepest, most sublime greatness lying dormant in the human heart, and only the righteous are worthy of it. The evil do not usually suffer. And when they do, it is often only at the end of a career of power, prestige, and desires fulfilled. Their suffering is more than likely a final punishment.

"When the wicked [and their wickedness] sprout like grass, it is only so that they should be cut down forever" (*Tehillim* 92:8). The initial pleasure and success that the wicked oftentimes experience are, in reality, part of their punishment. They are receiving full payment for the few good deeds they may have performed. When their account is paid, though, the punishment inflicted upon them is final.

On the other hand, when the righteous suffer, they are gaining. Their spiritual "bank account" is growing daily and accruing interest. The payoff will occur at some future date in a way they can benefit from forever.

Hashem can help the one who suffers and He can relieve suffering at any moment. However, the suffering is also a form of His help. It will make the good person better than he or she was.

If one stops and thinks, and hasn't already overdosed on tranquilizers, he will recognize that suffering, too, comes from Hashem. With this recognition, the first and perhaps most difficult obstacle is overcome. The pang may still remain, but the fatalistic feeling should not. Turn to Hashem to lighten or remove the suffering, but the point is: *turn to Hashem*. Do not overdose on tranquilizers. Realize that suffering has a purpose.

*   *   *

Generally speaking, a person is not allowed to ask for suffering nor may he seek ways to bring more suffering upon himself. However, when suffering is thrust upon us, we must know that it is an opportunity for more than "overcoming" — it is an opportunity to attain the heights of achievement. Of course, this is a high ideal (and that is why the judicious person does not ask for suffering). Nevertheless, when one realizes what stands to be gained with a moment of suffering, then he can clear his mind and focus only on the great reward that will ultimately accrue. That awareness blocks out even tremendous pain....

Thus, it is incumbent upon us to view every personal holocaust which Hashem weaves into our lives as an opportunity for personal redemption, as well as an opportunity to bring about the redemption of the world. (Reprinted with permission from *Darkness Before Dawn* by R. Ezriel Tauber, Shalheves, pp. 123-27.)

❧ True Faith Enables Acceptance of *Yissurim* with Love

> Our Sages taught: Hillel the Elder was coming down the road and heard the sound of crying in the city. He said, "I am certain that it is not in my house." About Hillel it was said: "He will not fear evil tidings; his heart is firm, trusting in Hashem" (*Tehillim* 112:7).
>
> Rava said, "This verse can be interpreted from beginning to end or from end to beginning. Either 'He will not fear evil tidings' because 'his heart is firm, trusting in Hashem;' or 'his heart is firm, trusting in Hashem,' because 'he does not fear evil tidings.' "
>
> (*Brachos* 60a)

R. Sender Erlanger שליט״א explains the difference between the two interpretations based on these words of the
Chazon Ish:

> The essential level of faith which for which a per-
> son should strive is complete acceptance of
> Hashem's conduct of the world for good or for
> bad, without resorting to misdirected and un-
> called for *hishtadlus* (human effort in the sphere of
> nature) but instead turning only to *tefilla* and
> *teshuva*.
>
> After achieving this level of *bitachon* (faith), a
> person may be granted the insight of *Ruach Ha-
> Kodesh*, a holy spirit which informs him that
> Hashem will help him. The verse, "If an enemy
> will besiege me, my heart will not fear; if a war
> arises against me — in this I will trust," refers to
> this. He is granted this awareness that no suffer-
> ing will befall him as a reward for his striving in
> *bitachon*.
>
> *(Emuna u'Bitachon)*

The words of the Chazon Ish teach us two levels of *bitachon*: the first is faith that whatever Hashem does is for the
ultimate good; the second is awareness of a promise from
Above that no evil will transpire, a promise at times given to
those who have already achieved the first level.

Rava finds two interpretations to Hillel's words: first,
Hillel taught his family to accept with quiet certainty that
whatever came upon them is all for the best, as the Gemara
says (*Berachos* 62a): "[the proper way of] accepting *yissurim* is
with silence and prayers for mercy." Hillel was sure that no
outcry would come from his house.

Second, since *Ruach HaKodesh* rested upon him, he felt
certain that no misfortune could have occurred in his house.

So the above-quoted verse can be read two ways. Reading the last phrase of the verse as a reason for the beginning, we can say that because a person's heart is firm in the belief that whatever Hashem does is for the best, he has no reason to fear any evil that may come upon him. Reading the beginning of the verse as explanation of the end, we find an allusion to the second type of *bitachon*, that which is given as a gift from Above. Thus he does not fear evil tidings because his heart is firm in the promise he has received that no evil will befall him.

Ideally, the difficult effort of striving for true trust in Hashem itself becomes transformed into the reward of *Ruach HaKodesh* promising that only good will occur.

How to Cope with Suffering

ושבתי אני ואראה... והנה דמעת העשוקים ואין להם מנחם....

"I turned and saw...and behold the tears of the oppressed; and they have no comforter..." (*Koheles* 4:1). R. Yehuda said, "This refers to children who are 'hidden away' due to the sins of their fathers; in the World to Come they will be in the company of the righteous."

(*Midrash Koheles Rabba* 4:1)

This midrash refers to those who pass away in childhood. We can, however, find allusion to children with physical or mental disabilities as well. They are often hidden within themselves, removed from regular interaction with society, and locked up in homes, institutions, or simply "locked" in their circumstances.

"Behold the tears of the oppressed," who suffer and moan, shedding tears inconsolably. "Why is my soul different, that it was put into a physically or mentally blemished body?"

"They have no comforter." With the limited insight of mortal man, there is no one to explain or to console. Only *"Adon Kol HaNeshamos"* — the Master of All Souls — knows the purpose.

Parents, family members, and friends who take it upon themselves to improve the lot of such children; those who bring some small comfort, who share in the suffering, and who wipe away the hard-to-hide tears can draw inspiration from the closing words of the midrash: "In the World to Come they will be in the company of the righteous," where their pain will have found meaning and ultimate reward. (Based on comments by R. Shemuel Wosner שליט״א, Rosh Yeshiva of Chachmei Lublin.)

🙙 Why Must Parents Suffer Their Children's Death?

Ilfa asked, "It is written, ורב חסד '[Hashem is] abundant with lovingkindness,' ואמת 'and truth.' Does Hashem act with lovingkindness *or* with strict truth?

"Initially He judges with truth and then with kindness. This can be likened to a king who was owed a thousand *zuz*. [The borrower] was pained [lacking money to pay]. What did the king do? He arose in the night, filled a purse with a thousand *zuz* and threw it into the borrower's window....

"He again sent a messenger [to collect the debt].... Thus the bill was paid and the king received his due.

"So too with human beings. A person commits a sin for which he deserves to be penalized with death. Hashem waits until he is married and a child is born to him, and then another child is born. Hashem then takes the child away. Thus he has paid his debt (received his punishment)...while his 'body' survives after Hashem has taken His due." (*Yalkut Shimoni, Shemos* 398.)

We can find here the possible answer to a painful and tragic question: Why must parents suffer the death of their children? Why must people bear the heartbreak of raising a handicapped or disadvantaged child?

As the *Etz Chaim* suggests in its explanation of the midrash, Hashem sends as a *gilgul* (reincarnation) one who deserved the death penalty in an earlier life, to these parents who themselves may deserve severe penalty. Hashem thus lightens the punishment to the parents, who would otherwise know even greater suffering.

This is the explanation of the verse (*Tehillim* 3:5): "He loves charity and justice; the kindness of Hashem fills the land." First He charitably bestows benefit, then He bestows justice, while leaving the sufferer with his life intact. Even in judgment "Hashem's kindness fills the world."

Parents of challenged children can find comfort knowing that these children bring benefit to their families, and that their reward is great in helping the soul find its rectification.

It has been asked, why do we desecrate the Shabbos to prolong the life of a child who is mortally injured, for the rule of "Desecrate one Shabbos in order that he may keep many" does not apply here?

R. Eliyahu Baal Shem explains that since every family, city, and country are judged based on the majority, this child can save an entire community. This child, being pure and righteous, can complete the majority, which will bring a decree of life to all those around him. Thus Hashem may give life even to those who are undeserving, through the merit of a sick or disabled child for whom they care.

Iyov comforted the unfortunate. He once asked a blind man, "If you built a house, would you not make windows in it? Similarly, Hashem will be praised through you, when He will give you sight in the future, as it is written, 'The eyes of the blind will be opened.' "

In other words, Iyov pointed out that just as the builder wants to build a perfect building, so Hashem wishes to create people without blemish. If He sometimes creates someone with an imperfection, it must be for his greater benefit. Your lack of sight, then, must be to rectify some earlier wrongdoing. If you will accept Hashem's decree willingly, you can fulfill your purpose and Hashem will then cure you and make you perfect, either in this world or in the World to Come.

The Vilna Gaon said that when a person is judged in Heaven at the end of his life, and discovers all that he could have accomplished and rectified in this world, he has a great desire to return again and *he is willing to accept all the suffering in the world* in order to do so. Our Sages comment on the words (*Tehillim* 42:12): הוחילי לאלוקים —"Hope to Hashem," that "if Hashem brings *yissurim* upon you do not 'kick' and reject them; instead, accept them with dancing" (interpreting *hochili* as related to the word *machol* which means "dance").

❧ The Loss Was Not in Vain

Upon suffering a miscarriage or stillbirth, Heaven forbid, a woman should not feel that her pregnancy was in vain or that her pain was for naught. The Talmud teaches (*Sanhedrin* 110b; *Kesubbos* 111a) that a person has a share in the World to Come from the time of conception. So a fetus, even in its earliest stages of development, already has a share in the World to Come, and, being unblemished by sin, will arise, without suffering, as a perfect *tzaddik* at the time of the Resurrection of the Dead. His mother, then, did him the greatest kindness in making possible the fulfillment of his purpose in Creation so that he could then receive the greatest reward.

Our Sages tell us (*Sota* 12a) that when Amram divorced his wife, Yocheved, as a result of Pharaoh's decree, his daughter, Miriam, said to him, "Your decree is worse than Pharaoh's — Pharaoh enacted an evil decree in this world only, but you have made a decree for this world and the World to

Come." Rashi explains that if a child is born and dies immediately, he then returns to live in the World to Come. But if he is never born, he can never go to the World to Come.

We see then, that it is worthwhile for a child to be born even if only to be thrown into the Nile to drown, and for parents to bear such suffering, so that the soul of this baby may receive its portion in the World to Come (*Toras Ha-Yoledes*, p. 173).

ೂ Special Children Are A Special Challenge

Educating special children is often accompanied by so much pain and disappointment that parents must first come to terms with their own inner selves, to learn how to cope inwardly with their plight, to accept it without feeling stigmatized and indeed to recognize their situation, however unwelcome, as one from which they themselves can and should derive spiritual growth.

It is this last point — spiritual growth — which requires above all else a Torah orientation; how to accept *tzar*, how to absorb anguish without becoming devastated, how to get up after having been knocked down. Emotional strength, and the strong supportive help of family and friends are, of course, indispensable elements in the recovery from the shock that one is the parent of a deficient child. But believers and Torah Jews have, or should have, something more at their command as an added resource. It is the realization that, in the face of their suffering, they have been given a special painful challenge by Hashem; that their tasks of education and love and care are those of special proportions; that *chesed* is to take on a new meaning in their lives.

The care and nurture of special children, and the needed assistance given to help them develop to their maximum potential is the most profound *chesed* one can contemplate...for it is *chesed* mixed with tears, *chesed* with a meager return. So when one is called upon by Hashem to be the vehicle of this kind of *chesed*, he or she must recognize it as a difficult, but sacred calling. Rising to the tasks of this calling is not only a measure of one's humanity, but is the very condition of one's being part of the Jewish people. This is a Jewish, holy task that parents and educators are performing, a task that bears eternal testimony to the fiber of our existence as a nation of givers of lovingkindness, children of givers of lovingkindness, who uphold the covenant of Avraham Avinu, גומלי חסדים בני גומלי חסדים המחזיקים בבריתו של אברהם אבינו.

Parenthood of special children is indeed a double *nisayon*, test. It is first of all a test of faith, a *nisayon* of *emuna* — being able to accept misfortune without having any complaints of Hashem. But it also entails another, more exacting *nisayon*: to convert misfortune into challenge, to reject despair and foster growth, to practice exceedingly love and *chesed* with that child who needs it most, so that he and his dear ones can be worthy of the love and *chesed* of Hashem.

Special children have special needs. It requires more than an ordinary intelligence to manage and oversee their educational development. You are all aware, I am sure, that mistakes can be very costly; that too much pressure can be as harmful as too little encouragement, that what one may consider a necessary encouragement is in truth really unnecessary pressure; that it requires sustained wisdom and unlimited patience, in addition to *siyatta d'shmaya* (Heavenly assistance) to raise a special child — and raise him right. And there is another dimension of the *nisayon*. I believe it to be an unspoken truth that the parents of the special child are simply expected to be better, more noble people than the parents of the regular child. Let me illustrate.

Anger, we all know, is an objectionable *mida*, trait, in any

person. It is detrimental to human relations. It is injurious to
education. But to the education of the special child, anger can
be fatal. Shalom, peace and herein I include *shalom bayis*,
marital harmony, is the basic ingredient of all human relations. The absence of parental *shalom bayis* is usually an insidi-
ous, hidden cause in the personality problems discovered in
people later in adult life. But in the home of the special child,
the absence of *shalom bayis* and a peaceful home atmosphere
or the existence of excessive sibling friction is poison to the
already fragile emotional structure of the special or disturbed
child.

So it is not at all an exaggeration to say that the home of
such a child is, of necessity, a home where peace and patience
and the practice of *midos tovos*, virtues, must be the norm of
everyday conduct. And if this becomes a joint effort of the
parents and the brothers and sisters of the child, you discover
that rather than having a pall of darkness descend over the
so-called afflicted family, on the contrary, the entire family,
parents and children both, have become spiritually uplifted
by the sacred challenge of caring for one who needs special
care. The *midos* of *chesed* and love and peace and patience
have been exemplified to the brothers and sisters of the special child and their education has become profoundly en-
riched.

One of the most inspiring sentences in all of the *sifrei
Mussar* is written by Rabbeinu Yonah in *Shaarei Teshuva*: "The
Jew who trusts in Hashem hopes in the seed of new light."
The passage continues: "Do not rejoice my enemies that I
have fallen, for I have also risen. If I sit in the darkness,
Hashem is a light unto me." Our Sages have commented
upon this: Had I not first fallen, I could not have risen. Were I
not to have tasted the darkness, I could not later appreciate
the light.

The trials and tribulations of having a special child are

many. They make demands on our bodies, on our time, on our emotions, and above all, on our endurance. But the measure of worthwhile living is the ability to endure *nisyonos*, tests. The word *nisayon* is derived from *nes*, a banner. The Ramban points out that not only was Avraham tested by the *Akeida*, but he was also changed and uplifted by it.

This is the Torah challenge to parents of special children. If the challenge is met not with sluggishness and despair, but with inspiration and *bitachon*, then the parents and the family have carried out a unique *shlichus* and special mission entrusted to them by Hashem. And this is another vital point in the understanding of one's role as a parent of any child. It is an axiom of education, a fundamental part of our *mesiras nefesh*, self-sacrifice. The education of our children is not merely a mitzva, or a task imposed from above. It is rather a mission, a *shlichus* of Hashem we are performing. It is His job we are doing. In, being, therefore, agents of mercy, שלוחי דרחמנא, one must be faithful and sensitive to the intentions of the Sender. Of course, each one of us would love to carry out this mission in the most enjoyable, successful way — *chinuch* coupled with an abundance of *nachas*. But if Divine Providence has appointed us to a service without too much *nachas*, we are not any less exempt from our mission. Every Jewish child born into this world, if at all able to absorb Torah and Yiddishkeit — at whatever level — is entitled to that privilege; and his and her parents have been charged with performing that service. It is a holy charge, a sacred duty.

Consider for a moment that the mitzva of educating one's children is given in the Torah in two familiar verses, but with a significant distinction between the two. In the first verse of the Shema we read: ושננתם לבניך ודברת בם בשבתך בביתך ובלכתך בדרך. In the second verse we read: ולמדתם אותם את בניכם לדבר בם. The first verse contains the word שננתם, *shinantam*, in which our Sages have seen the obligation to make our children proficient, sharp, and learned in Torah. *Shinun* means agility and sharpness. This implication, is, however, absent in the word found in the second verse, למדתם, *limadetem*, which means only to teach, to help study. And if one examines the *sugya* in *Kiddushin* (29), he sees that the basic obligation to teach Torah is derived not from the verse of *shinantam*, but from the verse of *limadetem*. Perhaps the message here is that even those children unable to master that level of intelligence, in whom we cannot carry out *shinantam*, are still not excluded from the precious privilege of studying and knowing and being taught. We are therefore told: *limadetem*, teach your children; teach them to the best of your and their ability. Do not stifle their souls with ignorance. Allow them too to enjoy at their pace and on their level the heritage of *kedusha*, holiness that we, the more fortunate ones, are better able to appreciate.

When we read about the *Mishkan* and all the sacred vessels that it was to hold, we should remember that *Klal Yisroel* is also compared to a *Mikdash*. If this is so, then each individual member of *Klal Yisroel* is likened to a holy vessel in the *Mikdash*. The *Mikdash* has many, many vessels. Some large, like the Altar and the Candelabra, and some small like the pots and pans, the spoons and forks. Some are made of gold and silver, others of copper and lead. But each of them is holy. If one violates their *kedusha*, holiness, he must bring a sacrifice.

All of us — old and young — are meant to be sacred vessels in Hashem's *Heichal*. We are each consecrated to the service of Hashem and He makes use of each and every vessel, be it made of gold, silver, or copper.

I think that it is a sign of real spiritual maturity that dedicated educators and Torah institutions have awakened to the crying need of many of the more unfortunate holy vessels. They will be blessed for the bold steps they have already taken to include these sacred vessels — these special children — along with all our children, and above all, for their ongoing concern and quest to discover still more and still better ways to help these children spiritually. The holy work of teaching and training these children, of helping even one of them emerge from the abyss of spiritual darkness, is beyond question in performance of "one who sustains a single Jewish soul it is if he has sustained the entire world." The parents and teachers of special children can therefore be special people, special great people. They can achieve heights of education and commitment that other people will never know. Their *nisyonos* can be banners of excellence of *midos tovos* and *mesiras nefesh* that other people will never achieve. And finally, ולפום צערא אגרא — the greater the effort, the greater the gain. The painful efforts and tearful labor that special people invest in special children will certainly invoke the *chasdei* Hashem of much *nachas* and happiness in their entire families, in all their children, לאורך ימים טובים. (An address given by R. Perlow, the Noveminsker Rebbe שליט"א, reprinted with kind permission from the Rebbe and P"TACH.)

⽊ The *Bris* of Binyomin Nesanel

Judy and I want to welcome you all to the *seudas mitzva* celebrating our son Binyomin Nesanel being inducted into the *bris* of Avraham Avinu.

At all joyous occasions we introduce a touch of sadness or discomfort to remind us of the *Churban* (the Destruction of the Temple). At a wedding we break a glass; at a *bris* we listen to speeches.

I didn't speak at any of our three previous *brisim*, and as many of you know, I'm a very reluctant speaker. However, special circumstances call for special responses, and there's much in my heart which has to be said. As you can well imagine, this is a very emotional time for Judy and me, and I know I'll be forgiven if mine show.

I took Judy to the hospital last Friday afternoon just before *licht benching*, and Binyomin was born shortly after Shabbos began. When the doctor told us that our baby had Down Syndrome, we were devastated. We had gone through a somewhat similar experience almost 22 years ago when Malka was born. We always felt we had paid our dues and it wouldn't happen to us again. Obviously, Hashem felt otherwise. That entire Shabbos we sat alone with each other and with our thoughts trying to understand why we were once again afflicted.

On Shabbos morning I went to shul near the hospital. Words and passages I had muttered all my life jumped off the page and confronted me, demanding to be understood.

In *Mizmor shir l'yom haShabbat*, I read, 'טוב להודות לה —"It is good to give thanks to Hashem," and I asked, "For what?" And when I read, 'מה גדלו מעשיך ה —"How good are Your works, Hashem," I cried. I asked myself, what meaning will the words have for me at the *bris* when I hear everyone cry out, כן יכנס לתורה ולחופה ולמעשים טובים —"So too may he enter Torah, marriage, and good deeds."

I was one of three new fathers who got *aliyas* that day and the congregation sang *siman tov u'mazal tov* to each of us in turn. I could not see how it was a *siman tov* for me.

I had lunch with the Rabbi and his wife. I shared their lunch and they shared my anguish.

Judy and I talked all that afternoon and we realized that it wasn't the end of the world. We told each other that if this is what Hashem wants for us, there must be a reason. We had learned a hard lesson in *bitachon* with Malka and now we tried to relearn it, or better, to reconfirm it. *Bitachon* in Hashem doesn't mean He will always do what you perceive is best for you. Rather, it's the belief that He knows what's best for the *Klal*, and we each have our own role to play. We're all soldiers in Hashem's army, and the success of the army often involves great sacrifice on the part of the individual soldier.

Many people told us that since we did such a good job with Malka, Hashem was giving us another challenge. It was comforting to hear, but we were willing to forgo the honor.

As many of you know, I had planned to retire next June and we were going to make *aliya* at the end of the summer. Binyomin's birth caused us to do a quick reevaluation. We had to find out if there were schools and programs in Israel to meet his needs. If, because of his condition, we could not make *aliya*, then it would truly be a tragedy. We're still checking, but preliminary indications are favorable and we plan to continue with our preparations.

Throughout our terrible ordeal last Shabbos, Judy and I had one great plus going for us, besides our faith. That was our strong love for each other. Countless times during that very long Shabbos we professed our abiding love for one another and our admiration. If helped pull us through that day.

During that Shabbos we made a conscious decision to be open about the baby's having Down Syndrome. We didn't want anyone to think we were ashamed or full of self-pity. We wanted to receive good wishes from everyone, not furtive glances. On *motzaei* Shabbos I called several friends and relatives and told them the whole story. It was one of the hardest things I ever had to do. I asked them to spread the word and to let people know that the news came directly from us. At the time, Judy and I felt it was the wise thing to do. Now we're sure of it.

We received many calls and a lot of support. The majority of people, however, did not know how to greet me when they saw me and I had to put them at ease. I don't blame anyone because I also never knew how to react in a similar situation. Let me now tell you how to act: Be happy for us. We're entitled to a wholehearted *mazal tov*. Ask us how the baby is coming along and share our ups and downs. That's what friends and relatives are for. By making the situation public we hoped to make the adjustment period easier for us, and it has worked.

Many, many people who have children with Down Syndrome got in touch with us and they all told us the same thing. They went through several stages — denial, terrible anguish, acceptance, and finally love and *nachas*. We are determined to eliminate or at least condense the first two stages into the shortest possible time. We're already well on the road and with Hashem's help we'll get there soon.

We don't know why Hashem chose us to be tested a second time. But we believe with *emuna sheleima* (complete faith) that He has His reasons and we have our roles to fulfill. In many ways we see parallels to the time when Malka was born. That too was a very difficult time for us, and whereas we accepted it quickly, it took us years to put it in perspective. At first I thought I was being punished for my sins. Then I came to see it as a test and a challenge. As she grew into the beautiful, wonderful and intelligent young woman that she is today, we understood Hashem's purpose. Malka was His special gift to us. When she was young I would repeat to myself the saying, וכשם שמברכין על הטוב כך מברכין על הרע —"Just as we must bless Hashem for the good He bestows upon us, so too must we bless Him the evil that befalls us," until I came to the realization that where Malka was concerned there was no evil. She has always brought us joy and *nachas*, and although sometimes she is a burden and a pain, it is only physical, never, never emotional.

I don't want to take anything away from our other terrific

children, each one of whom is very special and very much loved, but Malka has come so far with such determination, grace and humor that Judy and I sometimes just shake our heads in amazement and admiration.

So now we're being given another assignment — in some ways similar, in many ways different. We don't honestly know what lies ahead, but everyone we spoke to who either has a child with Down Syndrome or who deals with them tells us the same story. They are happy, lovable children, the focus of their families and fun to be with. There's no need to feel sorry for them and it's a total waste of time and energy to indulge in self-pity. We don't understand Hashem's ways, but we accept His challenge *b'ahava*, with love. Please be happy for us as we're happy for ourselves.

As I said, many people who have children with Down Syndrome spoke to me. I heard from several sources that the Chazon Ish would stand up when a person with Down Syndrome passed by, and the reason is that these people have a pure soul, a *neshama sheleima*. They are Hashem's special children. Rav Moshe Shapiro of Yerushalayim explained that people with Down Syndrome are always happy because their spirits are so pure.

We chose the name Binyomin for two reasons: One, we liked it all along and were considering it; and two, the Torah (*V'Zot HaBracha*) calls Binyomin "the beloved of Hashem." He will certainly be loved by us. Nesanel means "given by Hashem." Binyomin Nesanel is Hashem's gift to us.

In closing I want to extend my own good wish, to the בר הנימול, to my family and to myself — a wish that is part *bracha*, part *bakasha*, and part *haftacha*, a blessing , a prayer and a promise all rolled into one — three simple words uttered from the bottom of my heart and the depths of my soul: Next year in Yerushalayim! (Reprinted with kind permission from the family.)

ঽ A Mother's Letter

To tell you the truth, it is very difficult for me to put the following words on paper. On the other hand, since these words might be of help, I feel an obligation to overcome the difficulty and share them with those who may need them.

When we began to suspect that our daughter was brain damaged, we turned to a specialist in the field. After a thorough examination, he confirmed our suspicions. The spark of hope that had flickered in our hearts was dashed in a moment. Needless to say, it was a devastating blow.

We left the doctor's office and drove home as the sun was setting. I cried the whole way. Yet I felt uplifted, and throughout the ride home, I turned to Hashem with these words: "Master of the World! I simply thank You. Till today I did not know how I would go through life. Now I know that I am tied to You."

Strengthened by this exalted feeling, I entered the house. Since then, I have experienced times of discouragement and failure. Yet the feeling that all this is a gift from Hashem helps me cope and encourages me in difficult times.

Some other reflections from our visit to the doctor:

His diagnosis was that the situation was hopeless and he added a gloomy prediction of future developments. Nonetheless, he prescribed the usual series of exercises and treatments for such cases. When we rose to leave, I said to the doctor, "I do not believe your gloomy prediction; I hope that with the help of Hashem things will eventually work out. You can be pleased with my approach, because this belief of mine will give me the strength to keep up the exercises and treatments regularly."

He replied, "I envy you. Only religious people can respond like that."

A month later when we went to my husband's Rosh Yeshiva for a *Yom Tov* visit, I used the opportunity to pour out my feelings. I told him how hard it was for us to accept the Heavenly decree, and I shared with him the hidden guilt I was feeling for finding it so difficult.

How fortunate I was then to actually feel someone else share my load, and to have a chance to listen to the wisdom of a great Torah scholar. This is what he said:

"If it were easy, *tzaddikim* would ask for it for themselves. I do not see *tzaddikim* requesting something like this for themselves. Yet, some day you will see the hardship pass of itself."

A stone was lifted from my heart. I felt that someone understood my enormous pain, that someone genuinely shared my burden.

Another of my husband's teachers gave us a lot of encouragement with a short letter he sent:

"Your daughter is a princess who is loved dearly by her Father in Heaven. Every treatment given her brings happiness to her Father in Heaven, and the greatness of the reward is unimaginable."

In conclusion, I would like to tell you about a twenty-year-old girl I once met while we were vacationing. She was brain damaged, and although her behavior was very much out of order, her sister treated her with exceptional care. I was very impressed and could not refrain from commenting to the sister about the warmth and concern she showed. She responded sincerely, "What is the question? Hashem gave her to us, and because of her, we have the opportunity to do *chesed*. Can you imagine that we would not use this opportunity fully?"

*Go, My sons, console your brother
in his bereavement. Speak to his heart
and lighten his grief.*

Brief Words of Consolation

The traditional statement of consolation said to mourners is: "May *HaMakom* (the Omnipresent) console you, together with all who mourn Zion and Yerushalayim." R. Dessler explains that the ability to accept consolation after the death of a loved one is a direct gift to us from Hashem, Who Himself brings solace to the mourner. Although the words of consolation offered by our fellowman may be eloquent and heartfelt, it is only through a special miracle which Hashem performs for each and every mourner that he is enabled to accept consolation.

People think that time heals and consoles, that with the passage of time a person comes to accept his loss. But the view of our Sages is that consolation comes as a result of the Heavenly decree that the living eventually forget the departed. If a person is mistakenly thought to be dead, he is not forgotten, and his relatives are not genuinely comforted (Rashi, *Bereishis* 37:35). Yaakov remained in mourning for Yosef for twenty-two years, unable to accept consolation — a sign that his son was still alive.

It is important that mourners be taught to willingly accept the healing consolation that Hashem sends them and not grieve excessively, as people often do. They should know that they are not permitted to mourn beyond the reasonable limit, but should instead accept consolation as a gift from Hashem (*Michtav Me'Eliyahu*).

As R. Chaim Soloveitchik wrote in a letter of consolation: "May these words of consolation be accepted by you — since it is a mitzva to accept consolation and have faith — and may you be consoled in the rebuilding of Zion and Yerushalayim and in the salvation of Israel."

These thoughts are brought as a preface to the coming chapter, to help clarify the task of those who console, and the obligation of mourners to accept consolation.

❧ At the Edge of the Pit

It is related that when the students of the Talmud Torah in Kelm were taken to be murdered by the Nazis, their *menahel*, R. Daniel Movshovits זצ"ל הי"ד, one of Lithuania's most outstanding Torah scholars, asked to be allowed to say a few words. As the group stood at the edge of the pit in their final minutes of life, R. Daniel prepared to deliver his last address. Survivors speak of his amazing calmness and control. He stood on a slightly raised spot, straightened his tie, and looked exactly the way he always did when he stood in the *beis midrash* to give a talk to the students. This is what he said:

In the *piyut* of the Ten Martyrs recited on Yom Kippur, we are told that when the angels cried out, "Is this the reward for Torah?" they were silenced by a Heavenly voice saying, "If I hear another sound I will turn the world into water...."

Let us try to understand: Were these words intended simply to silence the angels? The point is this: If Hashem swore never again to destroy the world by flood, that implies that even though there could come a time when such destruction would be appropriate, Hashem would still not destroy the world in that way. So there must be some other means by which the world can be restored to order and its sins expiated. The death of the righteous is this means. Hashem therefore told the angels, "If these *tzaddikim* are not killed, I will have to bring a flood and turn the world into water."

ﻪۿ Why Did He Have to Die?

When the Chofetz Chaim's saintly and brilliant son-in-law, R. Tzvi Levinson ל״צז (Rosh Yeshiva of Radin), passed away, the Chofetz Chaim's wife mourned: "The world is so evil, with so many evil people walking around, why did the Attribute of Justice strike R. Tzvi of all people?"

The Chofetz Chaim answered: "Surely you understand that instead of one person like R. Tzvi, it would have been necessary to wipe out half the world, and that is impossible. R. Tzvi was taken in place of them." He then continued to explain the concept of: "Because of the evil, the *tzaddik* is taken" (*Yeshayahu* 57:1) (*The Chofetz Chaim — His Life and Work*, p. 434).

It is said that the Chofetz Chaim sensed the impending calamity that was to befall European Jewry and implied at the time that the decree was delayed for some years by the passing of R. Tzvi.

ﻪۿ Hashem Pities You More

The young widowed daughter of one of the *gedolim* of this generation was once asked, "How did your father comfort you after your husband's death?" She replied that after the *shiva* was over, her father said to her: "Did you notice how many people came to console you? Although it is true they all feel a great deal of pity for you, you should know that the Holy One, blessed is He, pities you more than all of them."

🍃 "A G-d Full of Mercy"

On the *yahrzeit* of his mother, an eighty-year-old Jew told the following story to his friends:

> Let me tell you the final words I heard from my mother, may she rest in peace. When my mother was on her deathbed, she called for me and told me: "Come close to me my child, and I will explain the meaning of the verse 'A G-d full of mercy.' When a cup is filled to the brim with water, the smallest touch is enough to cause the water to overflow. So it is with Hashem: All that is needed is the smallest 'touch', and a sea of mercy flows from Him."

These last words of a mother to her child were retold over seventy years later with the same emotion as on the day they were said.

🍃 No One Else Can Feel the Pain

R. Shemuel Rozovsky ל״צז, Rosh Yeshiva of Ponevezh, related that when his wife died, he received this letter of consolation from R. Chaim Shemuelevitz ל״צז, Rosh Yeshiva of the Mir Yeshiva:

> In order to properly console someone, it is necessary to feel the other person's pain. We have learned, however, that a wife only dies for her husband; no one else can feel the pain of a husband after his wife's death. Therefore, no person has the ability to console him. Only Hashem, blessed be He, senses and sees the total anguish, and therefore only *HaMakom yenachem eschem* — only Hashem Himself will be able to console you amongst the mourners of Zion and Yerushalayim.

❧ Like the Consolation of a Mother

"I bowed sorrowfully as one who mourns for his mother" (*Tehillim* 35:14). "What is unique about mourning for one's mother?" asks the Gaon R. Yechezkel Sarne צ״ל, outstanding Torah and *mussar* genius, founder and Rosh Yeshiva of Hebron Yeshiva (*Daliyos Yechezkel*, vol. II, p. 30). He cites an answer from a verse in *Yeshayahu* (66:13): "Like a man whose mother consoles him, so will I console you, and in Yerushalayim you shall be consoled." The prophet emphasizes a mother's consolation, indicating that a mother is the one most capable of consoling her children. When a mother dies, there is no solace, for along with her passing, the power to console dies with her. This, then, is why the verse in *Tehillim* considers mourning for one's mother unique.

❧ Why Did My Beloved Die First?

A Jew from Tel Aviv once came to the Steipler and poured out his tale of woe. The man said that his wife had died and life was now very bitter for him. The Steipler told him: "I too am in a situation similar to yours. I've been a widower for some time now. It is bitter for me as well. Although I am taken care of, there is no substitute for the original.

"I have given the matter much thought and have come to the conclusion that the Holy One, blessed be He, has set up nature so that couples don't die at the same time, but instead, one spouse dies first while the remaining one is left to suffer over the death. However, if we were asked for our opinion we would not have wanted it differently.... We must remain alive in order to thank Hashem that the order was not reversed!"

After hearing these words, the man left, encouraged.

*　　　*　　　*

The Steipler devoted many hours to encouraging others facing trials, explaining that *yissurim* are actually for our good. The simple faith he possessed and his constant awareness that all events were for his benefit illustrate the meaning of the blessing, "He has provided for *all* of my needs" — for no matter what my needs are, they will all be provided for.

*   *   *

The Saba of Novahrdok used to say:

All students of Torah know that when one studies the Rambam, it is essential to understand the deep meaning inherent in all his omissions. When the Rambam does not include a certain item in his discussion, it is cause for investigation. No one even considers the possibility that perhaps the Rambam omitted the item because he was preoccupied at the time, etc. Instead, everyone toils to clarify the underlying reason for the omission.

So too, we must try to understand the "omissions" of the Holy One Himself! Instead of complaining about Heaven, a person has an obligation to resolve these questions [by acknowledging that everything done to Man is certainly for his benefit]. The person who comes to terms with this issue feels the same pleasure as one who has just resolved a difficult Rambam (*Ashkavte d'Rebbi*).

*   *   *

At the end of the *shiva* of a great Rosh Yeshiva, R. Eliezer Menachem Shach said to the grieving sons of the deceased, "Our Sages teach us that Hashem is happy and rejoices when a pure and righteous soul returns to Him. If Hashem is happy, surely the deceased is also happy when he returns to Hashem."

On another occasion he remarked, "*Em is doch gut*" — for him, it is good.

To a father who lost children and asked how he could accept the loss, R. Shach replied, "You should feel as if they have traveled far away and for the present you cannot visit them. Eventually, you will be able to see them again."

In a short letter of consolation to someone close to him, he wrote:

"I heard of the great tragedy that has befallen you. Hashem's ways are far above ours, and we have no knowledge of why, or for what purpose this occurred. But this we do know: Hashem gave and Hashem took and He is good and does goodness; He is merciful and benevolent. May you find consolation in your important activities and Torah teaching. May you have no more reason for sorrow, and may you have much *nachas* from your children, in health and well-being, and be comforted among the mourners of Zion and Yerushalayim."

✒ It Is Impossible to Forget

R. Shlomo Zalman Auerbach, זצ"ל, Rosh Yeshiva of Kol Torah and one of the greatest halachic authorities of our generation, spoke these words of consolation to a young widow:

"People try to comfort you, saying that with the passage of time you will forget your pain. In truth, it is impossible to forget, and they are mistaken in telling you that you will forget. But you should live with it and continue to strengthen your faith, and Hashem will surely help you."

✒ Death Atones

After the murder of a G-d-fearing woman in a terrorist attack, R. Gedalya Eiseman שליט"א, *mashgiach* of Yeshivas Kol Torah, commented:

Our Sages say (*Moed Katan* 28a): "Why does the death of

Miriam appear next to the laws of the *parah adumah* (red heifer)? To teach that just as sacrifices atone, so does the death of a *tzaddik* atone."

Let us consider then why the Torah did not record Miriam's death together with the sacrifices intended primarily for atonement, such as the sin-offerings or burnt-offerings. Why was her death recorded adjacent to the *parah adumah* offering, which is essentially for *tahara*, ritual cleanliness? Perhaps it is because the *parah adumah* is the classic example of a mitzva whose reason and meaning are not known to us. We are taught that "It is a decree from before Me; you may have no doubts or questions about it!"

This also applies to the death of *tzaddikim*. Their death raises a question in our hearts: Why does tragedy befall them? Our only possible response is: "It is a decree from before Me; you may have no doubts or questions about it." Perhaps this is the deeper connection between the death of Miriam and the chapter of the *parah adumah*.

ࢠ When a Person Is Orphaned

A Rav gave these words of consolation to a young man whose parents both passed away within a short period of time:

Our Sages teach us that there are three partners in the creation of man: his father, his mother, and Hashem. What happens to a person when the first two partners leave this world and he is left feeling alone and forsaken? We find the answer in the words of King David (*Tehillim* 27:10): "When my father and mother abandon me, Hashem will gather me in." When a person is left behind by his parents, Hashem gathers him in. The hand of Hashem is stretched out to him and a door is opened to strengthen his connection with the Third Partner.

❧ Where Is Our Beloved Now?

"HaMakom" literally means *the place*. Perhaps we may understand this as alluding to *The Place* where the deceased has gone. If a mourner could see the place to which the deceased has gone, he could find consolation. Imagine receiving a letter from the departed with a description of his place in the World to Come, telling about all the angels who surround him and *tzaddikim* he sees there, of his joy in the profound awareness of Hashem which is achieved there. The letter would describe the wonders and secrets of the World to Come and explain that Hashem wishes that he remain there in order to receive full reward for all of his efforts in this world.

This is *The Place* which our limited mental powers can only try to imagine. That *Place* itself can be the consolation, reminding the mourners of the wonderful place to which the deceased has gone.

The phrase: "among the mourners of Zion and Yerushalayim," reminds us that all our exiles lead towards the ultimate salvation and Redemption we will eventually see. In the end, our eyes will be opened and we will see how all suffering not only led to good, but was Goodness in and of itself.

*For my father and mother have
forsaken me; G-d will gather me in.*

— *Tehillim*

Letters of Condolence

When the Saba of Kelm, R. Simcha Zissel Ziv, passed away in 1898, the leadership of his famed *yeshiva gedola*, the Talmud Torah of Kelm, passed to his nephew R. Tzvi Hirsh Broide. R. Tzvi Hirsh died tragically in mid-life some fifteen years later. The following is from a letter of condolence written by R. Nachum Zev, a son of the Saba, to his uncle, R. Leib, the father of R. Tzvi Hirsh:

> Allow me to make a small but highly significant comment regarding the death of Aharon's sons (on the day of the consecration of the *Mishkan*). In *Parashas Shemini* (*Vayikra* 10:3) it is written: "Moshe said to Aharon: 'This is what Hashem spoke, saying, "Through those close to Me I will be sanctified, and before the entire people I will be glorified." ' And Aharon was silent." Rashi explains: " 'Those close to Me' — my chosen ones: When Hashem punishes the righteous, He becomes feared, exalted, and praised. If so with the [punishment of the] righteous, even more so with the wicked, and so it is written: 'G-d, Your awe emanates from Your sanctuaries' (*Tehillim* 68:36). Read not ממקדשיך, 'from Your sanctuaries,' but rather, ממקודשיך, 'from those [people] made holy by You.' "

The purpose, then, of the punishment given to those chosen by Hashem is to arouse feelings of awe, exaltation, and praise of Hashem in others, thereby increasing fear and love of Hashem. It is of enormous benefit and a wonderful elevation for those chosen by Hashem, to receive immediate punishment. "Aharon was silent" — he accepted it. For a righteous, saintly person, the greatest consolation is the awareness that through his son's death, Hashem is more feared, glorified, and praised.

So, a G-d-fearing person's pain and sorrow should not exceed the Torah's rules and guidelines for mourning. Mourning should be an immense source of Fear of Heaven, and a glorification of His Name. Pain beyond this measure, as well as emotional and spiritual confusion, are nothing but veils which separate a person from that lofty goal, and can even make it appear as if he doubts the justice of Hashem's ways, Heaven forbid.

I discussed this in depth with the yeshiva students and it caused an increased spiritual resolve, which, *baruch Hashem*, continually grows.

Actually, among those of us here in the yeshiva, your beloved son, the great *tzaddik*, is still alive. He is alive in the *tefillos*, he is alive in the study of *mussar*, and he is alive in the atmosphere of the yeshiva and in every activity here. Since the passing of my father, it was your dear son, R. Tzvi, who spread his wings over this great house, expending the utmost effort towards the perfection and glorification of the yeshiva. He is still alive to us, and his name and memory are cherished.

The students and the guests who have come for the *Yamim Noraim*, study *mishnayos* (for his merit) every evening after *Ma'ariv*, with whatever depth is possible in the limited time available, and we say Kaddish *d'Rabbanan* and one Kaddish [for him] in the morning.

Without exaggeration, we can say that the result of the awesome tragedy was that Hashem, blessed be He, is more feared and exalted. This is the greatest consolation to all of us, and especially to you, my dear uncle, the father and teacher of a great son (Kelm, 26 Elul, 5673/1913).

❧ This World Is Only a Dream

R. Yehonason Eibeshitz, outstanding Torah genius in his generation two hundred years ago whose teachings were published as the *Urim veTumim*, writes:

> Peace to you, my sister-in-law, and to your sons. May *HaMakom* console you and spread His wings over you, to be a Father and Patron to you, and may He heal your crushed hearts.
>
> I cannot properly write to you because of my great grief and sorrow; actually, it is very difficult for me to console you and your beloved sons.... Many tears have flowed from my eyes, and my heart is hollow within me. Heaven bear witness that for my [other] deceased brother I did not feel as much grief and sorrow as I did for him [your husband]. Heaven testifies that on the anniversary of Moshe Rabbeinu's passing, when I delivered a *mussar* speech to my people, I alluded to him, and I have mourned privately for him.... Nonetheless, I cannot console you as the law demands, for my sighs have rendered me speechless.
>
> However, I do beg of you, give honor to Hashem, may He be blessed, and do not grieve excessively.
>
> You are weak without this [added strain], and now

you are in even greater need of strength than before,
[in order to] raise your children [properly]. So be
strong, and accept everything from Hashem lovingly
— "He crushes and He heals."

You have lost a father of flesh and blood, but you
have gained Hashem as your Father, for He is called
"The Father of orphans, and the Judge of widows" (Tehillim 68:6).

It is a fact that orphans are among the most successful in Torah [study], in wisdom, and in fear [of
Heaven]. This happens because Hashem watches over
them with special supervision, for He is compassionate to orphans.

How can people's wisdom be so clouded? What
reason do we have to cry over the deeds of Hashem?
Do we know what is good and what is bad? Are we as
merciful as He is? Do we bestow good as He does?
Pity orphans as He does? Do we love kindness and
mercy as He does? Can we foresee the future as He
can? Do we perform acts of righteousness as the Holy
One, blessed is He, does?! For He is the very essence
of Wisdom, Mercy, and Truth!

Certainly, if He, in His great wisdom, had determined that it was still possible for some benefit yet to
come [from the deceased], he would not have died, because even when there is mainly evil and only a portion of good in a person, the Holy One rejects the evil
and selects the good. That is why He is called "The
Good One," and is known as "He Who is Good, and
does good to both the bad and the good" (Siddur,
Yamim Noraim).

King David declared: "Hashem is good to all and
has mercy on all His creatures" (Tehillim 145:9) — there
are no exceptions! However, He is especially merciful
to the People which is close to Him, Yisrael; and is

even more merciful to the person whose conduct in
mitzva performance and whose deeds were done faithfully and unwaveringly, for the Holy One measures
every minute of the righteous individual's life with utmost precision, in order to extend his life. Hashem,
blessed is He and blessed is His Name, counts all the
minutes the righteous will live [or, all the minutes until the time comes for a *tzaddik* to be created], more
than the minutes until he leaves the world.

Furthermore, it is clear that Hashem, in His wisdom, has determined that death is the ultimate favor,
and that the death of the righteous is precious in the
eyes of Hashem (see *Tehillim* 116:15). So why should
we become upset? Don't we want to appreciate
Hashem's kindness? Does He pity the widow and the
young orphans, who are like sheep without a shepherd, any less than the grieving family pities them?!

Does the Holy One not grieve when a man is in sorrow and when widows and orphans are in sorrow?
Our Sages tell us (*Sanhedrin* 41a) that the Holy One laments and declares: "My head is heavy upon Me [with
sorrow]" when an idolater or a blasphemer is killed by
stoning by the *Beis Din*! And it is written: "In all their
troubles, it pains Him" (*Yeshayahu* 63:9).

Hashem, unlike man, can alter any situation, and
thereby nullify sorrow. It is therefore easy to understand that if He had not found this [death] to be a kindness and a perfect favor, He certainly would not have
caused such pain; rather, He knows this will lead only
to a good end, even if it is undoubtedly accompanied
by much suffering.

For example, when a patient undergoes a painful
medical procedure, he is certainly allowed to cry out
in pain, and everyone is obligated to share his pain.
Nevertheless, the treatment was done for his benefit,

and in this situation, mercy called for cruelty. The same is true of the King of Kings. The Holy One knew that this [death] should not be postponed because of the pain and worries that would follow, since it is for the benefit of the pure soul [of the deceased]. [It will even be] for the benefit of the orphans — whether we comprehend this or not — because we do not know what is good for us. Many mothers become ill, but when they recover, they are plagued with horrible suffering from their children, [to the point that] they wished they had died. Do their thoughts help them? Hashem has determined that for the time being it is better for them to suffer — perhaps to cleanse them of previous sins — and if He had determined otherwise, they would have died earlier.

How can a blind man complain that he was not led on a straight path, when his escort has vision and can see? Compared to Hashem, we are all blind, for He can see and foresee all future generations. What reason do we have for crying over a death? Did Hashem guarantee long life for anybody? Just as we are not beyond consolation when an eighty year old dies, likewise we should not mourn for a thirty year old, since it is all the same; even if Man were to live a thousand years, it would be as nothing.

Should one be upset about a dream? Some people sleep for a long time in a very pleasant dream, and some are awakened in the middle of their dreams. The person whose sleep was disturbed certainly would be upset, but not for long, because, after all, it was only a dream. This world too is only a dream; some of us are woken in the middle, some sleep for the entire dream, and some only sleep for most of it. But it really is all the same — a dream is a dream.

How can we, in the midst of our Exile, be upset

when an individual dies? Wherever we turn, we see anguish and sighing in our holy People, Yisrael. We wander as lost sheep from one end [of the world] to the other; our lives are like the trembling of a man being led to his death. We are walking corpses, for all we have in this world is fear, trouble, and panic. But when we die, we have redemption from the grave. This is what is known as the Resurrection of the Dead — we will be freed from ourselves and we will arrive alive in the True World, where everything is true and just. That is the world of happiness, where grief and sighing will be banished, where there is no weakness or weariness, and where all are illuminated by the light of the Living King.

Since ancient times, many gentiles took their own lives in the hope that they would thus be able to leave this dark world and reach a world filled with light. The Holy One forbade us to do so, however, as is written: "You shall guard your lives to the utmost" (Devarim 4:15). He knows when the proper time has arrived for life to begin and when it should end, and hence, we live and die in accordance with His Will alone.

Therefore, sister and children, watch over your health. This is more important than saying Kaddish for your father z"l — it is a greater mitzva. Accept everything from Hashem lovingly, for this receives His gracious approval.

A king who sends his servants to work in another land and sees that they still have work to be completed there would be foolish to recall them. But when he sees that their task has been accomplished, he will recall them at once. We are all here in this world to toil and perfect the holy work of Hashem; for this we were created. If the Holy One finds that a certain individual can still contribute to the holy work, He certainly will not recall the person to the World to Come. So why should we cry over his death? Do we not realize that the World to Come is better than this world? We must minimize our mourning as much as possible, since exchanging a passing world for an everlasting world is a good exchange.

Should we cry for the widow and the orphans? Can a mortal really save anyone? Can he save himself? What are we? What can we save? Man's salvation is false! If the Holy One saves, that is salvation, for He is everlasting. He does not need the help of human beings. He helps the widow and the orphans and does not need the support of the father.

And if the tears are for a different reason, namely, that we miss the deceased, this is truly the nature of the other nations, not of Yisrael, a nation whose salvation comes from Hashem...for we will yet be reunited in the "Land of the Living" (i.e., the World to Come).

A king who sends the children of his ministers to be educated in foreign lands does not keep them there for a long time. Bad children, however, are exiled for a long time. So it is with Hashem: Those whom He loves are called to Him earlier than the others, and this is why we say: "You are sons to Hashem your L-rd" (Devarim 14:1).

Eleven years ago when he [the brother] was very sick, he would have died if not for Hashem's great mercy. He would have been forgotten long ago. Dear sister, is Hashem not the same Merciful One as He was at that time? "I, Hashem, have not changed" (Malachi 3:6). Hashem is not a changing being, and therefore we can assume that He has deemed that the time for mercy has ended.

I ask of you, my sister, to be at peace, and Hashem will give you cause for rejoicing with your dear children, and your broken heart will be restored. Be consoled together with Zion and Yerushalayim, which we are obligated to mourn and remember all our days, as a woman cries for the husband of her youth. The "Husband" and "Father" of the Jewish people is as if no longer with us, and we are all orphans and widows.

The prophet Yirmiyahu laments: "We have become orphans with no father; our mothers are like widows" (*Eicha* 5:3). We wander in Exile without a leader, without the *Kohen Gadol, Sanhedrin,* Prophets, *Urim VeTumim,* or the *Mizbeiach,* and many other precious gifts that have been taken from us. The truth is, my sister, it is a wonder that anyone who is called a Jew does not take his own life at the thought of the destruction of Zion and Yerushalayim. For we have fallen from glory to degradation and into an Exile which has extended for so many years. However, we are forbidden [to take our own lives]. Meanwhile, we are consoled [with the knowledge] that Hashem will certainly redeem us when He consoles Zion, when the final time arrives. The Exile is a ripe fruit which spoils more slowly than fruit picked before it has ripened....

There is no doubt that Hashem will have pity on you, for He is merciful towards orphans, and He will not let you falter. Do not be upset over events in this world, which is in reality utter nothingness.

Darius was a great king and an only son. While still a young man, he became deathly ill. He told his wife and mother not to weep over him after his death; only if they heard of any bad deed he had committed were they to weep over his brief life.

After his death, they obeyed his wishes and held back their tears while they waited for someone to come and tell them of his bad deeds. But [as time passed] and no one reported any misdeeds, their urge to weep ceased. All the sages saw the great wisdom in

Darius' advice to his wife and mother. Death itself should not be cause for crying, only any wrong actions committed by the person. If someone without blemish dies, there is no reason for tears.

Therefore, dear sister and children, I would like to conclude with the following: Be happy that he died with a good name and no blemish, for "Who is a son of the World to Come? He who is honored by the elders" (*Bava Basra* 10b). If all the Torah scholars have only good words to say of him, then he has died in a good state. So why cry out and weep? Who knows, perhaps if he had lived longer, he might have lost his good state, for the righteous are compared to fine wine, which must be consumed before it sours. Only poor wine is left to stand a long time....

And so, dear sister, let us live with hope in Hashem: "Those who put their hope in Hashem will renew their vigor; they shall raise wings as eagles" (*Yeshayahu* 40:31).

❧ A Letter from Kelm

The last *menahel* of the Talmud Torah in Kelm, R. Daniel Movshovits, wrote this letter of condolence to R. Dessler when his father passed away:

My dear brother-in-law,

May consolation and salvation be yours in the future! What can I write, my beloved brother? How can I console you in your great anguish? It seems to me, based on the traditional words of consolation, "May Hashem comfort you among the mourners of Zion and Yerushalayim," that we pray that with the ultimate salvation and consolation, all individual suffering and grief will be assuaged.

Perhaps when we say "among the mourners of

Zion," we allude to the verse, "A song of ascent: When Hashem brings the return to Zion, we are as dreamers." At that time, the salvation will be so great that all suffering will seem to have been just a dream. Even more, it will be revealed that the suffering itself brought about the salvation. We say in the *Shemoneh Esrei:* "A King Who puts to death, and brings to life, and causes salvation to sprout forth." Hashem, in putting to death, plants seeds of salvation that will sprout forth at the time of the Resurrection. So we say that with the consolation of Zion and the return to life of those resting in the earth, every defect of the world will be rectified, bringing true and complete consolation to all the broken-hearted.

You may take comfort in many things — you were able to give your father comfort and take care of him until the day of his death, you never strayed from the proper path he taught you, and you continued the chain of Torah life and good deeds which will bring your father endless satisfaction and merit in the World of Truth. I am sure that you will be strong and take care not to let excessive mourning harm your health òr weaken your holy endeavors. As for B., you should make sure to see that she is given encouragement and does not become too grief-stricken, since she must guard her health. Who can even estimate the great merit of the constant care she gave your father throughout the years of his sufferings and illness. May He Who repays with kindness bring you all manner of salvation and consolation.

❧ From the Chofetz Chaim

The Chofetz Chaim wrote the following letter of condolence to his childhood friend, R. Chaim Leib HaKohen of

Tiktin, when his son, who had been a student in the Chofetz Chaim's yeshiva, passed away.

Tzom Gedalya, 5653/1892

Greetings and peace to Hashem's friend, and my good friend, outstanding in Torah and truly G-d-fearing, R. Chaim Leib HaKohen,

In response to your letter, I cannot say when I will next be in Bialystok. As for the matter of which you wrote, when I heard of your son's passing, I was very distressed.

My beloved friend — I understand your great and almost immeasurable pain. Yet we know from the holy Torah that the suffering of Jews is like the punishment one receives from a father. It is well known that Hashem loves each Jew more than that Jew loves himself. When He does bring suffering, it is at times only for the sake of the Jewish People. It is known that the *tzaddik* is taken because of the sins of the generation, as Moshe Rabbeinu said: "Erase me from The Book which You have written [to atone for the sin of the Golden Calf]."

Certainly if one suffers for the community and if, because of him, the community survives, then his reward is very great, for he has corrected far more than if he were just rectifying himself. So we find in *Pirkei Avos*: "If I am only for myself, what am I?" Thus we should not be overly concerned with matters like these.

My dear friend — I too was struck a blow this past winter with the loss of my son Avraham. He was great in Torah, with unusually profound understanding, and truly elevated in his natural kindness. But I take true comfort in the hope that I will not be shamed by him when I face judgment before the Throne of Glory after 120 years. You too can take solace [in this thought]. Your son was wonderful and beloved, and you will surely not be shamed by him in the World to Come. As for the ways of Hashem, what can we know?

...Who was greater than the sons of Aharon, as we read a number of times: "Speak to Aharon and his sons...." They were greater than the Elders and the leaders of the tribes, yet Aharon accepted their death, as is written: "Aharon was silent."

Therefore, my friend, we must be comforted for that which Hashem brought upon us. May Hashem console you among the mourners of Zion....

You wrote me your thoughts of sending your remaining son to the Yeshiva here. I do not think it would be correct, as the sign here is not good for him [i.e., his brother's passing does not bode well for him here]. It would be good if you could keep him at home.

May Hashem inscribe and seal you for good for the coming year and shower upon you His blessing from Above....

Yisrael Meir HaKohen

&❧ "I Feel Your Pain..."

R. Leib Chasman, ל״צז, *menahel ruchani* of Hebron Yeshiva, wrote to R. Nochum Yitzchak Broide, one of Kelm's *baalei mussar*:

To my dear friend,

Hashem strikes, and He commands, "Console My mourners...." Hashem brings suffering and He commands us to share in the burden of a fellow Jew's suffering. For Hashem's punishment is like a father's to his son; His only concern is for good and kindness. But if you, Man, see only the suffering and pain, and cannot perceive the true goodness therein, then you should take part in and personally share another's suffering.

The very mitzva of consoling mourners should be true consolation to the mourner — seeing that Hashem commands His friends and acquaintances: "Go, My sons, console your brother in his bereavement, speak to his heart and lighten his grief." Surely the mourner sees and hears the voice of our Father in Heaven: "You are sons to Hashem your G-d...you are a holy People..." (*Devarim* 14:1).

May it console you, my beloved friend, to know how much I feel your pain at this time when "your crown" (your dear parent) has been taken away....

May Hashem console you amongst the mourners of Zion and Yerushalayim,

Y.L. Chasman

≈ R. Yechezkel Levenstein Consoles His Daughters and Their Families

The first two of the following five letters were written in 5712/1952 upon the passing of R. Yechezkel Levenstein's daughter's young son.

Greetings and loving blessings,
"All that Hashem does is for the good" — even without understanding how it is for the good, it is a straightforward and easy task to bring this understanding close to one's heart. All we must know is that we are Hashem's children. Children entrust themselves completely to their father's care, knowing that his only concern is for their benefit. In the words of the Ibn Ezra (*Devarim* 14:1): "Know that you are children to Hashem and that He loves you more than a fa-

ther loves his son. Although you do not understand Him — as small children do not understand their father's actions, but simply trust him — so too, you shall trust Hashem." (See also the golden words of the Ramban on that verse.)

I contemplated the words of King David (II *Shemuel* 12:23). When he was told of the death of his son, he arose, washed himself, and changed his garments.... He came to his house and had food brought to him as if nothing had happened. He explained, "Is this a time for fasting? Behold, I am going towards him, but he will not return to me."

We will yet meet in Heaven, where he has gone. This is like one who sends his son from abroad to *Eretz Yisrael*, hoping that they will eventually be reunited there. So too with us. We hope to again meet with the deceased in the World to Come, where we will rejoice with him forever.

My dear children! If we were strong in faith, it would be easy for us to accept the decree of Heaven with love, for all the ways of Heaven are tests for Man. When Hashem acts, He has already planned the final result.

For a number of years, Hashem left this soul with us as a trust. This is the meaning of "Hashem gave and Hashem takes back." This child fulfilled his purpose in the world with the lesser degree of Torah and mitzvos which he achieved without sin, since there is no punishment for a child, although there is reward. The mitzvos he performed remain his completely, so his gain is great. He could not have made a better bargain! If we will but accept the Heavenly decree with love, we will withstand the test and thus merit the greatest good from our Father Above, just as Aharon's silence merited him the reward of seeing Hashem's Presence. We

will thus sanctify Hashem's Name publicly, since everyone will see that we truly believe in the Eternity of
Hashem.

I had a dream a few days earlier, before I received
the news, from which I understood what was to happen.

I intend to learn *mishnayos* for him....

Baruch Hashem, all is well with us, and we hope to
merit only glad tidings, for us and all of *Klal Yisrael*.

I hope very much that you will write to me that
you have accepted the tragedy with the true understanding that "All that Hashem does is for the good,"
in both worlds. "How great are Your deeds, Hashem.
How profoundly deep are Your thoughts. A boor will
not know, nor will a fool understand this."

*　　　*　　　*

Greetings and blessings,

Accept the judgment of Hashem with love, for no
evil comes from Him. This is intended only to test us.
We have the opportunity now to achieve everlasting
life in a brief hour, as we find: "Some acquire their
[share in the] World to Come in a single hour."

The Saba of Kelm once wrote in a letter of consolation: "Without a doubt, I can imagine that if a great
person like you is strong and firm in lovingly accepting the Heavenly decree, your reward will be greater
and greater. A person is naturally aroused to grief, but
if he overcomes his nature, thinking, 'For Hashem's
lovingkindness, I give song, and for His harsh judgment, I give song,' he will be amply rewarded. Why?
Because the punishment given by a father is surely
true compassion — for every such moment his reward
is exceedingly great."

Our Sages comment that in reward for Aharon's silence at the sudden death of his sons, Hashem spoke

to him directly. The chapter of "Those who drank wine" was taught by Hashem to Aharon (Rashi, *Parashas Shemini*). This is an instance where a person acquired his world in a single hour. Also, it should be understood that this also brought great merit to his sons, Nadav and Avihu, for having caused Aharon to achieve the honor of receiving Hashem's teaching directly. Who can imagine the enormous merit they had in causing so powerful a *kiddush Hashem*? As Hashem said: "Through those near to Me I will be sanctified."

So too, who can imagine the immense merit that will come to our deceased child if we accept the Divine decree with love. Who knows if he did not descend to this world only in order to understand what he could, and now, through him, we may achieve the great merit of accepting Hashem's judgment with love.

My dear children, our Sages say that if one grieves excessively, Hashem then says, "You do not have more mercy for him than I do" (*Moed Katan* 27b).

It is well known that the whole purpose of mourning is for the benefit of the living — to train us to constantly be aware of death. If not for that, mourning would be prohibited, for we should believe firmly that a Jewish soul does not die, it only returns to its Father in Heaven, as is written: "...the spirit will return to Hashem Who had given it" (*Koheles* 12:7).

My dear daughter, may your reward be great for your ability to be strong in a situation like this. May Hashem give us His mercy and say to us, "You are children to Hashem Your G-d." And may He say, "Death will stop forever" and that we will then merit only good and blessing.

*   *   *

The following three letters, dated 5720-23/1960-63, were written after the sudden passing of R. Yechezkel's son-in-law.

Condolences and blessings to my dear daughter and your dear children,

My beloved children, all we can do is accept the judgments of Hashem with love. Man was not created for the sake of this-worldly living. *Olam HaZeh* was created for the seventy nations of the world; for us, there is *Olam HaBa*, the World to Come, a world that exists forever. One hour of spiritual contentment in the World to Come is more desirable than all of life in this world. Ephraim Mordechai did not die; he returned to the world from which he came. That is the proper home for one who earns it with his Torah and mitzvos. He gave his life away for Torah — for himself and for others. He taught many students, so his place will surely be among the Torah greats.

For our part, we must help him the only way we can — by accepting the judgment with love. This is his request and desire now. My beloved grandchildren, you must now help your father, through your Torah and mitzvos. He gave so much of his time for you, now you can repay him with prayer and by saying Kaddish with deep concentration and meaning. Be sure to understand the words of Kaddish fully and to learn *mishnayos* every day for the benefit of his holy soul. Do not dwell on sadness. Instead, occupy yourselves with joyful learning, for we have a compassionate Father Who will surely have mercy upon you. With this you will make your mother happy.

Please devote yourselves to Torah study only, and give charity for his holy soul.

Please write to me about everything. I wait to hear from you. Hashem will not desert you, since He is the father of orphans and widows.

Your father who consoles himself, looking to Hashem for salvation,

*   *   *

Greetings and blessings,

"You are sons to Hashem your G-d" (*Devarim* 14:1). The *Ohr HaChaim* comments that one must realize that death is not a loss to the deceased — he has simply departed for a different place, like a person who travels abroad for an extended stay but expects to return and see his loved ones again. You should feel as though your father traveled to *Eretz Yisrael*.

Understandably, when one moves to a new place, he is a stranger. He meets acquaintances who help him find his place, after which he becomes comfortable in his new situation. Similarly, when one leaves this world, he may not feel at home for the first year, until he is purified by Heavenly retribution — Gehinnom.

How wonderful it is if he finds "friends and acquaintances" who speak on his behalf and save him from this punishment, be they his own good deeds, or the merit of mitzvos that his children and students do for him.

My dear children, the real truth is that your father is alive, living in a different place. He thinks of you, and desires your well-being, for your good is his good. May Hashem grant you growth in Torah and in Fear of Heaven, and then we will all prosper in both worlds.

Your father, who hopes for your well-being,

Yechezkel

*   *   *

The day after Yom Kippur, 5721

Blessings and greetings,

Surely you have read the *Igeres HaGra* [the letter written by the Gaon of Vilna to his family before he left for *Eretz Yisrael*]. It would be worthwhile to read over and over again that letter in which he writes his family: "How tragic that everyone thinks of leaving an inheritance for his children, when in fact the only help a person can give his children is through Torah and good deeds; their physical sustenance is decreed from Above."

Children have the power to elevate their parents from Gehinnom. Who is sure that he will not have to suffer in Gehinnom? Even great *tzaddikim* dreaded and feared Gehinnom. The purpose of saying Kaddish and learning *mishnayos* on behalf of the dead is to lighten their punishment after death. How great is the merit of parents when their children act properly, sanctifying Hashem's Name! And how foolish are those who worry about their children's physical needs! With these thoughts, they only acquire a place in Gehinnom, for no one has the ability to leave any wealth to his children. Hashem alone sustains and provides for all His creations. Man was not created in this world in order to keep alive his body, which today exists and tomorrow is in the grave. Besides which, you will cry tomorrow for what causes you happiness and laughter today.

How foolish is life in this world! Throughout life, we prepare ourselves a great share in Gehinnom, Heaven forbid, not only by our own actions but by the actions of our children if they do not act properly.

My dear daughter, it will soon be *Yom Tov*. Be happy, and know that the Creator of the world is our

Father, and He seeks to give us a world of eternity. We can easily merit everlasting reward by believing that all that has befallen us was decreed in Heaven, and by willingly accepting the Divine decree.

Wishing you and your children a joyous *Yom Tov* and a good year,

Yechezkel

(*Ohr Yechezkel,* letters 110, 111, 340, 349, 352)

✿ For Orphans

A student of R. Yerucham Levovitz, the Mirrer *mashgiach,* writes:

My dearly beloved children,

I write this hoping that you will first read it many years hence. I wish to console you when I will no longer be here. No one knows when his time will come. A day will come — may Hashem grant us long life! — when my place in the house will be vacated forever, and you will be orphans.

My children, I have observed many orphans. To most of them, the world has become dark, without hope or direction. Young orphans are full of envy — "Everyone else has a father and I don't." Older orphans are also shattered, as if their world had collapsed. Few that I observed were able to bear being orphans. I hope that I will be able to instruct you, so that my words will be understood, and a source of light for you.

The key to the mystery of life is belief in the Eternal One. A Divine Force gives life to all of Creation, to every blade of grass and every person. This life-force is the essence of everything, and is Man's spirit and soul.

I hope that I have succeeded in raising you with *emuna*. Strengthen yourselves in that *emuna* and know that in it lies the key to the riddle of death! If the cessation of the body were the cessation of man himself, there would be no consolation in mourning, but it is not so! The body ceases, but the person remains alive.

My teacher wrote in a letter of consolation, "We should perceive death as no more than a move from one city to another. In truth, your father did not die; he is alive in a different place. One who appreciates the subtlety of the matter knows that he is closer to us now than in his lifetime, since there are no barriers before him." This is amazing! Only a great, holy person like my rebbe could reveal to us such wonderful matters.

It is true: *Emuna* does not recognize death. The deceased is alive; he is aware and feels and is close to his relatives always.

But with all of this, you will not find comfort from the pain of parting. You are used to seeing your father, hearing his advice, and receiving his help. Even adult children who have built their own homes rely on their father and are strengthened by his presence. Who can fill this void?

But know, my dear children, if you truly loved me while I was with you, if your love was not superficial, then you will always be able to see me before your eyes and know what I would say and what I would advise. Let Yosef — who withstood his test by picturing his father before him — be an example for you. Each of you has in his heart the image of his father with which to strengthen and revive himself. And most important is the awareness that the essence of Man is his spiritual nature — and that remains alive forever.

I would also like, however, to tell you about my

thoughts when I was orphaned of my parents, may they rest in peace.

Every mourner feels the urge to come closer to mitzvos and good deeds. Even many completely irreligious people "keep Kaddish," going to *shul*, wearing *tallis* and putting on *tefillin*. What is the source of this urge?

Our Sages say, "There are three partners in the creation of man: his father, his mother, and G-d." One does not see the third partner. But when a person's parents leave him alone in this life, his heart tells him to throw his burdens upon Hashem, the Third Partner.

One whose belief is unshakable feels this with absolute certainty. "For my father and mother have forsaken me; G-d will gather me in" (*Tehillim* 27:10).

Actually, the physical father is only a representative of the true Father in Heaven. When the physical father completes his term as G-d's agent, the son becomes bound tightly to his Father Above, and "it is better to trust in G-d than to trust in man!"

These were my feelings in the days of my *shiva* for my parents, and this is what I pass on to you, my beloved children. But know this: What is most important for every person at every age, but especially for orphans, is to be firm in *emuna*, to really feel His Providence and how He leads and directs you every day, fulfilling your physical and spiritual needs so that you lack nothing — if only you are strong in *emuna*.

One can be consoled only if he lives with this belief.

Let me add that I have come to think differently about consolation, as well. A person's surroundings — his family, teachers, and friends — help him to hold on to his accomplishments and rise even higher. People always want to raise themselves up and not fall,

Heaven forbid. Yet when someone's relative is taken away, he lacks part of his spiritual support.

A person will be consoled when he merits finding someone else who can help him and support him in his spiritual awakening. The Torah tells us: "Yitzchak brought her [Rivka] to the tent of his mother Sarah, and he took Rivka as his wife, and he loved her, and Yitzchak was consoled for his mother." Rashi comments: "She was Sarah herself"; i.e., she was just like Sarah. During Sarah's lifetime, the lamp burned from *erev Shabbos* to *erev Shabbos*, there was blessing in the dough, and a cloud (symbolizing Divine Providence) hovered above the tent. Rivka caused all of these to return, and this re-creation of life as it used to be brought consolation to Yitzchak.

My dearly beloved, this is how you can comfort yourselves. Come close to each other, help each other, and give words of strength. Push sadness and despair far from your hearts. Make sure your friends are people who are firm in their faith, love Torah and study it. Always be a *ba letaken*, a person who strives to become purified and who is guaranteed help from Above. And know with absolute certainly that Hashem will console you and make it possible for you to continue in your path — our path — to be strong in *emuna* and Torah, and to build homes faithful to observance of Hashem's commandments. And from this I too will be helped, as our Sages say: "For one who leaves a worthy son, it is as if he did not die."

This is my advice, my request, and my final words to you: "Believe, and be faithful" and light will then shine upon your ways forever.

With love,
(*Alei Shur*, by R. Shlomo Wolbe, vol. I, p. 303,)

֍ Yisrael Lives Forever

R. Dessler writes about the destruction of the Yeshiva in Kelm during World War II:

> Not all departures are equal. There are different types of death. There is the "death of the dead" — one whose spirit, coarse and materialistic, is dead while yet alive, a person whose soul is buried within his body during his life of illusion. His departure from this world is total destruction — his existence then is emptiness, as it had been during his lifetime. His body is destroyed and his soul is consumed and they both turn to ashes, for they had been like dust in their "make-believe" life. He was nothing and he is now nothing. What, then, is his death? Only the destruction of the illusion, as we say: "all of the evil" — both body and soul —"will dissipate like smoke"— vanishing without a trace.
>
> Not so is the departure of "Men of Truth." Destruction cannot touch them. The outer garb falls, but the inner content lives and endures, being an integral part of the Above. The body falls away, like the cloak of Eliyahu, but the entire being, imbued with *kedusha*, rises to Heaven; it is no longer an outer garb, having become *kedusha* itself. "Our forefather Yaakov did not die" — Yisrael lives forever....
>
> The principle here is: Whoever has absorbed Truth into himself does not die; he merely removes his outermost garb and rises to a Heavenly status, becoming stronger and purer. In the words of our Sages: "The *tzaddikim* are greater in their death than in their lifetime" — greater in content, greater in their teaching, greater in their life of truth, that everlasting life that is within them.

‰ *Al Kiddush Hashem*

R. Yisrael Yaakov Kanievsky wrote the following letter of consolation to someone whose sister was killed *al kiddush Hashem*:

> I heard the shocking news about your sister whose merit is great, and I share in the anguish of your bereft parents, may Hashem console them.
>
> In truth, we need not worry for your sister herself, since she has already been wondrously lifted up to her resting place in her "three hundred and ten worlds." ("Hashem is destined to bequeath to every *tzaddik* three hundred and ten worlds.")
>
> She is far greater than a *tzaddik* who served Hashem in Torah and mitzvos for an entire lifetime, as it was said: "[As for] the Martyrs of Lod — no person can stand in their confines" (*Pesachim* 50a), because they were killed in sanctification of the Holy Name. It is clear that if she were now allowed to return to her earlier circumstances, she would have no desire to return. What interest could she have in a world filled with pain and anguish now that she is so fortunate as to be in the place of Heavenly joy, the sanctity of Heavenly Beings, and delight in Hashem's great love. The pain and heartache, however, are left to the bereft parents and the entire family who grieve over her.
>
> May Hashem, blessed be He, console them, and heal the entire family through all types of blessing and success; may they be satisfied with future happiness and tranquillity, long life, prosperity, and Heaven's help all arranged and guarded from Above....

> Yisrael Yaakov Kanievsky

?≈ For Bereft Parents

R. Shlomo Wolbe writes to the parents of a child who died by drowning:

> To my dear friends, parents in mourning, may
> Hashem console you amongst the mourners of Zion.
>   I join you in your anguish, though distance makes
> it impossible for me to come to the *shiva*. I come in-
> stead with the following inadequate words.
>   I can say only that the effort of raising your dear
> son was not in vain, for he is alive and not dead,
> Heaven forbid. This pure soul does not have to bear
> the suffering of perfecting himself and the world. Our
> Sages say (*Avoda Zara* 3b): "What does He do in the
> last three hours of the day? He sits and teaches chil-
> dren Torah" that they were not able to learn in this
> world! You son is now in the "*cheder*" of Hashem Him-
> self, learning Torah directly from Hashem and feeling
> the greatest joy. May you find consolation in the
> knowledge that your son indeed lives on!
>   Once a student in Kelm drowned. When the boy's
> father came to the funeral, the Saba asked to speak pri-
> vately with him. Since the father was a very simple
> person, the yeshiva students were surprised that the
> two spoke together for such a long time. After quite a
> while, the father came out of the Saba's office saying
> he was sure that his son was still alive and had just
> moved to a faraway place, that his son had gone to an-
> other world in which he lived a genuine and true life.
>   Your son continues to live! May Hashem grant that
> you should never again be caused grief.
>
>   Shlomo Wolbe

*   *   *

The boy passed away at eight years of age, on the day that he completed his studies with the verse, כי היום ה' נראה אליכם —"For today Hashem will be seen upon you" (*Vayikra* 9:4). The boy wrote an explanation in his notebook: "For today the glory of the Divine Presence will be revealed upon you."

The Shela HaKodesh notes that the letters forming the words נ-ר-א-ה א-ל-י-כ-ם can be rearranged to spell the names of Aharon and Michael, meaning that Aharon and his sons became like the angel Michael, who is considered a *Kohen Gadol* (High Priest) in Heaven.

The *Chacham HaRazim* writes: "Until the destruction of the *Beis HaMikdash*, the angel Michael brought sacrifices similar to those brought by Israel. After the Destruction, Hashem said to him, 'Do not offer before Me oxen, sheep and goats; rather, bring up the souls of the righteous and of children who have not sinned, and they will rise up to Me as a pleasing aroma.' " The Midrash *HaNe'elam* adds, "R. Chiya said, 'This is not like other sacrifices, but instead like a person who is allowed to bring a special gift directly to the king.' "

(Afikei Mayim)

⋙ Mourning for a Father

A Rav wrote to his student:

> I just received the bitter news of your father's passing. Knowing how close you were to him in heart and soul, and how concerned you were for his health, I can understand how difficult it was for you to accept and bear his death. In such instances, one is inclined to attempt to understand at least a bit of the ways of Hashem. But it is precisely in such circumstances that

we need to strengthen our faith and belief. We must understand that all our feelings of compassion and justice come only from Hashem, for all that we have is from Him. If we have feelings of compassion, and an understanding of justice, Hashem, Who is the Source of all that we have, has infinitely greater compassion and sense of justice.

It is known that everyone is in this world to rectify or accomplish certain things, based upon the nature of his soul or things he did in an earlier life (i.e., a previous *gilgul*; the Chofetz Chaim is known to have said that in our times almost everyone alive existed in an earlier *gilgul*). Thus, we can never know for what purpose and to overcome which tests we were brought to this world. A person may be brought to this world only in order to rectify a particular sin from the past or to suffer some pain or anguish and to sanctify the Name by bearing it with love.

Thus, there is no reason to ask why did this or that occur to so-and-so who is a great *tzaddik*, since only *HaKadosh Baruch Hu*, Who causes all events, knows what is good and proper and how events should occur.

This is the essence of the concept of *Tzidduk HaDin* — to believe that "all of His decrees are just," and not to say or even think, "What can you do?" One must rather believe that if he knew what Hashem knows, he would act in the same manner.

Aside from this, a person during his period of mourning should take to heart that the time of separation is short, for we are all children of Hashem and we will all sooner or later be reunited, returning home to our Father in Heaven, as the Ramban explains (*Devarim* 14:1). People do cry and suffer even for a temporary separation, and this is the only reason and justification for our crying and feeling pain over death.

As a son, you should help to bring merit to your father, for: "No man is perfectly righteous, without sin." Everyone is therefore obligated to do his utmost to bring merit to his parents, and this is part of the obligation of honoring one's parents.

I join in your sorrow and hope that Hashem will console you among the mourners of Zion and Yerushalayim.

(Afikei Mayim)

Hashem has given, and Hashem has taken;
may His Name be blessed.

Encouragement and Consolation

The essence of consolation is felt when the living person realizes that the deceased has merited receiving the goodness destined for the righteous, and that he has moved from this dark world to one of eternal light, as is written: "For one day in Your courts is better than a thousand." (*Tehillim* 84:11).

(*Kli Yakar, Bereishis* 37:35)

R Yehoshua ben Levi described the World to Come:
There are two gates made of rubies in Gan Eden, upon which there are six hundred thousand ministering angels whose faces shine like the brilliance of the firmament. When a *tzaddik* arrives, they remove the garments he wore in the grave and dress him in eight garments made from the Clouds of Glory. Then they place two crowns upon him, one of precious gems and pearls and the other of gold. Eight branches of myrtle are placed in his hands, while they all praise him and say, "Go eat your bread joyfully" (*Koheles* 9:7).

The angels then lead him to a place of flowing rivers. Eight hundred species of rose and myrtle surround this area. Each person is given a separate *chuppa* canopy, as is written,

"For in addition to all this honor, [there will be a] *chuppa*" (*Yeshayahu* 4:5). Four rivers flow there: one flows with milk, another with wine, the third with persimmon, and the fourth with honey. Upon each canopy there is a golden vine inlaid with thirty lustrous pearls. Each *chuppa* contains a table made of jewels. Sixty angels stand above each *tzaddik* and tell him: "Go eat honey, for you learned Torah, which is compared to honey, as is written: 'Sweeter than honey' (*Tehillim* 19:11), and go drink the wine aged since the Six Days of Creation, for you have studied the Torah, which is compared to wine, as it says, 'I would give you spiced wine' (*Shir HaShirim* 8:2)."

The least handsome among them are as beautiful as R. Akiva and R. Yochanan...and there is no night there, as is written: "And the light of *tzaddikim* is like the Glorious Light" (*Mishlei* 4:18).

The *tzaddikim* progress through three stages: During the first stage they become like children and enter the level where they are as happy as children. During the second stage they become young men and enter the level of young men, where they are as happy as young men; and during the last stage they become old men and are as happy as old men.

In Gan Eden there are eight hundred thousand species of trees; the least significant of them is more magnificent than the finest spice tree of our world. In every corner are six hundred thousand ministering angels, all singing pleasantly. The Tree of Life stands in the center of the Garden, its branches spreading out over the entire Garden. Five hundred thousand flavors can be detected in it, each possessing a different fragrance. Clouds of Glory are positioned above it, touching and shaking it from all sides, spreading the fragrance from one end of the world to the other. Beneath it sit *talmidei chachamim* expounding the Torah.

Each *tzaddik* has two canopies over him: one is made of stars, and the other, of the sun and the moon. Separating each of the canopies is a partition made by Clouds of Glory, and in the middle of each is Eden containing three hundred and ten worlds....

There are seven groups of *tzaddikim*: The first is comprised of the sainted martyrs, such as R. Akiva and his friends. The second is comprised of those drowned at sea [according to *Zayis Ra'anan*; this is a reference to the children who jumped into the sea, as recorded in the fifth chapter of *Gittin*].

R. Yochanan ben Zakkai and his disciples comprise the third group. What was his strength? He used to say: "If the Heavens were parchment, all men scribes, and all the forests pens, it would still not be possible to record all that I have learned from my teachers. And even that which I did absorb is only like what a dog could lick from the sea."

The fourth group is comprised of those for whom the Cloud descended and covered them [probably Moshe and Aharon — *Zayis Ra'anan*]. The fifth group is made up of *ba'alei teshuva* — in the place where *ba'alei teshuva* stand, perfect *tzaddikim* cannot. The sixth group comprises the unmarried men who never sinned. And the seventh group consists of the poor who possess *Mikra*, Mishna, and *Derech Eretz*. Of them, it is written: "All those who put their trust in You will rejoice and sing joyously forever" (*Tehillim* 5:12).

Hashem sits amidst them all teaching them Torah, as is written: "My eyes are upon the trustworthy of the land, that they may dwell with Me" (ibid. 101:6). However, Hashem did not reveal the full extent of the honor He has set aside for the *tzaddikim*: "No eye has ever seen what You will do for those who await You, besides You, Hashem" (*Yeshayahu* 64:3).

(*Yalkut Shimoni, Bereishis*, 20)

?◆ "You Are Children of Hashem"

בנים אתם לה' אלוקיכם, לא תתגודדו ולא תשימו קרחה בין
עיניכם למת כי עם קדוש אתה לה' אלוקיך....— "You are
children of Hashem your L-rd. Do not mutilate
yourselves and do not make a bald patch in the
middle of your head as a sign of mourning. You
are a nation consecrated to Hashem, your L-rd."

(*Devarim* 14:1-2)

Many of the Torah commentators derive from this verse a
lesson in the proper outlook on death. Their holy words are a
deep source of consolation and encouragement.

The *Da'as Zekeinim MiBa'alei HaTosafos* explains:

"You are children of Hashem," and therefore, if your father of flesh and blood dies, "Do not mutilate yourselves."
You have not been orphaned, for your Father in Heaven is
chai vekayam, alive and everlasting. But when a gentile's father passes away, he should mutilate himself, for the only
father he has left is made of wood and stone, as is written:
"They say to wood: 'You are our father,' and to the stone:
'You gave birth to us' " (*Yirmiyahu* 2:27).

The *Seforno* comments on this verse that one who still has
a relative who provides for him does not mourn as much as
one who lost his supporter. This, says the *Seforno*, is the message of the verse: "We should never be overly mournful, for
'We are children of Hashem' Who supports us; we still have a
Provider, and thus we should not be overcome with worries
after a death in the family" (*Seforno, Devarim* 14:1-2).

In the *Seforno*'s opinion, the latter part of the verse ad-
dresses another aspect of mourning. Many people upset
themselves by thinking that the deceased has in some way
suffered a loss. The Torah, however, reminds us that "We are
a nation consecrated to Hashem," a nation destined to live in

the World to Come. Every Jew has a portion in that world where even one breath is more pleasant then an entire lifetime in this world.

A similar thought is offered by the *Ohr HaChaim*, who says: "We should wonder why the Torah placed the thought of 'You are children' adjacent to 'Do not mutilate yourselves.' It seems that the Torah wanted to convey to us that when a person passes away, he suffers no loss; instead, he is like a son who was sent by his father on a business trip to a distant city. After some time had passed, the father called for his son to return home. Even though the son will no longer be found in the distant city once he leaves for home, he certainly still exists. In fact, it is for the son's benefit that he was recalled by his father, who is the source of his life.

"Therefore, it is not proper for us — Hashem's children — to mutilate ourselves, or to make a bald patch on our heads. The same is not true of the other nations, who are not called 'children of Hashem.' '*You* are children,' as opposed to the other nations of the world, whose mourners will cry on their days of death" (*Ohr HaChaim* 14:1).

The Alshich writes: "To what can death be compared? To a mother and son whose husband and father lived in a distant city for an extended period of time. During his sojourn there, the father amassed a fortune. One day, the son so longed for his father that he decided to join him. We can understand his mother's distress at the thought of her son leaving; yet the happiness she anticipates for her son when he rejoins his rich father's household brings her a joy which eclipses any sorrow.

"This idea is conveyed to us by Moshe Rabbeinu: 'You are *children* of Hashem,' and therefore, you should not become upset over being separated from the deceased, because the *child* has gone to his rich Father! The World to Come will be much better for him than this world; there, he will delight in

Hashem's Presence, and that is why 'you should not mutilate yourselves' " (ibid.).

*   *   *

There once lived a king who sent his son to learn in a distant village. When the son came of age and the king called him to return home to ascend the throne, all the villagers began to weep. Among them was one wise man who consoled them by saying: "My brothers, why are you crying? Don't you realize that the prince is only leaving us for his benefit — to reign over the entire land? You should rejoice in his happiness, not mourn!"

So too, the Creator, may His Name be blessed, sent Man to this world in order to occupy himself with Torah and mitzvos. When the time comes for a person to leave this world, his friends and relatives cry over his departure. A wise man arrives — Moshe Rabbeinu — who says: Why do you weep over him when it says, "You are children of Hashem!" Since your souls were taken from the highest of heavens and are parts of the Divine, they are certainly everlasting and do not die along with the body. Do not weep excessively, for that shows that you do not believe in the eternity of the soul, and makes it seem like you believe that the deceased goes to oblivion, Heaven forbid, like broken earthenware which cannot be repaired. The truth is, the soul is like gold and silver which can be repaired (*Zohar, Vayechi*).

❧ "You Have Less Pity Than I Do!"

Our Sages tell us (*Moed Katan* 27b) that the mourner should not weep for too long a time. Three days after the death are for crying, seven days are for eulogies, and thirty days are designated as days to refrain from ironing and haircuts. After this point the Holy One says: "You have less pity than I do!"

The Rambam explains that the above-mentioned periods are intended to calm the human urge to mourn. It is human nature for people to cry when their loved ones leave them, even when both people are still here on earth. If ordinary separation can arouse a person's feelings and cause tears, all the more so the separation of death. However, the truth is that the departed is going to his eternal home, *Olam HaBa*, where the fragrance alone is more pleasant than an entire lifetime in this world. (*Likutei Anshei Shem*, quoted in *Penei Baruch*.)

ᐛ For What Should the Living Mourn?

The *Pele Yoetz* explains that the mitzva of *gemilus chasadim* (doing kindness) includes, among other things, consoling mourners. Not only is consoling mourners a mitzva, but becoming close to and comforting anyone who suffers from *any* hardship is also a mitzva.

The realization that something worse could have happened can be a useful tool for consoling ourselves and others. We can thank Hashem for what has already occurred while at the same time praying to Him that nothing worse happen in the future. For instance, if someone suffers a financial loss, he should thank Hashem that he was not injured physically. If he was injured physically, he should be thankful that his life was spared. If he lost a loved one, he should take consolation in the fact that at least the person did not die an abnormal death, or that at least he left offspring after him. Above all else, we should be thankful for those remaining alive, and pray for their well-being.

At first glance it would seem that it is improper to cry at

all, since it is purposeless. Can it bring the dead back to life? This is, in fact, what King David said when one of his children died: "Now he is dead. Why should I fast? Can I now bring him back?" (II *Shemuel* 1:23). In any case, all we can do is follow the words of our Sages: "Three days are for crying," etc. The only time it is permissible to cry more than this is for a great *talmid chacham*, for we see that *Bnei Yisrael* cried for thirty days over Moshe Rabbeinu.

Even when a person cries, his motivation should not be the fact that the deceased has left him and that he misses the deceased, for that is foolish. This world is an illusory one — it is the World to Come that is the true world. So "for what should a living person mourn? For his sins" (*Eicha* 3:39). What is a real cause for crying and lamenting? The fact that, because of a person's sins, evil befell him, and he causes sorrow and anger to the Supreme King, Who does so much good. Also, the mourner should be upset that as a result of evil, the *tzaddik* was taken away and thereby prevented from continuing to be a source of pleasure to his Creator. This is the *Shechina*'s sorrow, too.

This is why a person should cry. He should resolve to repent, for that is the logical extension of "For what should a living person mourn?" as is clear from the next verse: "Let us search our ways, scrutinize them, and return to Hashem" (ibid. 40).

It should also occur to the mourner that perhaps the deceased is now suffering Heavenly justice. He should cry and imagine that he can see the deceased passing through flames. He should cry and plead for mercy for the deceased.

Our Sages said (*Devarim Rabba* 2:14): "The sorrow of others is a partial consolation." This saying can open up a window of consolation, when the mourner realizes that he is not alone in his suffering. Many good, noble and righteous people, with numerous good deeds to their credit, have suffered every imaginable hardship — you are no better than they.

Believe wholeheartedly that no evil comes from Above. Instead, realize that everything the Merciful One does is for the good!

Even if the Attribute of Justice strikes, causing death, we must remember that G-d gazes into the future, envisioning all events until the end of time, and counts all of man's deeds. Therefore, it is fitting to thank Hashem for the bad as well as the good, for there is no doubt that Hashem regarded it as for the good. When Moshe Rabbeinu killed the Egyptian, he looked to the future first [to make sure that no good would come of the fellow]. Likewise, the nations of Ammon and Moav were spared destruction until two righteous women, Ruth and Na'ama, came from them.

Just as it is mitzva to console others, so too, it is a mitzva to accept consolation and accept the Will of Heaven lovingly. After all, from Whom did the hardship emanate? From none other than the Master of the Universe, Who rules the world as He wills. We are the flock He pastures. We are obligated to bless Him and thank Him for everything. When a person allows himself to be consoled by others, and even more so, is able to console himself, he demonstrates his proper attitude, his perfect faith, and his clear thinking.

ਕ The Malbim on the Immortality of the Soul

> R. Elazar said: "How much ink is spilled and how many quills are broken in order to write 'The children of Cheis' ten times, parallel to the Ten Commandments! To teach you that when a person clarifies a *tzaddik*'s business transactions, it is the equivalent of fulfilling the Ten Commandments."
>
> (*Midrash Rabba, Bereishis* 58)

The Torah discussed this sale [the purchase of the Tomb of the Patriarchs] at such length and in such great detail because Avraham used the purchase to teach the nations one of the basic beliefs of our religion: the immortality of the soul. He taught the belief that the soul remains alive after the body's death, and also taught of the subsequent reward which both the soul and the body will receive. The bodies, which sleep in the earth, will awaken on the great Day of Judgment — some to everlasting life and others to everlasting shame. At that time, the *tzaddikim* will rise clothed in the garments — their physical bodies — which they wore during their first lifetime.

Therefore, it is necessary to prepare a choice burial place for the body amidst his family and righteous people. (A wicked person is not buried adjacent to a *tzaddik*, as seen in the story of the prophet Elisha.)

This information was unknown and strange to the children of Cheis, who believed that the dead never return, and that there is no reckoning and judgment in the netherworld. Thus, in their view, a grave is only needed temporarily, in order to prevent disgrace to the living, and for hygienic reasons. They used to empty the grave afterwards.

When Avraham bought a burial plot for a large sum, people were amazed. The entire community learned that even perfect, righteous people only have the four cubits of their burial plot — their entire lot in this life is nothingness.

This is why Avraham said, "I am a stranger and citizen," which was a reference to the phrase, "For I am a *stranger* with you; a *citizen* as all of my forefathers." Life in this world is the life of the stranger, where there is constant yearning to return to the original source of radiance.

Avraham also said: "Give me an *inheritance* of a grave"; the present burial of my dead is only *milefanai* (before me). But the truth is, this is not considered a burial, but more like someone who temporarily hides a precious object in a store-house to be protected until such time when it will be re-trieved.

But the children of Cheis who didn't believe in everlasting life insisted: "Use *any* of our graves." Why must it be for an inheritance?

That is why Avraham then asked for *Me'aras HaMachpela* (literally, "the double cave"), which had two floors, a meta-phor for Man's existence. This world is like the lower floor, while the higher world is like the upper floor of the cave. Even after death, when the body lays in its resting place, a person's spirit still hovers over him in the lower part of Gan Eden.

The cave that Avraham bought was at the end of the field, an allusion to the fact that the grave is the end point of Man's toil in this world. We are told that he bought it "for its full value," symbolizing the fact that all the material possessions of this world are not worth as much as this acquisition, which is the end of Man and all his hopes in this world.

Avraham clarified all these basic beliefs at the time of this purchase. That is why understanding this purchase is the equivalent of fulfilling the Ten Commandments, for in it lies the essence of faith, and the concept of reward and punishment.

❧ A Flower Plucked before Its Time

The Ben Ish Chai explained in the following speech how we can take comfort in knowing that those who die young have completed their mission here on earth:

Bnei Aharon, a commentary on R. Chaim Vital's *Sha'ar HaGilgulim*, was written by R. Shimon Agasi, whose son, Aharon, died close to his intended wedding day. In his intro-duction, R. Agasi describes the shock his son's death aroused in the community. People wondered: "What has Hashem done, to pick such a beautiful flower, to take such a pure soul before its time?" But when R. Chaim Vital spoke to the community and explained the concept of *gilgul* — reincarnation — they felt reassured. The following excerpt is part of his address:

The Midrash (*Midrash Mishlei* 31) says: One Shabbos afternoon, while R. Meir was delivering a discourse, two of his sons passed away. What did their mother do? She placed both of them on a bed and covered them with a sheet. When R. Meir returned home after Shabbos, he asked his wife, "Where are my two sons?"

"They went to the study hall," she answered.

"But I looked in the study hall and did not see them."

His wife placed the cup of wine for *Havdala* before him and he made *Havdala*. Then R. Meir repeated his question. "Where are my two sons?"

"Sometimes they go out. They'll return soon." She served a meal.

When her husband had finished eating, she said: "My master, I have a question to ask."

"Ask."

"The other day someone left a trust here, and now he wishes to take it back. Shall I return it?"

"My daughter, doesn't someone given a trust have to return it to its owner?"

"If not for your opinion, I would not have returned it." She led R. Meir to the room where the two boys were laying. She approached the bed and removed the sheet. R. Meir saw his sons and began to weep.

"My sons, my sons! My teachers, my teachers! My sons in the way of the world, and my teachers who enlightened me with their Torah!" he cried.

His wife then comforted him by saying gently, "My master, didn't you tell me that we must return the trust? So too, 'Hashem has given, and Hashem has taken; may His Name be blessed.' "

R. Chanina commented, "With this, she consoled him, and his mind was calmed." It is about behavior like hers that it is written: "Who can find a woman of valor?" (*Mishlei* 31:11).

What was it about his wife's parable that calmed R. Meir? He must still have been troubled, wondering why they had died prematurely before they had perfected themselves. If they had lived a normal life span, they would have learned a great deal of Torah and done numerous mitzvos. For this loss, it certainly is proper to cry and be full of sorrow. If so, how did the words of R. Meir's wife console him?

The answer is that some people who come to this world enter it for the first time, while others who have been here before have only returned to correct a previous deficiency. Those who enter for the first time will undoubtedly not die prematurely — if they remain perfectly righteous. But those who are returning as a *gilgul* to perfect a deficiency might possibly live for only a few years, since as soon as they accomplish their task, they immediately depart. Therefore, those who return as *gilgulim* do not all have a uniform life span. Instead, each one lives as long as is necessary to complete what he lacked in his first incarnation.

It is known that the soul which enters the body as a *gilgul* has the status of a "trust" in the body until it completes its deficiency. For souls, the first body is their main dwelling place. But with the second body, the soul is only there as a "trust."

R. Meir's wife was a wise woman. Her argument to her husband was that since their children were perfectly righteous, if this life had been their first, they would have lived the normal seventy or eighty years apportioned to all people. But since they did not, this must have been their second life. This proves that they were only like "trusts," who were here to correct the deficiency of their first lifetime. Since they completed their years and died when they were supposed to, why cry and be upset that they died at a young age?

She chose the form of a parable since this was a gentler way of revealing the truth. R. Meir understood, and was comforted.

With this idea in mind, another event can also be understood. It is told in *Avos d'Rabbi Nasan* that when R. Yochanan ben Zakkai's son died, four of his pupils attempted to console him, all without success. Then R. Elazar ben Arach came and consoled him.

R. Elazar entered his teacher's home, sat down, and began his consolation by saying: "Allow me to tell you a parable: To what can the matter be compared? To a person with whom the king left a trust. Each day the fellow cried and shouted, 'Woe to me! When will I escape the burden of this deposit in peace!' You too, Rebbi, had a son who studied Torah, Mishna, Laws, and *Aggados*, and he left this world without sin. You should accept consolation, for you have returned the 'trust' whole."

R. Yochanan replied, "R. Elazar, my son, you have consoled me."

In light of our previous explanation, it is clear why R. Elazar's parable appealed to R. Yochanan and brought him consolation. At first, he had been upset because he thought his son had died prematurely — he was worried that the boy had not completed his mission in life. R. Elazar wisely told him the parable of the trust, in order to allude to the concept of *gilgul neshamos*, reincarnation. Since his son had studied Torah, Mishna, and more, it was inconceivable that this was his first time on earth. It must have been his second or third time here, and he must have been born solely to perfect what he hadn't been able to the first time. If that were true, his soul didn't need the normal life span given to most people, but could complete its mission in as brief a time as necessary. His death came at the right time; it was not as if he had lost years. The truth of this realization consoled R. Yochanan.

The death of a young person often causes people to doubt Hashem. They wonder, "What sins could he have possibly done to deserve death at such a young age?" The more righteous and good the person, the greater the bitterness over his early death. Such criticism of Hashem's judgment is misguided and foolish. By understanding the concept of *gilgul*, the bereaved can take comfort in knowing that Hashem's judgments are true, and that He, may He be blessed, is "The faithful G-d, Who does no wrong."

❧ Now He Is Safe from All Harm

Man is not obligated to do more than the Torah commands. A man has an obligation to marry and bring children into the world. Regardless of whether or not the child lives, the father receives his reward. Hashem does as He wills for the man's benefit. Even if the son has gone to *his* world, he is not lost to our world. In the same way that if the child were to move to a distant city he would still remain his father's son, so too in this situation. In the end, the parents will be even closer to their son when they rejoin him in the World to Come for eternity.

Furthermore, it is comforting for parents to know that now their child is safe from all harm. It is possible that if their son had remained alive he might have fallen ill in some way, or perhaps strayed from the path. If that had happened, the parents would have preferred his absence from this world to a life of suffering. Now their son is safe, surrounded and protected from evil on all sides in Gan Eden.

Knowing this makes it easier to accept the limits to mourning specified by our Sages: "Three days for crying, seven for eulogies, and thirty days of no haircuts." Why transgress a Rabbinical prohibition? It is not even as if there is anything to be gained from excessive crying, for what has happened cannot be reversed... (*Shevet Mussar*, chap. 16).

ও How to Console and Be Consoled

The best way for someone to recover from mourning is to first pray to Hashem to raise his spirits, and then to rejoin the community. Within the community, the orphan may find his parents, parents may find their children, brothers their sisters, the widow her husband, and the husband may find the woman who will manage his home and be a mother to his children. It is the community's responsibility to make up for the losses of the individual, to be compassionate to orphans, and to do justice for the widow....

Those mourning children and those who have lost their place in this world — the very foundation for their endurance in this world — will also find consolation within the community. The community takes in our deeds like a flower we planted, and it continues the good we have started but did not finish. A person who belongs to the public and who lives as part of the community will never die! Therefore, the mourner should be made to feel more closely tied to the community. That way, he will begin to heal from his sorrow.

In the same spirit, the members of the community will come to visit him during the *shiva* period, and with the visit itself, they can give him the consoling feeling of being part of a community. They will also comfort him with true words of consolation, expressing to him the concept that life in all its vicissitudes is the task which our Father in Heaven has placed upon us in His mercy and compassion. If the mourner does not ask for words of comfort, then console him in silence, for your very presence is consolation. Once the mourner has indicated that the consolers may leave, they are not permitted to continue their visit (*Yoreh De'ah* 376).

Our Sages have ordained that we use the feelings of mourning as a source of consolation. But they also set limits to this mourning: "Three days are for mourning, seven days of lamentation, thirty days of not taking a haircut. After this the Holy One says: 'Are you more merciful than I?' " (*Moed Katan* 27b). He who adds to this is complaining. These are the words of our Sages, and how wise they were!

Do not tie yourself to anything transient, even if it may be the most precious item in the world, for its loss might lead to the grave. If you received the most beautiful gifts of kindness from Hashem, know that you should use them all for the service of Hashem, Who owns everything. But at all times be prepared to return them, for you never know when they will be demanded. And if He does take, then recognize that it was the hand of a loving Father Who took it, just as He had given it. Whatever He left for you, and in any situation in which you find yourself, rise to the occasion to live in accord with Hashem's Will, to thank Him, and to live to fulfill His Will, until you too are called to a different existence, to a new life. (From *Horeb* by R. Shimshon Rafael Hirsch.)

∂ “If Not for Torah, My Delight...”

A broken-hearted young Torah scholar went to see the Chazon Ish on the day he got up from sitting *shiva* for his young daughter. He wanted to express his feelings of pain and sorrow, in the hope that he would hear some words of consolation from the great sage. When the young man entered, though, the Chazon Ish immediately began a Torah discussion with him. When they had concluded discussing one issue, the young mourner tried to talk about his problem. But the Chazon Ish started discussing yet a different topic, and again the two became engrossed in Torah thoughts. Thus they went from one issue to another, but the conversation about sorrow and mourning never began.

When the young man left the Chazon Ish's house, he felt that the Chazon Ish was giving him the message that his task was to be engrossed in learning — that would be his consolation. "If not for Torah — my delight — I would be lost in my affliction" (Tehillim 119:92).

ঙ He Gives and He Takes

R. Tzvi Pesach Frank זצ"ל, Rav of Yerushalayim and outstanding halachic authority (Shevivei Ohr), points to the importance of elevating our perception of suffering:

Your choice of words concerning the tragedy in our family is in the style of simple people. But he who sustains himself with the light of Torah understands that everything that was done, or will be done, comes from Divine Providence — He gives and takes life. No creature can fathom the depths of the judgment, for there is no fathoming His wisdom. "The Rock, His deeds are perfect and all His ways are just. He is a faithful G-d; there is no injustice, He is righteous and straight" (Devarim 32:4).

In the End of Days, which will surely come soon, Hashem's justice will be clear to all. His great mercy extends as the waters cover the sea.

*   *   *

This world, as pleasant as it may be, is but a passing

shadow, a spent cloud, a fleeting dream. But there is another world — the world of reward — where each person receives payment for his deeds. The World to Come is set aside only for the righteous. All the anguish and suffering that the Jewish People suffer in this world will one day be seen clearly by all as really being for their good. All their hardship was experienced so that their reward may be multiplied in the World to Come. All the nations, with all their wealth and temporary success, will fade and cease, as if they had never been.

*   *   *

Man must understand that everything that happens is by Hashem's Divine Providence, that all comes from the One Who is righteous in all His ways, and that it is forbidden to complain about His ways. R. Yehoshua Leib Diskin, a Torah genius in his generation, *av beis din* of Shklov, Lomza, Kovno, Brisk and Yerushalayim, and well known as the Brisker Rav, used to say that the confession על חטא שחטאנו לפניך בתמהון לבב —"(We confess) for the sin of wonderment of the heart," refers to those times when a tragedy befalls someone and the person wonders, "Why did Hashem do this?" This is what is meant by the expression "wonderment of the heart."

❧ From a Eulogy by R. Yechezkel Levenstein

The Saba of Kelm used to say that when someone becomes ill everyone wonders why it happened. But the truth is, our question should be the opposite. When someone is *not* ill, we should wonder "How can anyone be healthy?"

So too, in this terrible situation. When someone like this passes away, we wonder how could such a good and righteous person be punished. What we should really wonder is: How does everybody live in tranquillity? Logic dictates that a person should receive his punishment immediately after he commits a sin. Hashem's justice is clear and straightforward. The wonder is when there is no strict judgment....

Hashem desires perfection and expects righteous people to achieve it. The Creation, the Torah, and Divine Providence are complete and perfect. Perfection is essential for eternity.

Lastly, Man questions because he believes there is something real about this world, that it is lasting. In fact, this world is empty and imaginary.

๊๛ Encouragement from the Chazon Ish

The Gemara in tractate *Berachos* says: "If a person sees that *yissurim* befall him, he should examine his deeds. If he inspected them but found nothing wrong, he should attribute them to *bitul Torah*, wasting time from studying Torah." Rashi explains that the words "but found nothing wrong" indicate that he found no sin that would warrant this punishment. Since we know that Hashem punishes *mida k'neged mida*, measure for measure in accord with the sin, a person should find the sin that matches and warrants the punishment he received.

The Chazon Ish ruled that the above was only said concerning events in the time of the Gemara, but that in our era, we are not worthy of conducting this type of self-examination. On the contrary, a person might arrive at an incorrect conclusion. Obviously, if the problem is self-evident, or if the person feels that some of his ways need correction, he certainly should rectify those things. If he doesn't, it will be held against him.

๊๛ We Are All Suffering

R. Eliezer Menachem Shach told a Torah scholar whose sister was near death:

240 Encouragement and Consolation

We should not think that affliction is the trouble of the individual. Ever since World War I the Jewish People have been suffering. There is no moment of rest, only persecution and tribulation. "[Hashem] is slow to anger, but [ultimately] collects payment." Affliction of the individual actually indicates that he is a detail within the totality of the People, because *yissurim* are the lot of the People until the coming of *Mashiach*. So there is even reason to rejoice in suffering and to accept it lovingly.

In the *Tochacha* (Rebuke) section of the Torah, it is written: "If after all this you still are not disciplined by Me, and you treat My acts as accidents, *keri*, then I will respond with 'randomness' " (*Vayikra* 26:23-24). We know that all events come from Hashem and are not accidental. While animals and plants are not under *Hashgacha Pratis*, individual Divine Providence, man is. There is a directing hand at work. There *is* a purpose for everything. "All that the Merciful One does is for the good."

We see that Hashem strikes specifically at the most righteous among us, and none of us can fathom the reasons for it. Certainly we don't even know what will happen tomorrow, for any day may bring a war, Heaven forbid, and the fate of the entire Nation hangs in the balance. The streets are no longer safe, for terrorist attacks and traffic accidents are commonplace. With all these uncertainties, who can say he knows what is good for man?

So, an individual must accept all events given to him by the Holy One, and realize that he is being watched and taken care of at every moment by *Hashem Yisbarach*, unlike the animals, which are only under general supervision.

It is clear that as long as a person is alive he must not refrain from asking for mercy. Even if a sharp sword is lying on a person's throat, he must not despair. Even the worst situations must be viewed with the correct attitude of acceptance and an awareness of how upset to be over them. We who are *bnei Torah* want to live according to the Torah's outlook, which guides us. This is why we must contemplate events in the manner mentioned above.

In previous eras, every individual felt that he was part of the whole, so he viewed his personal troubles as part of the suffering of the entire Jewish People, not only as his own. This is correct and the way a person should relate to the matter.

✒ Our Vision Is Limited

R. Shach consoled a widow and her young orphans by saying:

It is forbidden to mourn too much. What happened was decreed, and it is impossible to know what would have been if not for the decree. Man does not know the future. Even when the entire family is alive and well, it is impossible to know what will be in the future. Only Hashem knows! We all pray each day, "Our Father, the merciful Father...." We talk to the Holy One and say: "Father, You have mercy on us, You are the most merciful to us." A father always looks after the well-being of his children.

We do not know the future, nor can we see it, for our vision is limited. But the Holy One has no limitations — He sees and He knows. We have to mourn just as the Torah commands us to, but not more than that. Life must return to normal, and Hashem will help. He will help each and every one of you.

It is written in the Torah: "You are children to Hashem your G-d; do not cut yourselves and do not make a bald patch between your eyes [in mourning] over the dead" (*Devarim* 14:1). When a gentile dies, the mourners tear their flesh. But the Torah forbids us to do so, for we are children of Hashem. The Ramban explains that when we mourn the death of a relative, even that of a father, whose loss is most painful, we must remember that we have a Father in Heaven — "You are *children* to Hashem." Our Father in Heaven is alive and eternal.

Yes, we must mourn as the Torah commands. But after we have fulfilled our duty, we must place our trust in Hashem. The older boys and the students in the family should return to their studies, and Hashem will have mercy on their mother. I tell you that he [the father] knows that he has left behind a family which is continuing in his ways and will continue learning. Once he knows that his family is in faithful hands and that it will continue in his way, he is full of happiness, as our Sages have told us.

Therefore, I bless you that you should be consoled, and may each one of you return to tranquillity. You should return to a normal life. Let the mother educate the older and younger children, may she merit to live until a hundred and twenty...deriving *nachas* from all of them.

❧ Your Father Is Happy in the World to Come

R. Meir Chodosh,ל״צז, *mashgiach* in Hebron Yeshiva and in Ateret Yisrael Yeshiva, consoled a son who mourned his father by explaining the verse: "You are formed against your will, you are born against your will, you live against your will, and you will die against your will" (*Avos* 4:22).

"What is meant by 'against your will'? Force is used only when persuasion fails. So it is clear that preceding each stage mentioned in the above Mishna, an attempt is made to convince the person that it is worthwhile for him to go on to the next stage. What is the person told? What do they tell the baby before birth?

"Most likely they explain to the fetus: 'What do you have to do in your mother's womb anyway? It's dark and crowded in there. It will be better for you to emerge into the big world where the sun shines, where you can enjoy yourself and do as your Father in Heaven wishes of you.'

"But the fetus answers: 'I don't want to leave — it's good for me here. All my needs are fulfilled here.'

"Eventually, only after several attempts are made to convince him to leave and he still refuses, he is born 'against his will.'

"Now, let us make a calculation concerning this concept: Imagine if they came to the child a few days *after* he was born, and offered to return him to the womb. They might suggest: 'Didn't you want to stay inside? You argued that it was better for you in there. Well, we've found a way for you to return!'

"What would the child say? 'That's madness!' he would cry in alarm. 'You expect me to reenter that dark, crowded place?'

"The same is true about the phrase 'and you will die against your will.' When a person arrives in the World to Come and sees how wonderful it is — that he merits being close to Hashem — he has no desire to return to this world."

At this point, R. Meir Chodosh turned to the orphan and said: "Your father z"l has certainly merited entrance into the World to Come, for he raised good children who toil in Torah faithfully and contribute to the good of the community, and he himself spent his life in the tents of Torah. If they would now say to him, 'You didn't want to leave the world and you had all sorts of reasons not to leave the world. Now we've found a way for you to return to your old world,' your father would most certainly refuse the offer, just as a child would refuse to return to the womb.

"This is your consolation — that your father's soul is enjoying unimaginable delight. The loss of your father pains you, but he has found eternal rest. It is good for him in his new world, and there he will speak on your behalf.

"May *Hashem Yisbarach* bring *Mashiach* and may we all merit the Resurrection, speedily in our days."

ès Why Didn't His Good Deeds Protect Him?

R. Chaim Pinchas Scheinberg שליט״א, Rosh Yeshiva of Torah Ore, eulogized a young woman:

We have found that the death of the righteous is more difficult for Hashem than the "hundred rebukes minus two" that are recorded in the *Mishna Torah* (*Devarim*), and the destruction of the Temple. In the verses on rebuke it is written: "Your blows will be a wonder," while concerning the destruction of the *Beis HaMikdash*, it is written: "You have descended wondrously." But concerning the death of the righteous, it is written: "Therefore I will add wonderment upon this nation, wonderment upon wonderment" (*Midrash Eicha* 1:39).

When the Holy One removes a righteous person from this world, it is more difficult than other destructions, for the death of a *tzaddik* raises many questions and doubts. The destruction of the *Beis HaMikdash* caused the nations of the world to wonder, "Is it possible that the Jewish people can suffer such devastation?" But the death of righteous people causes even more questions. There is no answer to the many questions those deaths evoke, especially when we see so many wicked people in the world. An example of this is the case of the master killer [Hitler], may his name be blotted out. Many holy, righteous people and great sages perished, while so many wicked people remained alive. This causes many people to stray from the straight path, for they ask: "A person lived his entire life in holiness and purity! Why didn't his good deeds protect him?"

This is indeed a question that the human mind cannot resolve, especially the tragedy that we are facing today. She [the deceased] worked hard during her brief time, and she merited to raise two precious children. It is indeed a wonder that such a young sacrifice should perish. We wonder and wonder and continue to wonder: How can it be? Where is the *Ribbono shel Olam*'s mercy? Where is mercy for the children, the husband, the parents? We fail to comprehend.

Hashem's ways are beyond our comprehension, as our Sages say: " 'Hashem saves man and beast.' This refers to cunning people, who make themselves like beasts" (*Chullin* 5b). Rashi explains that these people are smart in the way that Adam was smart. Despite his lofty, almost angel-like level, he nevertheless, at times, had to submit himself like a beast concerning Hashem's judgments — into Whose workings it is forbidden to inquire — just like an animal that has no understanding but simply follows his master as it is led and directed. So too, with man, *l'havdil*. He must allow himself to be led without asking questions, and to accept lovingly all that happens to him. This is the meaning of the verse: "Your judgments are as the great depths — Hashem saves man and beast." Hashem's judgments are deep like the depths and are impossible to fathom. Man must therefore act like a dumb animal when it comes to inquiring into Hashem's ways.

But it must be remembered that "Your righteousness is like mighty mountains." There *is* great justice here. The Dubno Maggid said concerning the verse: "He is a faithful G-d; there is no injustice — He is just and straight," that when a human judges someone, even if the defendant receives the proper sentence, his children and wife suffer unjustly. But when Hashem passes sentence, there is no injustice, because all those affected also receive only what they deserve. It is true that the blow is terrible, but it is all justice and kindness. And, as the Chofetz Chaim said, "True, hardship is a bitter medicine, but it is not 'bad' — whatever Hashem does is for the good."

"May You Plant but Not Harvest..."

R. Gedalya Eiseman, *mashgiach* of Yeshivas Kol Torah in Yerushalayim, gave the following encouragement to mourners:

R. Shimon bar Yochai told his son to approach two of his disciples whom he considered men of character and ask them for a blessing. His son was puzzled when he heard the two disciples bless him: "May it be the Divine Will that you should plant but not harvest; gather but not send out; send out but not gather; that your house should be destroyed but your lodging place established; that your table should be in disarray; and may you not see a new year."

R. Shimon's son returned to his father and said, "Not only did they not bless me, but they even cursed me."

"What did they tell you?" asked R. Shimon. When his son repeated the blessing, R. Shimon explained: "All their words were blessings. *Plant but not harvest* means have children, but may they not die; *gather but do not send out* means gather daughters-in-law into your home, but may your sons not die, causing them to leave; *send out but do not gather* means your daughters' husbands should not die, causing your daughters to return to you; *your house should be destroyed but your lodging place be established* means this world, which is a temporary lodging place, should last, but your grave should be destroyed [i.e., you should merit long life]; *your table should be in disarray* — from sons and daughters; *and may you not see a new year* — that your wife not die and you remarry" (*Moed Katan* 9b).

The Maharal's brother (*Sefer HaChaim*, Part II, chap. 6) considers why these wise men gave a blessing which sounded like a curse, and explains that they spoke this way to hint that this world is the world of hardship and *yissurim*, and that it is normal for every individual to experience hardship. When they said *May it be the will*, they did not mean may it be Hashem's Will, but rather may all this be *your* will, namely, that you should desire these problems and prepare yourself for any eventuality, for that is the way of the world.

R. Eiseman commented that most of the damage caused by hardship comes from not anticipating it. If people would prepare themselves for possible hardship and accept the fact that trials and tribulations are part of normal living, realizing that everyone suffers in some way, they would have an easier time coping with adversity.

Obviously, intellectually understanding this truth is not enough — one's whole life should be lived with this understanding in mind. Reaching such a level of acceptance requires a great deal of self-discipline and practice. The Saba of Kelm listed among his goals for character perfection the resolution to train himself not to expect everything to go his way.

‏&ہ Sharing the Burden

> R. Pinchas ben Chama expounded: "What is meant in the verse: 'Hadad heard in Egypt that David rested with his ancestors and that Yoav the general died' (I *Melachim* 11:21)? Why is the term 'rested' used concerning David, while 'died' is used for Yoav? David, who was survived by a son like himself, is only at rest; but Yoav, whose son was not like him, is considered dead."
>
> (*Bava Basra* 116a)

What a wonderful thought! If we were to tell a mourning son: "Listen, there is a way to return your father to life if you are willing to pay a certain amount — are you willing to do

248 Encouragement and Consolation

it?" the son would definitely give all he owned to do so. This Gemara, though, says that when a child follows his father's ways it is considered as if the father had never even died, but is only "resting"! (What is meant here is that the *yissurim* and judgments associated with death are decreased.) In brief, when a son exerts himself to raise his level and become spiritually like his father, then it is possible to say that the son has lessened his father's death!

It is common for children in mourning to be filled with ideas about creating a suitable remembrance for their departed parent. Our Sages here teach us that each child can help his parent best by emulating him spiritually, actually giving him "life."

The verse says: "Hashem said to Shemuel: 'How long will you mourn for Shaul? Fill your horn with oil and go to the house of Yishai of Bethlehem, for I have seen a king among his sons' " (I *Shemuel* 16:1). Why did Hashem link the cessation of mourning with the anointing of King David?

It is well known that when someone shares the burden of his fellowman he helps to lighten his load. When Shemuel mourned for Shaul, sharing Shaul's tragic loss of the monarchy, he lessened the loss of the monarchy, making it incomplete. This prevented King David's reign from beginning, since "two kings cannot use the same crown." Only when Shemuel would cease mourning over Shaul would it then be possible to anoint David.

The Saba of Kelm explained that mourning is a form of sharing — sharing the burden of the deceased. This explains the various levels of mourning. From the first day until the third day is the hardest stage; another stage begins after three days, the next after seven days, and the final stage begins after thirty days and lasts until the end of the first year. Sharing the deceased father's burden progressively eases the father's hardship. (Heard from R. Gedalya Eiseman.)

ᴣ᷑ Contemplate the Day of Death

> Among the reasons a person is duty-bound to re-
> member the day of death is so that he won't be-
> come negligent, and so that he won't weaken in
> his service to the Blessed One. Let sleep wander
> from his eyes so that he may labor in Torah, reflect
> upon the fear of Hashem, correct his character
> traits, and attain fear and love of Hashem.
>
> (*Sha'arei Teshuva*, Feldheim, p. 111)

The *Sha'arei Teshuva* (2:17) also says that whoever wants to
enjoy the World to Come when he dies must remember death
while he is still alive, and set aside his earthly desires. Death
will be very difficult for anyone who does not do so, as our
Sages said: "If you wish not to die, then die before you die!"
(*Maseches Derech Eretz*).

We find this same concept powerfully elaborated in the
words of the Alshich on the same verse: "Which man lives
and never sees death, and rescues his soul from the grave?"
(*Tehillim* 89:49). The simple meaning of the verse is "who can
escape death?" But the Alshich explains the verse as follows:
"Who can live his life without anticipating the day of death,
yet still expect to be spared from the judgment of Gehinnom?"

The Maharal points out that the mourner's silence stems
from his closeness to the deceased, who is now silent. The
mourner behaves like the deceased because he feels that the
deceased was a part of himself. The Rashbam explained that
"and half its flesh was consumed" (*Bamidbar* 12:12), refers
to Moshe, who, because of his closeness to his sister
Miriam, felt that half of his own flesh had been consumed
when she was afflicted with *tzara'as*. Closeness to the deceased and being one with the deceased can help a person

experience the sense of the day of his own death, because the mourner is confronted with the reality of death. It is self-understood, then, that it is a great merit for the deceased if his relatives begin to think about the day of death.

❧ A Lesson from the Wild Rooster, the *Duchifas*

> And the *duchifas*—the mountain-carpenter
> (*Onkelos* to *Vayikra* 11:19).

> This refers to the wild rooster which has two
> combs (Rashi, ibid.).

According to Rashi's explanation, says R. Yitzchak Zilberstein, the name *duchifas* is understandable, for it comes from the word *du* (two) *kippos* (head covers), referring to the two combs on its head. But Onkelos' definition requires thought: Why is it called "the mountain-carpenter"?

An explanation can be formed based on the Gemara in *Gittin* (68b) which discusses the *shamir* creature, which was created at the end of the sixth day of Creation. (The *shamir* was capable, despite its barley-sized body, of splitting any object in the world [*Sota* 48b].) At first, the *shamir* was given to the Angel of the Sea for safekeeping, because if it had been given to any land creature, the *shamir* would have destroyed the world. The Angel of the Sea subsequently passed it on to the wild rooster, known for being utterly faithful in keeping its oaths, who gave an oath not to pass it on to any other land creature. The wild rooster then took the *shamir* to an uninhabited mountainous area, where the *shamir* would cut a crack in the mountain. The wild rooster would then place a tree seed in the crack, thus cultivating the area. Hence the name "mountain-carpenter," for the wild rooster used the *shamir* in "sawing" the mountains just as the carpenter saws wood.

This is possibly also the origin of the name *duchifas*—two *kippos*, or domes, referring to dome-like mountain tops. But we now come to an obvious question: If the wild rooster keeps its word so faithfully, guarding the *shamir* until the *shamir* was needed for the construction of the *Beis HaMikdash*, why isn't it listed in the Torah among the kosher birds?

Perhaps the answer can be found further on in that same Gemara in *Gittin*. When Benayahu ben Yehoyada, King Solomon's general, discovered that the *shamir* was to be found with the wild rooster, he went and found the nest of the wild rooster and devised a scheme to capture the *shamir*. Benayahu took a sheet of white glass and placed it over the nest. When the wild rooster returned and found its nest covered by the glass, it went and got the *shamir* and placed it on the glass in order to split the glass in two. At that moment Benayahu shouted loudly, scaring away the wild rooster. When the *shamir* fell from its grasp, Benayahu snatched the *shamir* and brought it back to King Solomon to be used for the construction of the *Beis HaMikdash*. The Gemara relates that the wild rooster then went and choked itself to death, for breaking its oath.

Let us give a little thought to this story. Was the wild rooster correct in committing suicide? Obviously it was wrong, for until this moment it had loyally guarded the *shamir*. Now that the time had come to give the *shamir* to King Solomon, the *duchifas* was not allowed to hold on to it any longer. In fact, if he had succeeded in using the *shamir* for his own purposes, it would have been an illegal use of an entrusted object. The wild rooster, then, was doubly wrong: 1) It lacked knowledge. It did not know that the time for King Solomon to take the *shamir* — a time destined since the Six Days of Creation — had arrived; 2) It erred in faith — it was loyal, but not faithful.

To explain what is meant by "not faithful" let us contrast

the wild rooster with the dove, which is a kosher bird. The dove stretches out its neck for slaughter in submission and faith to its Creator. But the wild rooster has no faith in his Creator. If it had faith, it wouldn't have committed suicide. Instead it would have and should have accepted the fact that the time had come for it to relinquish its guardianship over the *shamir*. Then the wild rooster would have willfully let the *shamir* be used for the purpose for which it had been created. On the one hand, the wild rooster is very loyal; but on the other, it is too haughty and lacks faith in its Creator. When it doesn't understand something, or if unexpected events unfold, the wild rooster feels that it must commit suicide. Perhaps this is why it is not a kosher bird.

Human beings may not follow the way of the wild rooster. When calamity strikes ח״ו we should remember two things. First, we should consider the person who passed away as being like the *shamir*, in the sense that his time has come to fulfill the task for which he was destined; he is now moving towards the lofty goal intended for him, just as if he were leaving the *duchifas* and going to King Solomon. Secondly, we must have faith in our Creator. A person who complains against Hashem's judgment is like the *duchifas* which committed suicide when something happened which its mind couldn't accept.

The Jewish People is compared to the dove, not the wild rooster. Just as the dove faithfully and submissively stretches out its neck for slaughter, so too, believing Jews accept Heaven's judgment lovingly and submissively. This befits a nation called "children of Hashem."

Letters of Consolation

❧ Leaving the Sea of Grief and Returning to Life

A Torah scholar writes:

> My dear and esteemed friend, Rabbi ...,
>
> I feel it proper to share with you a few thoughts that were difficult for me to express in person.
>
> Actually, my intention is not to try to console you, because we say, may *HaMakom*, Hashem Himself, console you. If only Hashem can console, how can a mere human being even attempt to console someone upon the death of a wife, who is part of her husband's very being. Therefore, I do not attempt in this letter to console you, or to dull the terrible anguish you feel upon the death of your righteous wife, may she rest in peace, but rather to share with you some of my own experiences when my wife, may she rest in peace, passed away, and to tell you some of the thoughts that gave me strength and encouragement at that time.
>
> When I got up from *shiva*, I felt a terrible void in my life; I did not know where I and my seven young children were headed. I contemplated embracing Despair and finding consolation there. But then, in the

midst of my thoughts, the verse at the end of *Parashas Nitzavim* came to mind: "See, I have placed before you today life and good, death and evil. Choose life!" I thought to myself that although this verse is a command which was given for all aspects of life, nevertheless the simple meaning of the verse is that it refers to a person standing at a crossroads where one path will lead him to life and the other to death and evil. I asked myself, what situation is there where a person would be facing such a difficult decision and would be given this commandment? The answer came readily. Obviously the reference is to a person in my situation, when one choice is to fall into the arms of Despair — death and evil — which is the easy way out, and the other way, the hard way, is to choose life and to pull one's self together, to build a new life. That is when the person is commanded "Choose life!" I realized that it was for this moment that the Creator commanded me to "Choose life!"

You have no idea how much strength and encouragement I drew from the feeling that I was on the path of life. I pulled myself together and went to the *beis midrash,* where I sat and learned for a few hours. Since then I have continued my learning sessions regularly, and the Holy One has showered me with Divine help, enabling me to continue to learn and study the holy Torah.

But at the end of the day, when I went to bed at night, my conscience bothered me and sleep eluded me. I felt lonely and cut off from Heaven. I found no solace for my soul. Until Hashem placed a thought from the *Mesillas Yesharim* in my heart, a thought that helped my stormy soul see things differently.

The *Mesillas Yesharim* writes in Chapter One that all aspects of life are tests for Man. Poverty is a test for one person, and wealth for another. Tranquillity and *yissurim* — wherever a person turns, he is faced with a battle. If so, I thought to myself, there is no reason why I should view myself as being excommunicated in Heaven, Heaven forbid. Rather, if until today I had been given the test of tranquillity, then today my test is *yissurim* and hardship. (Note that the greatest sufferer, Iyov, clearly received *yissurim* only as a test and not as a punishment.)

A careful reading of the Ramban's commentary on *Bereishis* (35:18) will demonstrate that this thought lies at the heart of his explanation of the verse where Rachel called her son *ben oni*, son of my mourning, while his father called him *ben yamin*, son of power and strength. The Ramban explains that "he [Yaakov] wanted to name his son the same name that she (Rachel) had given...but he gave it a positive interpretation." What did the Ramban mean by "he wanted to name his son the *same* name, etc."? Yaakov interpreted *ben oni* in a positive sense, namely that the Holy One had challenged him with a new, more difficult test; therefore Yaakov hoped that Hashem would give him new strength as well, in order to withstand the test.

I return again to what I wrote in the beginning of the letter. My intention is not to console, for that is not in my power. My only purpose is to encourage you in preparation for the difficult emotional and mental battle facing you — may you be a winning soldier in this difficult battle.

I will conclude with the blessing, "May *HaMakom* console you among all other mourners of Zion and Yerushalayim" and may Hashem help you in all your endeavors.

Your friend,

*   *   *

R. Shach relates that just when the Chofetz Chaim finished writing one of the volumes of the *Mishna Berura*, his granddaughter suddenly passed away shortly before her wedding. The family's grief was understandably great, and the saintly grandfather was troubled by the tragedy.

He was overheard saying to himself, "Satan, Satan, I know you want to confuse me so that I should not complete the *Mishna Berura*, but know that nothing will help you. I will strengthen myself and I'll complete the entire *Mishna Berura*."

ৰ Acceptance Is the Cure for Suffering

My dear friend,

I cannot withhold my words. As a continuation to my previous letter, I feel compelled to focus on a different thought which accompanies me constantly.

It is common for people in the midst of trials and tribulations given by Hashem to occasionally feel embittered over their situation. They ask, "Why did Hashem do this to me?" and other similar questions. (Parenthetically, let me reassure you that these are, generally speaking, not serious questions which would reflect the person's true attitudes, but rather these are questions that simply surface on their own and cannot be avoided. Nevertheless, this does not exempt us from finding the proper response to them.)

Our holy Torah provides us with a way to deal with these thoughts. In *Bereishis* (41:52) we read: "The second one he named Efraim, for G-d has made me fruitful in the land of my poverty and affliction." Let us picture what Yosef meant when he called Egypt "the land of my poverty and affliction." From sitting like a prince at his father Yaakov's table, Yosef was cast down to the lowest depths. He was sold as a slave

to the lowliest of nations, he lived for many years totally cut off from his family, he was abused by his master's wife, and he suffered from all sorts of trials which
were his lot. There is no doubt that the suffering of
Yosef's soul was very great, yet he was still able to see
Hashem's kindness which accompanied him on his
hard and afflicted path.

He expressed those feelings in the name he gave
his son. "G-d has made me fruitful" although "I am in
the land of my affliction." The name Efraim was intended to remind him at all times that even when he
faces hardship and *yissurim*, nevertheless, G-d's kindness does not forsake him.

This thought should accompany us in all our endeavors. G-d has surely given us *yissurim*, but there is
no room for doubt. We need only open our eyes and
see His daily kindness.

Even stronger words can be found in the *Ohr
HaChaim HaKadosh*, which adds an important point: that
the acceptance of *yissurim* without second thoughts
serves as a cause for the *yissurim* to be removed.

Know, my brother, that whenever my questions
tormented me, these words calmed me and were like
cool water on a tired soul.

৵ Accept the Decree Willingly

And they arrived in Egypt, Yaakov and all his
descendants with him; his sons and grandsons
with him; his daughters and sons' daughters and
all his descendants he brought with him to Egypt.
(Bereishis 46:6-7)

Once the verse mentioned "Yaakov and all his descendants," it was unnecessary to say again "his sons and grand-

sons," etc. Furthermore, why is the clause "his sons" separated from "his daughters" by the phrase "with him"? Was the end of the sentence "he brought with him to Egypt" insufficient?

The explanation is that this verse differentiates between the various children Yaakov had. There were differences among his children in the way they went down to Egypt. Some went willingly, accepting the Will of the King, but others were hesitant to go down to the "Iron Furnace" that was Egypt. Those who went down willingly, the verse describes as going down "with him." In other words, just as Yaakov went down willingly, so too, his sons went down willingly. Yaakov did not have to "bring them down." The verse continues, listing those who Yaakov had to bring with him forcefully. "His daughters and son's daughters and all his descendants he brought with him to Egypt." These children he "brought," for they did not want to come of their own free will.

I took notice of our Sages' words (*Shemos Rabba* 1:8) which stated that as long as one of the original group that went down into Egypt was still alive, the bondage did not begin. It says, "And Yosef died and that entire generation died...." Only then did the bondage begin. Perhaps this was as a reward for accepting the decree of the King [Hashem] willingly; in this merit He exempted them from bondage, for the healing of *yissurim* depends on acceptance. The proof for this is that Yocheved and Serach *bas* Asher were members of the original group that entered Egypt, yet the bondage began while they were still alive. The explanation is that Yaakov forced them to come against their will — they had no protection from the decree. (*Ohr HaChaim, Bereishis* 46:6,7.)

֍ You Have a Living Father in Heaven

The verse says: "You are children to Hashem your G-d; do not mutilate yourselves and do not make a bald patch between your eyes for the dead." The *Ba'alei Tosafos* comments here: "You are children to Hashem your G-d; therefore, if your father of flesh and blood dies, do not mutilate yourselves, for you are not orphans, since you have a living Father, may His Name be praised and exalted. But when a gentile's father dies, he does have cause to mutilate himself, for he no longer has a father."

You have a living Father Who will stay by your side with every step you take. Every Jew senses that he is a son of Hashem, but Hashem's fatherhood expresses itself especially to the broken-hearted, the bereft, and the orphans. As the Torah says, "Do not cause anguish to any widow or orphan...for if he will cry out to Me, I will certainly hear his voice" (*Shemos* 22:21-22). The Ramban explains, "Even if the orphan only cries out to Me, I will immediately hear his cry. He does not need to do anything else, for I will save him. The orphan is helped more than anyone else, for other people toil to find saviors to rescue them and other helpers to take revenge; but these helpers may not help and will not save. But this orphan with his cry alone is saved by Hashem...for he has a mighty Redeemer and Hashem is closer to him than to any other person."

This is a clear promise given from the Supreme One to the orphan and widow: they have a Savior Who is closer to them than to any other. They are helped more than any other, for they do not need anything — if they will only call out, Hashem will answer! All the inhabitants of the world have to exert their energies to succeed and build, yet despite all their efforts they might not succeed and will not be helped. Even when they turn their eyes Heavenward, they have no guarantee that their prayers will be answered. But any widow or orphan is guaranteed by Hashem that their cries alone will bring them help and rescue them.

True, you and the children have suffered a terrible blow, but at the same time you have received a Redeemer Who is closer to you than to any other. You have a living Father Who is omnipotent — everything comes from Him. Further, He has promised you that from this day onwards you will lack nothing. Just call out and He will answer. From Him you will receive everlasting salvation.

So accept consolation, my loved ones, and know with surety that *HaMakom* will console you. He knows how to console and is able to, and you are assured by Him that you will receive goodness and pleasantness. He is your saving Father, your Supporter. His hand will guide you and His right arm will support you and lead you on straight paths until you merit to witness the consolation of Zion and Yerushalayim. May those who sleep in earth awaken and be rejuvenated; and in the cities of Yehuda and in byways of Yerushalayim may the sounds of joy and happiness be heard. May the Redeemer come to Zion.

Writing to you tearfully, broken-hearted, but hoping for salvation,

❧ On the Tragic Death of Your Sister

My dear esteemed friend...*shlita*,

May *HaMakom* console you among all other mourners of Zion and Yerushalayim.

All eyes weep and all happiness turns to sorrow

upon hearing of the tragic death of your righteous sister. Whose heart does not shudder knowing that Death has crept in through our windows? Which heart does not share the grief of the honored family and the young orphans she left behind?

My dear friend, let me tell you from my experience, to my great sorrow, that despite all the explanations and clarification — some based on the words of our Sages — nevertheless, there is no better measure than what is written in the Shema: "Love Hashem with all your heart, with all your being, and with all your means." This must be your main source of strength in order to accept the judgment lovingly, and to know that the Rock, His actions are perfect, for all His ways are just. We have no understanding of Hashem's ways and our thoughts are unlike His thoughts. Do we really understand anything in Creation? Hashem's ways are in accord with the loftiest of calculations, and with depths that cannot be fathomed: "Your thoughts are great, and Your deeds are numerous; Your eyes are open to [observe] all of Man's ways in order to give each person [payment] in accord with his ways and the fruit of his deeds" (Yirmiyahu 32:19).

With the power of simple and pure faith the Jewish people have survived terrible tragedies and rivers of blood. Children of those who questioned and argued, left the Jewish people. Only those who walked with faith and accepted everything lovingly are still alive today as Jews.

May it be Hashem's Will that you suffer no more grief, and that only good news and glad tidings be heard in your family. May we soon merit the revelation of Hashem's glory with the coming of the true Redeemer at the time of the Resurrection, speedily in our days, Amen.

From your friend who shares your pain, writing to you with sorrow and tears,

ঌ The Gates of Tears Are Never Locked

"May it be the Will of the One Who listens to the sound of our cries, that You collect our tears so they are not lost; save us from all cruel decrees, for our eyes are turned to You alone" (*Selichos*).

We all feel like soldiers who have returned from the battlefield, a battlefield where many of our people — men, women and children — all joined together to beg their Creator to revoke the decree. But they were unable to have the decree revoked. I cannot recall, in the span of many years, a personality that merited such attention from the *gedolei hador*, teachers and children, families, and from the various educational institutes. Everyone shared the prayer: "Our Father, our King, send a complete recovery to the sick of your people, and specifically to...."

Have we returned from the battle in apparent defeat? No! We certainly hoped and looked to Hashem, as watchmen longing for dawn. The awaited morning did not arrive, but we have not been defeated. On the contrary, all those who cried out gained great merit; yet, even greater merit was gained by the one who was prayed for. For "greater is the one who causes the deed more than the doer." Our beloved had the merit of inspiring the community to draw closer to our Creator, blessed is His Name, with the closeness of union with G-d through saying *Tehillim* and increased devotion in prayer. The departed also has the merit of being the cause of an arousal to *teshuva*, which expressed itself in public fasts and a resolve to improve ourselves and increase our Torah study. Furthermore, who knows how much forgiveness has come down to this world and how many decrees were annulled in his behalf?

All of the above point to a victory of Good over Evil. Good has won. Faith has increased, and Heaven's Name and service of Hashem were sanctified. We can say that if it was decreed upon him — and upon you — whatever was decreed, fortunate is he that these merits paved the way for him to enter the gates of Gan Eden, to reach the place of those who sanctify the Name of Heaven and contribute to the public good.

I know that my words are insufficient to console your broken hearts, but I could not keep from expressing my feelings. If anybody wants to know where all those tears and prayers went, the answer is: The hot tears evaporated and became clouds of glory which joined together with his many merits. Together they will rise before the Throne of Glory to praise our unforgettable loved one, bringing him to his resting place in Gan Eden.

I have no words to console you, but I do have a blessing and a prayer: be blessed in the Great Light which is the Light of Hashem's Countenance which encompasses everything, as is written: "For in Your Light You have given us, Hashem our G-d, a Torah of life and loving-kindness, righteousness, blessing, mercy, life, and peace" (*Siddur*). May *HaMakom* console you among all mourners of Zion and Yerushalayim.

Signing in tears,

❧ "But I Am a Widow..."

My dearest one,

A cruel and unbearably painful reality has arisen. I'm still in shock, my soul is torn and broken, and only his precious, dear children bring me back to reality. Thanks to them, I feel myself as still belonging to this world. I must carry my suffering deep within me for their sake, so that they may grow as their father had wished and so that he may be proud of them up Above.

One thing I know, I must not rob them of their precious childhood nor their days of maturity by my constant crying and poisoning of the atmosphere in the house. My objective is so clear, but the strength needed for the task is still beyond me. My hope to Hashem is that He should strengthen me and give me the power necessary to fulfill my life's purpose, which has not changed, but which now seems so difficult to achieve.

These words fall on the paper, written with the tears and blood of my heart. They are the first lines I've written since that Monday. One of the children said to me as we accompanied him on his last length of the road to the eternal world: "Ima, why are you crying and why are you upset? It's better for Abba now. He has gotten there already and for sure he is in Gan Eden. We still have a long way to go...who knows how long and who knows when we will get there?"

That is the truth — I felt it with my whole being. There is nothing in our world beside the eternal, and the passageway is so tiny! A few minutes earlier we talked to each other, his face was so clear, and his words were so normal, when suddenly he belonged entirely to the spiritual world and his life on earth had ended. I am full of pain and suffering — I don't have the strength to continue my letter. I would be so happy if you could be here by my side, because there are certain things that must be discussed. Each passing day the loneliness increases. I have to reach the point quickly where the "I" in me takes up no space, and then it will be easier for me to fulfill, with Hashem's help, my great task.

I feel the friendship which surrounds me from all sides. I feel all the tears that were shed and have joined with my own. I know I am not alone in my infinite sorrow, but it is bad and bitter for me, and only my faith and confidence can bring me back to a sense of equilibrium.

Write to me and the children.

Yours,

❧ Nevertheless

I was recently in the home of a young widow, the mother of young orphans. I saw her surrounded by friends who came to console and encourage her. "You have to accept the judgment with happiness and love," they said. "Whatever Hashem does is for the good!" Their words, however true, and however innocently said and well meant, upset me terribly.

The poor, suffering girl was sitting there in shock. Her entire world had turned black.

She suppressed the pain searing her heart, pushed it further within her, and swallowed her tears bitterly. Isn't she allowed to cry?!

She looked at me with questioning, wondering eyes. I answered her with my thoughts, for I am experienced in this — I've felt it myself: Yes, the hand of

Hashem has struck at me too. The pain is very great. I can't deny it and I don't want to. This is reality.

You, too, know that the blow is almost unbearable. It is extremely difficult to carry the burden of widowhood.

You are allowed to recognize this. It doesn't show any lack of faith and it doesn't negate the knowledge that everything is from Hashem, that everything is for the good! As King David said: "Even as I walk in the valley shadowed by Death." Widowhood is walking in that valley of Death.

Even so! "Even as I walk in the valley shadowed by Death, I will not fear evil, for You are with me!" Even in my most difficult moments, actually at all times, I felt and still feel that He is with me. A hand is holding me, leading me, and directing me to a safe and secure place.

You too, my dear one. Hold Hashem's hand, which is outstretched to you! Lean on Him and place all your hope and trust in Him. You will still recognize, as I have, that, literally, Hashem is with you every step of the way. I witnessed amazing revelations of Divine help, and I have no doubt that you will have the same experience. May the Father of orphans and the Judge of widows come to your help.

"Even as I walk in the valley shadowed by Death, I will not fear evil, for You are with me!"

✤ A Daughter Consoles Her Mother

The following letter was written by a young girl of fifteen to her mother upon the death of her grandfather. Twelve years later, the now-married young woman herself passed away, and her letter of pure faith became a source of consolation to her family.

Dear Mother,

I write to you with a wondering and unbelieving heart. But some things are very real, despite our refusal to accept them and despite our feeling that "things should have been different."

Hashem's directing hand is behind all events and all His deeds are only good. He does nothing bad, and even when He decrees one thing or another, it is for the good of all of us — even though at the moment we feel pain and bitterness.

It is good for the person who leaves this illusory world, even though it is hard for relatives — it hurts so much to lose a loved one.

It is good for him to have left this narrow "entryway," grand as it may seem to us. After all, what is it in comparison to the eternal life which follows?

Leaving is difficult, but now he has crossed the narrow bridge of this world. He was only here for a few short years, but they were the preparation for his real life.

True, the thought that he is gone pains us, but our feelings are only based on our physical view, for he does still exist, and he is even closer to us than he was before. Only his outer form is missing — he himself is still here. What value is there to an outer form if there is nothing inside? The core is the essential part of his being, and the core will remain with us forever.

The road was difficult, strewn with obstacles; the bridge was narrow and dangerous. He crossed the bridge and now he has crossed it safely.

But as he enters the "palace," he is checked by the guards at the gate to see whether he will be allowed in or, Heaven forbid, not. That is why our hearts are troubled; we are in pain, we cry out of fear of that "maybe." So we try to help the soul enter that World of Good.

With our tears we can make a small opening for the soul, the portion of the Divine which soared after completing its task in this world. The soul first presents an accounting to its Master, and then rests and enjoys the radiance of the Divine Presence in a world that is all good.

So please be consoled upon your great loss. The trust has been returned to its Owner, to its place, and to its home.

Yours, with love,

Rachel

ಈ Is It All Right to Cry?

Many mourners wonder if it is all right for them to cry and mourn. They think that because our Sages teach us that we should say a blessing for the bad just as we would for the good, that crying and mourning go against full acceptance of Heaven's judgment. "A person should accustom himself to say, 'Whatever the Merciful One does is for the good' " (*Berachos* 60b). Mourners feel they are obligated to control themselves, to stifle their tears and suppress their natural emotions. There even seems to be some support for this notion in halacha: "Three days are for crying" (*Shulchan Aruch, Yoreh Deah* 394:1), as if to say, "three days and no more."

This question bothered us when we sat *shiva* for our beloved, may he rest in peace. The pain was indescribable. If a substantial monetary loss is painful, how much more so this! But, on the other hand, we were troubled: Aren't we believers, children of believers, who believe with perfect faith that everything is decreed in Heaven, and that the Holy One knows what is good for each person? We believe that what Hashem does is good. If so, perhaps we should overcome our natural inclination to grieve? Perhaps, we wondered, the correct way is that we should not cry at all? Maybe our Sages meant that it is all right to cry *only* during the first three days and that after that it is forbidden to shed even one tear.

We discussed our confusion with a number of great Torah personalities who helped us clarify the issue as follows:

The Midrash says, "When Avraham went to sacrifice Yitzchak, he cried, but his heart was happy" (*Bereishis Rabba* 56:8). The *Avodas HaGershuni* [written by a grandson of the Vilna Gaon] records an explanation of this Midrash given by the Gaon: It is hard to accept that Avraham, so perfectly righteous, would have cried when performing this service to Hashem. It is also difficult to understand how his heart could be happy if he was crying. It must be that this Midrash is praising Avraham's greatness. By looking closely at this description, we can learn the proper approach to serving G-d.

Because of Avraham's burning love of Hashem, everything usually valued in this world was meaningless compared with his love. When Hashem said to him, "Please take your son," and added, "your only son," He let Avraham know that no matter how precious Yitzchak was to him, he should still disregard personal emotion — this was part of the test. Since Avraham had mastered the art of subjugating his will to Hashem's, he had no sense of loss. Rather, in order to increase the value of his obedience, he strove to create an inner will opposed to Hashem's, so that he would later be able to break it for Hashem's sake.

Avraham began by remembering things that would increase his love for his son. He thought of how precious this only child was. He pictured his and his wife's years of prayer and supplication before they were finally blessed with a son in their old age. He thought too of the anguish he and Sarah would feel without Yitzchak. Avraham continued thinking this way until he began to weep from sorrow. At that point, he turned his thoughts to G-d and felt a great love and a desire to do His Will. These feelings — that he was about to fulfill G-d's command with joy and that he was breaking his own will to do so — brought Avraham great happiness. That is why he felt happy while he wept.

These words explain how we can accept death and they teach us how we should act. Not only is it *all right* to feel sad and to cry, it is even desirable, for it increases our love of Hashem. We can even develop stronger faith. It is obvious that the intense emotions that follow the loss of a child, G-d forbid, or other relatives, emotions that at times become so intense that the person cries even after the first three days, are in no way a violation of the halachic dictum of "three days for crying." Our Sages never intended that crying that stems from natural emotions suppressed.

A mourner should channel and direct his feelings in the right way, by encouraging himself and his family to accept the Will of Heaven in strengthened faith. They should keep in mind that there is nothing besides Hashem. They should reinforce within themselves the knowledge that all the pain and suffering they are experiencing comes directly from Him. Since it is His Will to bestow good to His creatures, surely all is for the best. With this understanding, they will accept their portion of suffering lovingly, and their anguish and tears will be transformed into an integral part of their service to Hashem.

This is surely Hashem's Will. If we act like this, we will elevate ourselves. If instead we suppress our emotions, we cut ourselves off from reality. If that happens, our potential for growth, for accepting the judgment of Heaven, and for being in harmony with true faith becomes blocked.

Hashem's desire is that we emulate Avraham, whose heart was joyous although he cried. It must be emphasized, though, *that we should not try to increase our anguish as he did.*

That was Avraham's unique striving for perfection at the time of the *Akeida*. Our job is to use our inherent emotion of sorrow to serve Hashem and to accept Heaven's judgment.

ت Our Son Is Gone!

These lines are written the day after we got up from sitting *shiva* for our precious son, whose delicate soul and good heart were filled only with the longing to learn Torah. He was called to Heaven to bask in the radiance of the *Shechina* and to learn from His mouth, so to speak, as our Sages say (*Avoda Zara*, 3b): "The Holy One sits and learns Torah with schoolchildren who have passed away."

We felt it was our duty to make sure the days of mourning wouldn't be wasted, but would be used as days of spiritual growth and acceptance of Heaven's judgment. The greatest kindness for us was the feeling that we can continue to do good for our son Eliyahu Yosef, may he rest in peace. In this way, we feel he is still alive, and as parents, we can continue to help our child.

We feel that we are escorting our son's precious soul on its way to basking in the *Shechina*'s light, leading to its purification. It is our duty to escort it so that it will benefit from our combined merit. That is why it is best to use these days in a way that will be the most useful accompaniment to the departed — not to engage in meaningless chatter during the *shiva*, but to only matters of spiritual encouragement.

May we merit *Techiyas HaMeisim*, the Resurrection of the Dead, soon, in our days, Amen. And may it be Hashem's Will that we grieve no more.

❧ Hashem, Do As You See Fit

Why should we grieve? Don't we believe that everything Hashem does is for the good? We certainly do believe in this with complete faith. The proof is that if Hashem had revealed Himself to us and had informed us ahead of time, "Know, My children, that it is for so-and-so's benefit to die," and had He also given us the opportunity to change the edict, would we have done so? Certainly not. We would have accepted the Will of Heaven lovingly, saying, "Let Hashem do what is best in His eyes."

So, let us ask again, why should we grieve? Is it just because He gathered in the soul of the deceased without giving us the chance to say, "Hashem, do as You see fit"? This is not the way of believers. We want to increase our faith and feel wholeheartedly — no matter how difficult it is — that G-d intended it for the good!

When our Father in Heaven sees us withstanding the test, strong in our faith, we will surely find favor in His eyes. The merits of the deceased — merits the soul needs so much when it stands before the Heavenly Court — will increase. May Hashem console the bereaved among all other mourners of Zion and Yerushalayim.

❧ Couldn't We Have Prevented What Happened?

Many mourners torture themselves with the question: "Did I do everything in my power to save my beloved from death? Couldn't I have done more?"

If we examine these questions from the Torah perspective, we will see that these guilt feelings are out of place. We must all believe with complete and sincere faith that everything that was done or not done to save the life of the deceased was part of the Heavenly plan. As long as our loved one was still alive, it was our obligation to do whatever was in our power to help him. But now that he has returned his soul to the Creator, it is our duty to feel confident that there was nothing else that could have been done to lengthen his life, not even for one more moment.

In a way, thinking about what could have been done to save his life — although appropriate, and even a mitzva as long as the person was still alive — is, from the moment of death, considered absolutely wrong! In retrospect, everything we did or did not do was really not in our hands at all, but was under the control of the Master of all souls. Of the mistakes that were made (if they were mistakes), the Maharam Chagiz said: *Shigegas rofeh, kavanas borei*—"The doctor's mistake, the Creator's intention." Included in the category of doctors' "mistakes" are our errors concerning which doctor to go to and other decisions we made.

That is why it is to our benefit to constantly keep in mind and sincerely believe that "Hashem gave and Hashem takes — may Hashem's Name be blessed."

𝕰 "For My Thoughts Are Not Like Your Thoughts"

When we open the door to a home where a family is mourning, we see the bereaved family sitting solemnly, burdened with feelings of loss. Their hearts are breaking as they remember what once was, and at the same time, they worry over what will be. There are fleeting moments of distraction, of kind words, healing and consolation, but the relentless pain of the present always returns.

This very human scene is normal and makes sense when the response to what happened is based on what meets the human eye and on what the human mind can understand. But the picture changes as soon as events are viewed from a higher, Heavenly perspective, as the following episode from the Torah teaches us:

> At that time, Yehuda descended from his brothers (*Bereishis* 38:1). R. Shimon ben Gamliel began: "For I know My thoughts concerning you," said Hashem; "thoughts of peace, not of evil, in order to give you hope and a future" (*Yirmiyahu* 29:11). The brothers were busy with the sale of Yosef, and Yosef was occupied with his sackcloth and fasting. Reuven was occupied with his sackcloth and fasting. Yaakov was occupied with his sackcloth and fasting, and the Holy One, blessed is He, was occupied with creating the light of *Mashiach*."
>
> (*Bereishis Rabba* 81:1)

At the very moment when the human eye could only see Yaakov, Reuven, and Yosef busy with their sackcloth and fasting, the Holy One was preparing the birth of *Mashiach*. About this the prophet says: "For My thoughts are not like your thoughts, nor are your ways Mine, said Hashem" (*Yeshayahu* 55:8).

This idea sheds light on the Mishna which says: "A person is obligated to make a blessing over the bad like he would for the good" (*Berachos* 54a). The Gemara adds: "To accept it with joy."

In his work *Ohel Yaakov*, the Dubno Maggid describes the way Hashem governs the world, explaining that He bestows good on Man in one of two ways: 1) in a revealed flow of goodness, as when a person is blessed with wealth, honor, property, etc.; and 2) by hiding the flow, in which case a person experiences things which seem to be only detrimental, such as hardship, poverty, and pain. Actually, these two ways parallel each other. But while we feel confident that all is for the best when things seem to go well, only Hashem can see the ultimate good destined to result from difficulties.

This can be compared to the skill of a tailor. When the tailor takes up a piece of fine silk material and begins to cut it into pieces, the fool starts yelling and shouting that the tailor is "destroying" a good piece of material. But the knowledgeable person understands that this is the only way to make a garment.

The same is true about suffering. Hashem Who is the Ultimate Source of all that happens, and Whose understanding is infinite, does things that seem to be bad and harsh. But the truth is that, just as plowing and planting precede a harvest, seemingly destructive events bring all the blessings and good things which follow. Since what we see as "bad" is really preparation for ultimate good, we can say that it is part of that good. That is why we should be able to and are able to bless the "bad" with the same joy with which we bless the good.

If the tailor had listened to the fool, he would have put down the cut pieces and run away in fear. Only useless scraps of material would have been left. This same fate could befall people who complain about the way Hashem runs the world. If Hashem would leave them alone and not complete His plan, they would be left with only the misfortune, and none of the intended benefits. The opposite happens when a person joyfully accepts what seems bad. When he shows how much he trusts Hashem and believes that Hashem wants only what is good for him, then he allows the work to continue. Hashem will complete what He began and will bestow all the good He had originally intended.

Once we know this, when hardship strikes, we can think to ourselves that no matter how "bad" and bitter things seem to be, it is only the material being cut up for the beautiful garment being made. Although our limited human understanding cannot imagine the eventual good, we can still believe with complete faith that this good will yet come. Knowing this brings comfort and solace, and helps us accept the decree with joy.

*May His great Name be glorified
and sanctified.*

— Kaddish

Bringing Merit to the Deceased

The Sages of Israel have compared the separation caused by death to the separation caused by travel abroad. The comparison appears many times in this book, since it is a true source of consolation. There is another dimension to this analogy which also brings solace, and this is the concept of *bera mezakei abba*, a son brings merit to his father.

Let us consider the example of a mother sending her son away to yeshiva. From the moment he leaves, her heart longs to see him again, but he is too far away to visit. What can she do to satisfy her desire to be close to him? The simplest solution is to send him a package of his favorite foods once a week. This way she stays in contact with her son and feels less lonely knowing that she is doing something for him even from a distance.

When a loved one passes away, the survivors often feel an intense desire to somehow find a way to help the deceased, to keep some kind of connection with him. If only they could continue to give to him, their yearnings for closeness would be satisfied and they would be partially consoled.

The rule *bera mezakei abba* is itself of great significance, as we shall see. It is also the way Hashem makes it possible for us to help those who have departed this world. It is therefore fitting in this book about consolation to devote a chapter to that concept.

R. Yechezkel Levenstein related that within the first year of mourning for the Saba of Slobodka, the Saba visited his son, R. Eliezer Yehuda Finkel ל״צז, Rosh Yeshiva of the Mir Yeshiva, in a dream and requested: *Shick mir pekalach*—"Send me packages, especially on *motzaei Shabbos!*" He meant, of course, "packages" of Torah and good deeds, of Kaddish and *mishnayos*, presents from afar which bring immeasurable relief and salvation to the deceased.

Mourners will be consoled knowing that their relationship with the deceased still exists and that they can bring priceless benefit to their loved ones who are no longer in this world.

ᔍ Honoring Parents after Their Death

Our Sages teach us (*Sanhedrin* 104a) that a son brings merit to his father. Any mitzva a son does after the death of his parents is accredited to their Heavenly account. Rabbeinu Yonah writes (*Igeres HaTeshuva*, Part III, day 6; 59): "The main merit of a mother in the World to Come comes when her sons serve Hashem, do His Will, and fear Him. If, after her death, her children are *yirei shamayim*, if they fear Heaven and are involved in Torah and good deeds, she is considered to be alive and performing all the commandments. She is elevated to the highest levels in the World to Come."

"Good deeds performed by a son...expiate the sins of his father" (*Yeish Nochalin*, written by the father of the Shela HaKadosh, quoted by the Chofetz Chaim).

The Shela adds that a son not only saves his father from the judgment and suffering of Gehinnom, but can even cause him to enter into Gan Eden and lead him to the section reserved for the perfectly righteous. As the *Zohar* (end of *Vayikra*) teaches: "A son honors his father. Even though his father has passed away, the son has a strong obligation to honor him. If he falls into evil ways, he most certainly brings disgrace to his father. But if the son walks in the path of the good and behaves as he should, he honors his father in the eyes of people in this world, and also in the eyes of Hashem in the World to Come. Then Hashem acts with mercy towards the father and seats him in a place of honor."

The Chofetz Chaim continues: "Imagine if a person is thrown into a burning fire or suffers terrible pains. How he would wish that his children save him from the agony! And how hard his children would try to help him, sparing no effort! This thought should arouse a person to do all in his power to save his parents' souls from the punishment of their sins, especially during the seven- and thirty-day mourning periods, when Divine Judgment is particularly severe. During these days a son should make the greatest efforts to increase his Torah study, charity, and acts of kindness for his parents' benefit."

The *Pele Yoetz*, discussing the obligation to honor parents, says: "The greatest honor is the honor given after the parents' death. Every day a son should do everything in his power to bring peace to his parents' souls. It is useful and appropriate for a son to visualize his father's face before him, to picture his father calling out from a burning fire, 'My dear son! Help me! Save my soul from the sword; save my very being from predators!'

"If a son believes his father was a perfect *tzaddik* who will receive no punishment in the World to Come, he should still see himself as bestowing blessings and benefits upon his father, increasing his father's spiritual delight through his own good deeds. How good is it for a son to pray daily, 'May it be

Your Will, my G-d and the G-d of my fathers, that you accept with compassion and goodwill my every good deed, word, and thought as a source of merit, tranquillity, and benefit to the spirit and souls of my parents and parents-in-law. And may it be Your Will that their souls be bound in the bond of Eternal Life.' If he acts in this way, he will be blessed by Hashem and by his parents in Heaven."

R. Eliyahu Lopian related that due to the severe famine during World War I, many of his neighbors called their sons home from Yeshiva so that they could help support their families ward off starvation. Although R. Lopian had nine sons studying in yeshiva, he and his wife refused to interrupt their studies and call them home. Their neighbors, who saw the depth of their deprivation, asked the Rebbetzin, "Why don't you call two or three of your sons home to help support you and relieve your hunger?" To which she replied with strength and conviction, "I don't want my sons' help now, for a time will come — in the World to Come — when I shall very much need their help. I prefer that they remain in yeshiva now, so they will be able to help me then, when I will truly need their help!"

ܐ Avoiding *Loshon Hora* Brings Merit to the Deceased

The Saba of Kelm wrote the following letter of condolence to his brother when their mother passed away:

Greetings of peace to my dear brother,
Your pleasant words reached me. I was very pleased to hear that you are afraid that we have not done enough to honor our mother. The obligation to honor parents is awesome and demanding, may the All-Compassionate One forgive us. All of us, my dear brother, must now honor her by atoning for her, by

bringing her as much merit as possible by devoting set times daily for studying Torah and *mussar*. We should try to study Torah for its own sake, with no ulterior motive, as the *Nefesh HaChaim* writes, and to refrain from any *loshon hora* (derogatory speech.)

I have therefore written to you, my brother, suggesting that at every meal — and especially on Shabbos — you study a bit of the *Alim l'Terufa* by the Vilna Gaon. Praised be Hashem that He prepared for us the holy *sefer*, *Tomer Devorah*, which is of great help in developing love for one's fellowman, and all good character traits, as well as in helping to avoid the harsh sin of *loshon hora* over which one cries bitterly when his time comes. Let us build strong barriers to protect ourselves from this sin, and be as strict as we are in our Yom Kippur resolutions. If we can accustom ourselves to this, we can feel wonderfully blessed, and it will be of great merit to our righteous mother, may she rest in peace.

May the All-Merciful One help us realize how strictly and precisely man is judged, for it is truly awesome and frightening. "Your judgment is like the great abyss" (*Tehillim* 36:7). If even the greatest, most righteous and holy people are judged with the utmost precision, what can we ordinary people expect? This should be discussed at great length, but it is difficult for me to write now.

Our mother, may she rest in peace, was indeed known to all as a great *tzaddekes*. Yet my heart is afraid — who knows the extent of the Divine judgment of man? Her illness made a strong impact upon me, when I saw how precise Divine judgment is. May we merit that this lesson be of lasting benefit.

❧ Only Torah Study and Good Deeds Help

It is a long-standing custom for every Jew to leave instructions to his children and family which are to be carried out after he has departed. This ancient custom comes from a reliable source, our forefather Avraham, as we find (*Bereishis* 18:19): "He will instruct his children and household after him...."

With the passing of generations, our hearts have become smaller due to our many sins, and in our times, most wills are about the division of wealth and possessions. Although this is important in order to avoid later disagreements among one's inheritors, it was not the type of will left by Avraham. His final command was that "they guard the way of Hashem." This is the essence of the inheritance and last will that a person must bequeath his children. Only in this way does he benefit his children, and do they in turn bestow merit upon him.

Our Sages say, *bera mezakei abba*—"a son brings merit to his father." Woe to a father who has not prepared himself through Torah and good deeds in this world, and must rely on his children's help to save him from judgment in Heaven. Yet, his children should not feel that their father is somehow diminishing their reward; they are helping him while acting for their own benefit. We are taught (*Kiddushin* 40a) that a person should always see himself and the entire world as being perfectly balanced between good and evil deeds, so that if he performs a single mitzva he tips the scales for himself and the entire world. Everyone is happy to save the entire world through a mitzva that he does for himself. How much more should a son try to improve himself with Torah and good deeds, and thus bring eternal benefit to himself *and* to his father. As true as this is with regard to simply adding to his father's merit, it is even more so if he can save his father from distress while helping himself.

To you, my dear sons, this comment should suffice.

Therefore, my dearly beloved children...imagine this scene. The simplest person, seeing his father wounded and tortured, beaten mercilessly, would surely be unable to stand by passively. He would certainly spare no expense, and would surmount any difficulty — even at the risk of his own life — to save his father. Likewise you, my beloved sons, whom I always cared for and brought up, sending you to *yeshivas*, educating you to follow the Torah, and instilling in you fear of Heaven, you whose souls are bound with mine through bonds of love, surely you will not stand by when you can save your beloved father from suffering.

Well do you know the words of King Solomon (*Koheles* 4:1): "I have seen the tears of the oppressed...and they are not consolable." (See Rashi on this verse: "I saw through *Ruach HaKodesh*, Divine inspiration, those who suffer in Gehinnom because of what they did instead of following the Torah. Behold, they cry for their souls that are oppressed by Angels of Destruction.") How can you deliver your father from such anguish? Only through Torah and good deeds. Whenever you give charity, or perform a kind act, please say explicitly, at least during the first year, "I am doing this for the sake of my father's soul."

Please read this letter daily throughout the first month [after my passing]; afterwards, please read it at least once a week for the remainder of the first year. Thereafter, please read it from time to time, so that you will always remember me.

(From the will of R. Leib Broide, the brother of the Saba of Kelm and one of the first *baalei mussar*.)

ن A Son Is His Father's Leg

The Sages say a son is the leg of his father. Why the leg and not the hand? This is because people in this world are called "goers" (מהלכים), while souls and angels Above are called "standers" (עומדים), as we read in *Zecharia* (3:7): "I will grant you *movement* among those who *stand*."

The dead are free — free of mitzvos. But without mitzvos there is no upward movement, there is only standing, staying at the same level. The leg is the limb that gives movement to men. That is why a son is called the *leg* of his father. Once he is in the World to Come, the father cannot move, but his son, with his actions, can become his father's leg and move him.

I pray that the air of *Eretz Yisrael* will give you wisdom and that you will rise ever higher in Torah, service of Hashem, and acts of kindness, so that you will transfer your ability to move and rise to your father who is now amongst those standing.

May *HaMakom* console you amongst the mourners of Zion and Yerushalayim.

Yitzchak Hutner
(*Pachad Yitzchak,* "Letters," p. 242)

ن The Importance of Studying *Mishnayos*

The Shela HaKadosh writes of the importance of studying *mishnayos*, of knowing the six orders of Mishna fluently by heart, for in this way a person can make a ladder for his soul to climb to a lofty level. The Hebrew letters that spell Mishna (*mem, shin, nun, heh*), when rearranged, spell *neshama*, soul.

Many Torah scholars left written requests of their children, students, and friends asking them to study *mishnayos* for the merit of their souls after death. The great R. Akiva Eiger wrote in his will: "When I die...my death should be announced in newspapers with the note that I request that my students and friends learn a chapter of Mishna on my behalf, every day for the first year, and every year on my *yahrzeit*."

R. Yechezkel Levenstein wrote in a condolence letter to his grandchildren upon the passing of their father: "My dear grandchildren, it is now your obligation to be engaged in Torah and mitzvos in order to help your father who gave so much of his time for you. Please repay him. Make sure that your prayers are said with proper concentration. Be sure that you know the meaning of Kaddish and recite it with deep concentration. Also learn *mishnayos* every day on behalf of his holy soul...."

The *Penei Baruch* (on the laws of mourning), in writing on the importance of *mishnayos* to the souls of the deceased, quotes our Sages who tell us that Asher, Yaakov's son, sits at the gates of Gehinnom and saves anyone who studied *mishnayos* (or anyone in whose name *mishnayos* were studied). This is alluded to in the verse (*Bereishis* 49:20) which says of Asher that "his bread is fat." The Hebrew word used here for fat, *shmena*, is made up of the same letters as *neshama*.

The *Penei Baruch* quotes the *Torah Ohr*, which states that studying *mishnayos* is of greater benefit to the deceased than leading prayers. Similarly, the *Yosef Ometz* writes that the practice of leading prayers and reciting Kaddish for the deceased was enacted essentially for unlearned people. For someone, though, who can learn, Torah study is far more useful to the departed. Torah study brings the soul into Gan Eden. And if the son brings to light previously hidden aspects of the Torah, his father receives incomparable honor in the *Yeshiva shel Ma'ala*, the Heavenly Yeshiva.

❧ Saying Kaddish Brings Merit to the Deceased

The Midrashim speak about saying Kaddish for one's parents. It is therefore customary to recite Kaddish for one's father and mother for the first year. It is also customary to read the *maftir* on their *yahrzeit* day and to lead the evening prayer on the preceding *motzaei Shabbos*.

Whenever a son leads the prayers and recites Kaddish publicly, he redeems his father and mother from Gehinnom (Rema, *Yoreh Deah* 376:4).

The *Ohr Zarua* tells us a true incident in the life of R. Akiva which powerfully illustrates this fact:

Once R. Akiva saw a person who was naked and as black as coal carrying on his head a load equal to ten loads and running like a horse. R. Akiva ordered him to halt and asked, "Why do you do such difficult labor? If you are a slave and your master forces you to work this way, I will redeem you from him. If you are impoverished, I will give you wealth."

The figure replied, "Please do not restrain me, lest those who are appointed over me become angry."

"What is this for? What are your deeds?"

"I am a dead person. Every day I am sent to chop wood and I am burnt along with it."

"My son, what were your actions in the world from which you came?"

"I was a tax collector who showed favor to the rich and killed the poor."

R. Akiva then asked him: "Did you hear from those in charge of you how you can repair your soul?"

Again the man pleaded, "Please do not restrain me, lest the agents of punishment be angry at me, for there is no salvation for me!

"I did hear them say that there is one way my soul can be redeemed and released from this torture, but it is an impossibility: They said that if I had a son who would stand before the congregation and say, 'Bless Hashem, the Blessed One' and the people would respond, 'Blessed be Hashem Who is blessed eternally,' or if the son would say 'yisgadal' and the congregation would respond, 'May the great Name be blessed,' I would be immediately freed from punishment. But I left behind no son. My wife was pregnant, and if she did bear a son, I do not know who would teach him, for I have no friend in the world."

R. Akiva decided then that he would take responsibility for finding out if a son had been born so that he could teach him Torah and show him how to lead the congregation in prayer. So R. Akiva asked the man, "What is your name?"

"Akiva."

"And your wife's name?"

"Shoshniva."

"And your town?"

"Ludkia."

Even though the journey was long and arduous, R. Akiva immediately set out to locate the man's child. When he reached the town the soul had named, he asked about the dead man. The people answered, "May the bones of that evil person be ground to bits."

When he asked about the wife of the deceased, they answered, "May her name be blotted from the face of the earth."

"And what of the child?"

"The boy is uncircumcised. We did not even make a *bris* for him."

R. Akiva immediately took the boy and circumcised him. He sat the child down in front of him, but the boy could not grasp the teachings of the Torah. Only after R. Akiva fasted forty days for the boy did a Heavenly voice call out, "R. Akiva, go and teach him!"

R. Akiva taught him Torah, the Shema, *Shemoneh Esrei*,

and *Birkas HaMazon*. Then he stood the boy before the congregation so that he could say, "Bless Hashem, the Blessed One," while the congregation responded, "Blessed be Hashem Who is blessed eternally," "*Yisgadal*," and "*yehei shemei rabba*."

The dead man was immediately released from his punishment. He then appeared to R. Akiva in a dream and said, "May it be the Will of Heaven that you should rest in Gan Eden, because you saved me from the punishment of Gehinnom."

R. Akiva then said, " 'Hashem' is Your Name forever, 'Hashem' is Your memorial for every generation."

The *Tanna d'Vei Eliyahu Rabba* tells us: "When a child says *yisgadal*, his father is saved from punishment" (*Ohr Zarua*, sec. 2, "Shabbos," sec. 50).

The *Zohar Chadash* writes that when the man reappeared before R. Akiva, he told him: "When my son recited the *Haftara*, my punishment in Gehinnom was lightened. When my son led the congregation in prayer and said Kaddish, the decree against me was torn up completely, and when he became wise and achieved Torah knowledge, I was given a share in Gan Eden."

ﻙ Your Father Waits for Your Kaddish

A G-d-fearing young man passed away, leaving a five-year-old son. Despite all entreaties and promises made to him, the child was embarrassed to say Kaddish. The worried family consulted the Steipler Gaon, who asked that the child be brought to him. The Steipler prefaced his talk with the child by saying that although he had no experience in such matters, Hashem would help.

The Steipler spoke warmly to the boy, saying, "Your father is now in the World of Truth. Nothing is of value there, and even if he were given all the money in the world, it would be worthless to him. The only thing of value to your father is the Kaddish you can say for him. Do you know how he waits for your Kaddish? It is very good for you to say Kaddish, because that brings the biggest pleasure to your father." Then he told the child the story of how R. Akiva had taught a boy to say Kaddish for his father and how that son's prayer had saved his father from Gehinnom.

The Steipler's heartfelt words impressed the boy, who began saying Kaddish and continued to do so every day for the rest of the year of mourning.

৯ৡ Mourner's Kaddish

Recitation of Kaddish has enormous power to protect and save the soul of the deceased. It is not actually a prayer for the soul of the deceased, but is really praise of Hashem and a prayer that His Name be glorified and sanctified. There are, though, two places in the Kaddish where a person can include a request on behalf of the deceased. When reciting the words "May there be great peace...upon all of Israel," one can also mentally include among all of Israel "the soul of so-and-so." Also, when saying the words "He Who makes peace in His Heavens," a worshipper can mentally phrase a request that the soul of the deceased be blessed with peace.

The *Sefer HaChaim* speaks of another theme in the Kaddish prayer: the acceptance of the validity of Divine justice. Death is always caused by sin, most often the sin of *chillul Hashem* (desecration of Hashem's Name), for which death alone can atone. When Hashem punishes the sinner, His Name is sanctified, as it is written: "I will judge," and then, "I will be glorified and sanctified."

When a son declares, "May His great Name be glorified

and sanctified," he is in effect saying, "I am comforted for the loss of my parent in the knowledge that the Name of my Father in Heaven was glorified through my parent's death."

Thus his father's sin of *chillul Hashem* is atoned for. This is similar to the comment made by the relatives of a person put to death by a Jewish court when they say to the judges, "You have judged properly," thus showing that they accept the verdict of the Rabbinical court without complaint. (Based on *Olas Tamid*, by R. Shemuel Houminer זצ"ל.)

❧ Kaddish Is Sanctification of Hashem's Name

From the famous story of R. Akiva quoted in the *Ohr Zarua*, we may infer that Kaddish is not a prayer for life in the World to Come or a prayer for the souls of the deceased, as many people mistakenly assume. There is no hint in the Kaddish prayer of such requests, or of requests for leniency or forgiveness for the dead.

Kaddish is, in fact, solely a sanctification of Hashem's Name. The son of the deceased, by inviting the congregation to publicly bless Hashem and by their responding to the words of Kaddish, brings about a *kiddush Hashem*, which proves that the parent's life was worthwhile, since he merited having such a son. Through this son the deceased has a share in the *kiddush Hashem* he brought about, which can positively affect the judgment he receives from Hashem, the true Judge. (Based on *World of Prayer*, by R. Munk.)

❧ Kaddish Can Lessen the Suffering of the Departed

The two central themes of Kaddish — *kiddush Hashem* in the present, and the prayer for the universal recognition of Hashem in the future — give Kaddish its central place in our prayers and arouse our deepest feelings. The prayer of *Aleinu*, which closes every prayer service, teaches us the centrality of these two ideas. In its first section, we express our obligation to sanctify Hashem's Name in the present. In its second half, *Al ken nekaveh*, we express our great yearning for the ultimate recognition of Hashem's sovereignty by all mankind. These two ideas form the song of the Jewish People. The saying of Kaddish has withstood the test of time for generations because it expresses our deepest commitment and yearning. Because it gives voice to our unbroken commitment and hope, it is the greatest means by which the living bring merit to the dead.

When a parent dies, a child feels an acute sense of loss. He realizes how much he received from his parent and how little he gave in return. In his heartache, he looks for ways to express his gratitude and love. Since he knows that good deeds are the true accomplishment of his loved one, he shows his love by continuing their noble deeds. In this way, a child brings merit to a parent who has once again become a source of inspiration to do good.

Since the paramount goal of a Jew should be to sanctify Hashem's Name, the child continues to express that goal when he recites Kaddish, saying: *Yisgadal veyiskadash shemei rabba*—"May His great Name be glorified and sanctified."

Echoing his parent's innermost spirit, the son leads the congregation with: *Yehei shemei rabba*—"May the great Name be blessed for ever and ever."

Since Kaddish is, in a sense, a continuation of the deceased's worship of Hashem, even though it is a prayer said by the living, it is also a prayer of the dead.

According to our tradition, the soul reaches its final rest under the wings of the Divine Presence only after a period of purification. The journey from this world of falsehood to the World of Truth takes the soul through a tortuous path of retribution which cleanses it of sin.

This is why a son should always try to help minimize his parents' suffering, especially in the year of mourning and on the day of the *yahrzeit*. Through his merit, the son can lessen the amount of suffering needed for purification.

Let the son continue in the proper way, for which his parents were a wonderful example. Let him devote his time to Torah, just as his father would want. Let the son lead the congregation in prayer and recitation of Kaddish, not by rote, but with the intention of arousing the community to sanctify Hashem's Name. Only in this manner will he bring merit to his parents' souls. Then Kaddish can become a prayer for both the living and the departed. (Based on *Tefillas HaKaddish*, by R. B.Z. Jacobson.)

?❧ It Is Important to Understand the Words

Kaddish is one of the few prayers recited in Aramaic. *Tosafos* (*Berachos* 3a) gives two reasons for this: 1) Since Kaddish is an exceptional praise of Hashem, we recite it in Aramaic, a language the angels do not understand, so they will not envy us; 2) Because many people do not understand Hebrew, our Sages instructed that it be recited in Aramaic, so that everyone could understand it.

Now that Aramaic is not commonly spoken, we should make certain to study the meaning of Kaddish until we thoroughly understand it, especially since our Sages felt it was so important for this prayer to be universally understood.

?❧ A Yeshiva Says Kaddish

There once lived in Pressburg a righteous wealthy woman. For many years she made contributions to support the famous Pressburg Yeshiva, always stipulating that Kaddish be said for all those unfortunate people who had died without leaving anyone behind to say Kaddish for them.

After her husband passed away, their business began to falter, and eventually the widow was forced to close it entirely. Her economic situation went from bad to worse, and in addition she was soon faced with another burden, the marriage of her two daughters. Where would she find the money to marry them off?

The woman bore her suffering silently, and courageously accepted her fate. One thing bothered her constantly, though, and that was the thought that the Yeshiva might stop saying Kaddish. She went to the Yeshiva's administration and begged them to continue the recitation of Kaddish. She told them that even though she could no longer contribute, she hoped and prayed that at some time in the future she would be able to.

The *Rashei Yeshiva* were very touched by her sincerity and righteousness, and they promised that the students would continue to say Kaddish. Reassured by their promise, she left with a renewed sense of hope. She no longer felt the pain of her personal difficulties because at least Kaddish would continue. As for her daughters, she put faith in Hashem, the Father of orphans and the Judge of widows. Surely He would see their plight and arrange proper matches for them.

On her way home, she was greeted by a regal-looking elderly Jew with a long white beard. The woman was surprised by the courteous greeting this elderly stranger gave her. She was even more surprised when he drew her into conversation and asked her how she was managing.

The woman sighed deeply and told him all about her difficult situation, about how she had once been quite wealthy but was now poverty stricken, lacking even funds to marry off her daughters. When she had finished speaking, the distinguished gentleman asked her how much money she needed.

She told him and watched in astonishment as the stranger took out his checkbook and wrote out a check for the amount she had mentioned. Before signing the check, he made one request: Since it was a large sum of money, it would be better if he signed the check in front of two witnesses who would then be able to verify that he had, in fact, signed the check himself.

Excited and amazed by the fortunate turn of events, the woman rushed over to the yeshiva and asked two students if they could please be witnesses to the signing. The elderly gentleman asked the two witnesses to note carefully how he signed the check and, as an added proof, he gave them a copy of his signature on a blank piece of paper. He told the widow to go to the bank early the next morning to cash the check.

With a trembling heart, she rose early the next morning and went straight to the bank.

The bank teller took the check and quickly glanced up at the woman in front of him. He examined the check again carefully and asked her to wait for a moment while he showed the check to the bank's manager. When the manager saw the check, he fainted.

The bank was in an uproar. Bank officials suspected a trick, and took the woman into a side office where she was guarded to make sure she did not leave.

Once the manager recovered, he asked to see the woman who had presented the check. When she entered his office, he asked her in confusion when and where she had received the check. She explained that she had received it the day before from a distinguished-looking elderly Jew, and that there were witnesses who had watched him sign it.

"Could you identify the man if you saw his picture?" the manager asked.

"I certainly could, and I am sure the two witnesses could as well," she replied.

He then showed her a picture of his late father, whom she identified without hesitation. The bank manager told the teller to cash the check for the full amount and the woman went home filled with joy.

The manager then explained to his staff what had happened. The man who had given the widow the check was none other than his father, who had passed away some ten years earlier! The previous night his father had appeared to him in a dream and told him: "You should know that from the time you stopped being religious and married a non-Jewish woman and no longer said Kaddish, my soul knew no rest. Then, one day, this kind-hearted woman arranged for Kaddish to be said on behalf of those who have no one else to recite it for them. The Kaddish recited in the Yeshiva at her behest elevated my soul and brought me peace. That woman will appear in your bank tomorrow with the check I gave her to cover the wedding expenses of her two daughters."

"I woke up this morning and repeated the dream to my wife, who scoffed at the whole thing. When that woman brought the check into the bank, I realized the dream was true."

The man became a *ba'al teshuva*, his wife converted to Judaism, and they raised a fine Jewish family.

R. Yosef Chaim Sonnenfeld זצ״ל, Rav of Yerushalayim noted for his exceptional piety and Torah wisdom, finished telling the story and told his rapt listeners, "Do you know who the two students were? My friend, R. Yehuda Greenwald, and myself!"

❧ Kaddish in the Capital

A group of four *frum* (religiously observant) businessmen from Cleveland had arranged to travel together by plane early one Sunday morning to a New York City trade show. It was *Rosh Chodesh Elul* and R. Mordechai, one of the business-men, had assured the others that, provided their plane landed on time at LaGuardia Airport in New York City, they would be able to catch any of a number of *minyanim* for *Shacharis* in Manhattan and still be at the trade show when it opened at 9:00 a.m.

R. Mordechai was supposed to pick up the others at 5:00 a.m. to catch the flight an hour later. But he overslept, and at 5:30 his brother, a second member of the group, came frantic-ally to his house to see what had happened. R. Mordechai awoke with a start and told his brother to get the others and go without him; he himself would have to make the next plane. The three others made their way to the airport as R. Mordechai frantically put his things together, dashing around to find his *tallis*, *tefillin*, attache case, trade samples and car keys. Equipped with a cup of coffee and his radar detector, he drove with abandon and got to the plane just as the doors were about to be closed. The others were surprised that he had made it.

The plane took off from Cleveland's Hopkins Airport in perfect weather. But shortly after the flight was in progress the captain announced that he had just been informed that there was a thick blanket of clouds and fog enveloping the New York City area. He promised the passengers to keep them informed of any developments. The men began to get apprehensive, for they had not really left much time to get from the airport to a *minyan* and still be on time to the trade show.

The flight continued as passengers tried to figure out alternate ways of getting to their destinations if they couldn't land in New York. Soon the captain's voice came over the intercom again. The news was not good, he announced. The fog had traveled westward over the New Jersey border, and not only was it impossible to land in New York, it would be dangerous even to attempt a landing at Newark Airport. They would have to land further south — in Washington, D.C.

On board with these businessmen was a small group of *chassidim*. They had come to spend Shabbos in Cleveland Heights with their rebbe, R. Mechele, and were returning to New York this morning as well. When the plane landed in Dulles Airport, in the nation's capital, the *chassidim* and the businessmen decided that perhaps they had better form a *minyan* right there, for by the time they could catch a connecting flight and land in New York, the time for reciting *Shema* would be long gone. They counted to see if they had ten. Indeed, the *chassidim* were six, and then they counted the businessmen: one, two, three — and R. Mordechai made four! They had their *minyan* — and only because R. Mordechai had caught the plane!

A member of the airline personnel designated a corner of the waiting room where they could say their morning prayers. The ten men congregated there, each in his *tallis* and *tefillin*. All this was in perfect view of any passersby who could watch the proceedings through the glass partition behind which the *mispalelim* stood.

As they were saying *Hallel*, a well-dressed man slowly and hesitantly walked into the area where they were *davening*. A few heads turned to see what he wanted. "Would you mind if I said Kaddish?" the man asked softly.

One of the businessmen, R. Yankel, was taken aback. The man hardly looked Jewish. How did he even know about Kaddish, and what did he want with it? It was then that R.

Yankel noticed that the man was wearing a black ribbon on his lapel. (Numerous Reform Jews who do not observe the ritual of rending a garment as a sign of mourning wear a black ribbon instead.)

R. Yankel motioned to the man to wait for a few moments and he did so. At the appropriate time R. Yankel went over to the man, gave him a *siddur* and a *yarmulke*, helped him don a pair of *tefillin* and said, "You may begin the Kaddish." The man looked around uneasily, then began. "*Yisgadal ve-yiskadash*..." he whispered, and burst into tears. He regained his composure and continued, "...*shmei rabba*...." The men answered *Amen* with reverence. The gentleman struggled through the remainder of the words, as the men of the *minyan* helped him get through the entire Kaddish.

When he finished, he nodded his head in thanks and asked, "Is there another one to recite later?" They told him that there was. He waited patiently and then after the *davening* they motioned to him once again to begin. And once again as he said the Kaddish he burst into tears. All in the *minyan* could not help but be touched by the sensitivity and sadness of the man.

When *Shacharis* ended, one of the *chassidim* went over to the gentleman and introduced himself. After a few moments of conversation the *chassid* said, "I couldn't help but notice that you were so emotionally torn as you prayed. Is everything all right with you?"

It was then that the gentleman told this incredible story.

"You see," he began, "my father died just a few days ago, and last night he came to me in a dream and said to me, 'Robert, how come you're not saying Kaddish for me?'

"In my dream I replied, 'Dad, I hardly know how to say Kaddish, and besides, there are no synagogues where I live and I am always traveling.'

" 'I need you to say Kaddish,' my father insisted to me. I

kept repeating that I just could not get to a place where I could say Kaddish for him. It was then that he asked me, 'But what if I send you a *minyan*? Would you then say Kaddish?'

" 'Of course I would,' I replied, and that's when I woke up. I couldn't believe that dream. I was trembling as I awakened. As I was getting dressed I managed to convince myself that there was really nothing to that dream. But then I came to the airport to catch a flight, and there, to my unbelieving eyes, were all of you praying in a *minyan* — in the *minyan* that was obviously meant for me!" (Reprinted with permission from *Around the Maggid's Table* by Rabbi Paysach J. Krohn, Artscroll/Mesorah Publications.)

Take this amulet...

— Ramban

Accepting Divine Judgment

When the Ramban visited a student who had become ill and saw that his end was near, he gave him the following instructions:

"In Heaven there is an upper sanctuary where thrones of judgment surround the Divine Presence. Take this amulet — with it, the gates of all the Heavenly sanctuaries will be opened before you and you will eventually reach the uppermost sanctuary. When you get there, ask these questions — important questions concerning the Jewish People — which I have written on this piece of paper. Please return to me in a dream with the answers you receive there."

Some time after the student passed away, his image appeared before the Ramban and spoke: "Wherever I went with the amulet, gates were opened before me and I was allowed to rise higher and higher, finally reaching the sanctuary you described. But as I prepared to ask the questions you had asked, I immediately realized that in the World Above, those questions are not questions at all, for it is a World of Truth, where the justice and correctness of all events is clearly understood." (*Me'am Loez, Parashas Shoftim.*)

◆ A Single Tear

The following is from a letter by the Chasam Sofer about his teacher, R. Noson Adler:

> When I studied under my master, R. Noson Adler, when he first moved to Boskovitz, his only children were a small son and a twelve-year-old daughter, whom he dearly loved. She was a wonderful girl, just like her mother — it's impossible to describe all her good qualities. Although, due to our many sins, she died there, her father did not cry. He accepted the judgment with a happiness so boundless that not even on *Simchas Torah* did I see him so happy.
>
> That Shabbos he was called up to read the *Haftara*, as was his custom. While he read, he shed one tear, which he caught in his hand. His expression instantly changed and he never again showed any sign of sadness, nor did he mention her name at all.
>
> He never had another child and he did not make any special efforts [i.e., through prayer] to be granted another child. Perhaps his wife could no longer bear children and he did not wish to trouble Heaven to alter nature, fearing that it might bring an early death to his wife.
>
> For that reason, I never asked my teacher to pray and beg for mercy from Above for my first wife.
>
> A person who does not "press" the hour (contend with Heaven to receive what he wants) will not be "repulsed" by the hour (by having misfortune befall him before his time). There is much relief and salvation from Him. May He Who cures the broken-hearted and binds their sorrows close the breach in your lives, and rebuild your family with no more sadness.
>
> Moshe Sofer

‰ Ease My Suffering

When R. Nochum Zev, the Saba of Kelm's son, was ill and suffered intense pain, his sister overheard him praying for his suffering to be lessened. When she asked him why he didn't pray for his suffering to cease completely, he replied, "It is true that I am not on the level of accepting suffering with joy. Yet Heaven forbid that I should detest it or deny its value. It is enough for me that my suffering be eased a little." (*Kisvei HaSaba MiKelm.*)

‰ "My Head Is Heavy..."

R. Meir Robman זצ"ל, founder and Rosh Yeshiva of Tiferet Yisroel Yeshiva, and a student of R. Nochum Zev, quoted his teacher's explanation of the insight in the Gemara (*Sanhedrin 46a*): "What does the Divine Presence say when a person is in pain? My head is heavy, My arm is heavy."

> Hashem does only good, constantly seeking ways to save us so that no Jew will perish. That is why He brings suffering — to arouse us to repentance. When someone reacts to his suffering only with emotional pain and sadness, he shows that he doesn't appreciate the meaning of his trials and has still not repented. The Divine Presence then says, "My head is heavy" — like one who made great plans which weren't successful, and "My arm is heavy" — like one who expended great effort without results.

‰ Suffering Is Never As Crushing As It Seems

R. Nochum Zev's daughter wrote in her diary (17 Teves

5676/1915) about her father's last days:

> Father spoke about *yissurim*, about how they must be accepted willingly. Even more, that they should be accepted happily, since they come from Hashem's kindness. Hashem's mercy and kindness are always increasing, so we should realize that suffering, which comes from Him, is never as crushing as it may seem.
>
> Father gave himself over to Hashem's protection completely and accepted the Divine Will. Because of this, he was able to restrain his weeping.
>
> He also repeated the parable about a doctor who amputates a limb to save the life of his patient.

❧ He Waited Two Days

In the preface to *Toras Avraham* by R. Avraham Grodzinsky, his children tell us how their father accepted the news of their mother's passing:

> Father was a *baal yissurim* (a person of great suffering) from earliest childhood. His troubles, though, never broke his spirit. On the contrary, he drew strength from his suffering and became a greater person.
>
> After being appointed *mashgiach* of the yeshiva, he was struck by waves of *yissurim*. His wife passed away, leaving him to care for eight young children — the two smallest were only one and two years old.
>
> It was characteristic of our father that he did not recite the required blessing of *Dayan HaEmes* (Blessed be the Judge of Truth) immediately upon

hearing the terrible news, for he had always fought against performing mitzvas by rote. Now he was about to perform *tzidduk hadin*, proclaiming the justness of the punishment, about which Rava said one must accept the evil decree with happiness (*Berachos* 60b). Indeed, he waited two days and then recited the blessing properly, with complete intent and awareness.

❧ Am I Better Than Aharon?

R. Nochum of Horodna was struck again and again by the Divine hand of punishment. Although his prayers had saved many people, he was unable to save the lives of his own sons. His wife complained bitterly, yet he remained silent. After the seven days of mourning were over, he soothed her with these words of consolation: "Am I better than Aharon, whose righteous sons Nadav and Avihu died in his lifetime? Am I better than R. Yochanan who lost ten sons? Hashem sanctifies His Name through those close to Him, and this will atone for the many sins we have committed in His presence.

"In addition, the secrets of all generations are revealed to Him. If any righteous and good person were destined to come from these children, they would not have died. But it was known before the Throne of Glory that they would have no holy or righteous descendant. Blessed be Hashem Who took them to Heaven, plucking them before their petals opened. Let us lovingly accept the suffering cast upon us by Hashem and be grateful that He has taken our sons to Gan Eden, where their souls will repose in purity among the righteous of the world, and where they will constantly enjoy the pleasantness of Hashem. May His great Name be blessed forever!"

When R. Nochum's seventeenth son passed away, many people came to console and comfort him. He then spoke of

how a believing, G-d-fearing person should accept his suffering and pain with love and should feel happy with his lot.
Since Hashem punishes those He loves, suffering is a good
sign. However, a person should trust that Hashem will not
bring more suffering upon him, lest his faith be weakened,
Heaven forbid. R. Nochum explained this thought with a
parable about a man whose business expanded. Although the
businessman feels happy and secure, he should be careful not
to overextend himself in a way that could endanger his entire
fortune. As King David said in *Tehillim*: "Suffering has expanded my awareness and sensitivity — it is a good sign for
me; please, though, rescue me from my troubles."

ਵੈ Accepting Heaven's Judgment with Love

R. Moshe Yashar, in his biography of the Chofetz Chaim,
writes about the death of the Chofetz Chaim's son, R. Avraham z"l:

Even as a child, R. Avraham's outstanding
abilities were recognized. *Gedolim* were amazed at
his depth of thought, his quickness of mind, his
acuity, and the profundity of his logic. His powers
of memory and concentration were exceptional.
His study methods were like those of the *Rishonim*. His brilliance was especially noticeable
when he grappled with complex Talmudic sub-
jects. With rare breadth and penetration, he would
illuminate every matter under discussion.

The Chofetz Chaim wasn't home when his
precious son departed at the age of twenty-three,
on Shabbos, the twentieth of Kislev 5652. After
Shabbos, the Chofetz Chaim received a telegram
urging him to return home immediately. When he

arrived the next day and alit from the wagon, he saw a crowd of mourners returning from the local cemetery and understood what had happened.

The Chofetz Chaim entered his house in a controlled, restrained manner to sit *shiva*. Not a tear was seen on his face; no sigh was heard from his lips.

"In truth," he said, "a great genius has perished. When R. Avraham was barely sixteen, he innovated *chiddushei Torah* like one of the *Gedolim*." The Chofetz Chaim concluded, "Hashem has given, and Hashem has taken, may Hashem's Name be blessed for ever. Now I know that I am a Jew."

He explained this comment by relating an event (*Toldos Am Olam*, chap. 16) that happened during the Spanish Inquisition in the year 5252/1492. When the vicious murderers slaughtered one mother's beloved children before her eyes, that woman of valor raised her eyes Heavenward and whispered fearlessly: "Master of the Universe! I have always loved You, but as long as I had my precious children, my heart was divided in two. Now that my children are no longer here, my whole heart has become a torch of flaming love for You. Now I can truly fulfill the mitzva of 'You shall love Hashem *Elokecha* with all your heart and with all your soul.' "

After telling this story, the Chofetz Chaim declared: "Master of the Universe! All the love I used to feel for my son I now transfer to You."

The Chofetz Chaim's eldest son, R. Leib, said that his father later told him, "My transgressions caused it. When the severity of his condition became known to me in Warsaw, I rushed home.

But, through an act of Satan, I missed the express train and was forced to travel on a local. My journey was delayed from Above. It is possible that, had I still found him alive — if I had prayed and recalled the few merits I possess — it might have helped. I might not have been turned away empty-handed...and he might have remained alive. But 'Hashem is the G-d of all knowledge....' Who knows what sort of soul his was and what his purpose was in this world? It is very possible that in his brief lifetime he achieved all that was necessary for him." (*The Chofetz Chaim — His Life and Work*, vol. I, p. 248.)

ॐ Bless the Bad Like the Good

R. Shlomo Zalman Auerbach told about R. Avraham Dovid Rabinowitz-Tumim (known by the acronym "Aderes"), Rav of Yerushalayim, who had a daughter who died in her youth. Knowing the Rav's extreme punctuality, the *Chevra Kaddisha* burial society came at the appointed time and waited for the funeral to begin. To their surprise, the Aderes remained in his room, coming out only after a twenty-minute delay.

Later, he explained the delay as follows: "We are commanded to make a blessing over bad news 'like' we make a blessing over good news. The Gemara uses the word כשם, 'like,' to mean that a person should accept evil tidings with the same gladness he accepts good news. When I prepared to recite the blessing of *Baruch Dayan HaEmes*, Blessed be the True Judge, I did not feel that level of acceptance. So I remained alone until I could arouse in myself the same sense of joy I had felt at my daughter's birth. Only then could I properly bless Hashem for His true judgment."

❧ When Words Fail Us

In the Israeli War of Independence, R. Yitzchak Eisen, זצ״ל, lost seven members of his family to Arab artillery. Even so, he remained unshaken, despite the river of blood and the waves of suffering which flowed over him. The future Slonimer Rebbe, R. Shalom Noach Brezovsky, שליט״א, was the first person to enter R. Yitzchak's house on that terrible day. He found R. Yitzchak covered by the blood of his sons and daughters, sitting alone in the only corner of the room spared destruction. The young Rebbe stood silent, swallowing his sighs and suppressing his tears. Finally he said, "My dear R. Yitzchak — I have no words to console you. I have searched the entire *Book of Iyov*, but I find nothing to say."

After a long silence, R. Yitzchak replied, "Surely you recall the words of the pious man quoted in the *Chovos HaLevavos*: 'Hashem, You have left me starved and unclothed in the darkness of night and You have shown me Your strength and glory. If You devour me in flames, I will only increase my love for You and my joy in Your Presence, as is written (*Iyov* 13:15), "Behold, if He will slay me, yet I will trust in Him." ' "

Thus R. Yitzchak accepted the judgment in all its severity. (Told by his son R. Avraham Eisen.)

❧ Feeling Hashem's Pain

As a young man, R. Yitzchak Eisen had studied together with other gifted students under the tutelage of R. Dovid Dubiner *z"l*, an outstanding holy scholar, in his hometown of Tzefas.

For many years, R. Dovid was not blessed with children. When a son was finally born to him, the whole town rejoiced with him. This son was raised in the study of Torah and *avodas Hashem,* and at the young age of sixteen or seventeen was engaged to be married. Suddenly, after a brief illness, he passed away.

All of Tzefas was shocked by the news and attended the funeral. Everyone wept at the youth's untimely death and the terrible grief it brought to his father. Only one person present did not cry — R. Dovid himself. He accompanied his son to his final resting place without shedding a tear. For the first three days of the *shiva* he remained silent. His many visitors mourned his loss, but R. Dovid did not cry. Then, on the fourth day, he began crying and continued to weep for the remainder of the *shiva*.

He later explained his behavior: "I believe wholeheartedly that Hashem, Who gave me a son, took back that son with complete justice. That is why I was quiet and did not 'protest' by shedding tears. By the fourth day, I became calm enough to reflect on what had happened and decide how I should react.

"My thoughts were as follows: Hashem is surely right in punishing me so severely. True, I have been struck a terrible blow. But I must accept it unquestioningly. This is why I shed no tears for three days. On the fourth day I reflected on the fact that when a father is forced to hit one of his children to correct his behavior, the father's pain is greater than the son's. I realized that Hashem's 'pain' in having to punish me so severely was far greater than my own. For this great pain of the *Shechina*, I cried." (Told by R. Avraham Eisen, who heard it from his father, R. Yitzchak Eisen.)

✽ Just Being Alive Is Enough

R. Meir Feist, צ״ל, was confined to a wheelchair from the age of four, when both of his legs became paralyzed. He suffered a number of other chronic diseases as well. For more than half of his life he lived alone in the world, without parents or family.

His doctors were always amazed that he remained alive. One doctor even said that from a medical standpoint he could not be expected to live beyond the age of forty. Yet he lived to the age of sixty-eight and passed away from an illness unrelated to his chronic ill-health!

Due to his heavy burden, R. Meir could have become depressed and bitter. He could have been jealous of all those more fortunate than he. He might have lost all will to continue living. Yet the opposite was true. R. Meir was always happy, displaying patience, tranquillity, and a sense of good fortune. He was full of hope and encouragement, sharing in the joy of others as if it were his own. His face radiated happiness at all times and in all circumstances. It could be said that happiness was an integral part of his being.

How did he come to such a state of happiness and great desire for life?

King David says in *Tehillim* (84:11): "One day in Your courtyard is better than a thousand...." Rashi explains: "It is better to be in Your courtyard and die the next day than to live a thousand years in any other place." Since the destruction of the *Beis HaMikdash*, Hashem's courtyard is the yeshivas and study halls where Torah is studied. So, living as a *ben Torah* for a single day is more rewarding than living a life of pleasure for a thousand years.

This was the secret of R. Meir's success and joy in life. He understood that every day he lived in *avodas Hashem* and Torah study was endlessly valuable. Only in this way could he be full of happiness despite his many difficulties.

Our Sages comment on the verse (*Eicha* 3:39), "For what should the living man complain," that just being alive is reason enough for a person not to complain. R. Meir exemplified the meaning of this wisdom. For him, just being alive, even without any of the pleasures of life that most people take for granted, was enough. His desire to live, and his love of life were that much greater, because he knew the true value of life and how to use it properly. (*Penei Meir*, the biography of R. Meir Feist *z"l.*)

‏ Shabbos Is Not for Crying Out in Pain

On Shabbos it is prohibited to cry out. Yet the Rema (*Orach Chaim* 288:2) writes, "One who feels pleasure [i.e., finds relief] if he cries in order to assuage his heart's pain may cry on Shabbos." (There are, however, varying opinions as to the intent and applicability of this ruling; see the *Mishna Berura* and the *Shulchan Aruch* there.) Nonetheless, great and simple Jews throughout all generations rose above their natural emotions to follow the letter and spirit of the halacha, not expressing their grief and not allowing their personal tragedy to disturb the joy and sanctity of Shabbos. The following two true incidents illustrate this theme:

As night falls one Friday evening in Yerushalayim, Aharon Meir Auerbach lays in Hadassah hospital suffering indescribable pain. Hundreds of splinters of glass riddle his body, terrible burns torture his skin, and blood loss is continuous.

In a nearby room, R. Raphael Dovid Auerbach, the wounded boy's father, welcomes in Shabbos. From the moment the siren sounded announcing the beginning of Shabbos in Yerushalayim, there has been no sign of worry on his face.

News of the explosion that shook Yerushalayim that Friday afternoon had worried R. Raphael. He knew that his son would be on his way home at exactly that time. After long hours of worry and uncertainty, his fears were confirmed: his son lay mortally wounded in Hadassah. When he rushed to the hospital he was met by doctors who told him there was no hope for his son's life. Tens of yeshiva students arrived to donate blood for their friend. Then, in a small room near his son's, R. Raphael had donned his Shabbos clothes, put on his *shtreimel*, and welcomed Shabbos with joy.

"Shabbos is not for crying out," he says to those around him, his voice full of faith and reassurance. He eats his Shabbos meal, enthusiastically singing the traditional Shabbos melodies, his face radiant with the joy of the mitzva.

The hospital staff peers into the room with wonder. Minutes before they had seen R. Raphael pale with worry and anguish over his son's condition. How could his mood have changed so completely?

R. Raphael conducts the Shabbos meal exactly as he always does at home. Seeing a cloud of worry shadow the face of a family member, he says, "It is Shabbos! We must eat our Shabbos meal and sing with joy — on Shabbos we do not cry out."

After the meal R. Raphael returns to his son's bedside, praying silently. Throughout the long night he stands there, only leaving his son's side to help patients.

In a nearby room, another victim of the explosion, the holy martyr Aryeh Yosef Sheinfeld, breathes his last. His friends stand by in shocked silence, not knowing what to do. R. Raphael hurries over to calm them and tells them how to move the body on Shabbos, accompanying them on the long walk to the hospital morgue.

In the morning, the doctors' expressionless faces inform R. Raphael that they can do no more. Standing at their son's bedside, R. Raphael and his wife recite *Shema Yisrael*, as their son's pure and holy soul rises and soars to Heaven.

R. Raphael again shows inner strength and rock-like faith. "It is prohibited to cry," he calls to those present.

Locking within him the pain he feels, he begins singing a fervent prayer:

Ein k'Elokeinu — There is none like our G-d;
There is none like our Master;
There is none like our King;
There is none like our Savior.

Memories rise up before him. For fifteen years he had raised and cared for this beloved son who was so much like him. Aharon Meir had been such a happy child, so full of life, with such enthusiasm for everything holy. He was an exceptional student, and since he had left home for yeshiva, his father's pride in him had grown. Aharon Meir had taken his studies seriously; he had learned hundreds of pages of Gemara and his teachers envisioned a great future for him. Now, his brief life was over.

Yet R. Raphael's deep faith is not shaken in the slightest. His voice continues firmly:

Mi k'Elokeinu — Who is like our G-d;
Who is like our Master;
Who is like our King;
Who is like our Savior.

R. Raphael's older son arrives in the hospital after a long walk, but is too late to see his beloved brother. His father greets him with the bitter news, adding immediately, "Restrain yourself — it is prohibited to cry. Today is Shabbos!"

The hours move slowly, but R. Raphael continues to contain his emotions. He eats the third Shabbos meal, fulfilling *halacha*, as he always does.

"It is Shabbos."

Only with the exit of Shabbos did the fountain of tears stream forth.

❧ A Woman of Valor

Friday night in the house of the famed *tzaddik*, R. Aryeh Levin, finds his Rebbetzin, Zipporah Chana, sitting by the candles, hands over her eyes, immersed in prayer. Family members used to say that "anyone who did not see the Rebbetzin in prayer does not know what true prayer is."

This time she prayed for the life of her three-year-old son who lay prostrate and pale in a corner of the room. Hundreds of people were dying in the terrible famine sweeping *Eretz Yisrael* at that time during World War I. Many children were victims of the disease which spread quickly from house to house. Now the Levin's precious son had been struck in one of these epidemics. His illness grew worse. The doctor who visited him that Friday night said quietly, "There is nothing for me to do. Only Hashem can help."

The next morning the child returned his soul to his Maker. His mother stood at his bedside and bit her lips. It is Shabbos! She will not cry.

With super-human strength, she comforted and encouraged her family members. The sound of Shabbos songs came from R. Aryeh's house and the neighbors remained unaware of what had happened. A neighbor who visited was not told the tragic news.

"It was Shabbos. How could I cause pain to our neighbors?" the Rebbetzin explained afterwards.

*   *   *

R. Aryeh and his wife lost three more children in the diseases and hunger of the first World War. The hardest blow came with the passing of their year-and-a-half-old Avraham Binyamin. He had been a true wonder-child. He began speaking when he was only a few months old. At the age of nine months, he began to recite the blessing *Shehakol* before nursing. People were amazed at his intelligence.

Alas, this treasure was also taken from them.

During the *shiva*, two new immigrants from Russia came to offer condolences. The Rebbetzin stood in prayer at the time, a look of angelic serenity on her face.

The two women, knowing of her many misfortunes, remarked to each other in Russian that she must have become unbalanced from her sufferings. Unaware that she understood Russian, they continued to talk of how they had never seen someone so serene during a *shiva*, and decided that she must have lost touch with reality.

Rebbetzin Levin was fluent in many languages, including Russian. Softly, she said to them, "My dear friends, my mind is clear. I accept the decree of Heaven with love. If I had merited, my son would have studied in a yeshiva in this world. Since I did not have that merit, he will study in the *Yeshiva shel Maala*, the Heavenly Yeshiva."

❧ The Value of Suffering

There was once a person whose life was constantly beset by misfortune, poverty, and illness. One day he decided to travel to the great *tzaddik* and *mekubbal*, R. Shalom Sharabi, to ask him for advice and a blessing to ease his heavy burden. When he arrived at the *tzaddik*'s home he was asked to wait until he could be received. He sat down, exhausted from his journey, and soon fell into a deep sleep.

He dreamed that he arrived in Heaven. A desolate path stretched in front of him. A heavy silence prevailed, with not a soul in sight. Slowly and carefully he began to walk forward on the path. Suddenly he heard loud noises coming from behind. A chariot full of snow-white angels passed by quickly and disappeared beyond the horizon. Silence returned to the scene and he continued on his way. Again and again he was passed by chariots full of white angels, some large and powerful, some small and weak. After the caravan of white angels passed by, there began a massive procession of chariots filled with terrible black angels. His curiosity was aroused, and he quickened his pace. A short time later, he reached a large clearing where he saw all the chariots standing. All the angels descended and climbed onto a large set of scales in the center of the clearing.

At first the man was confused, but he was given to understand that the scene before him was his judgment in the Heavenly Court. As is true for all men, he was told, each angel he saw had been created by an action of his. The strong and healthy white angels were created when he did a mitzva properly, with enthusiasm and joy. The weak, blemished white angels were the result of the mitzvos he had performed improperly. The same was true for the black angels of destruction — the large and terrible ones were created by his misdeeds, from intentional, premeditated sins, while the stunted, weaker ones came from the unintentional sins and the ones which brought little pleasure.

After receiving this explanation, the man looked again at the scales. He saw that every angel bore a sign identifying the act from which it had been created. Upon the white angels were written: "Torah Study," "Prayer," "Honoring Parents," "Kindness," etc., while the black angels bore the inscriptions: "Desecration of Shabbos," "*Loshon Hora*," "Jealousy," "Stealing," and the like.

As the scales filled up, black on one side and white on the other, he was shocked and frightened to see that the black angels were weighing down their side of the scale more than the white angels. He shuddered to think what would happen if the black angels won in the end — he would be sentenced to Gehinnom with the other sinners!

A call went forth asking if there were any more angels. None came forward.

Another call went forth. Perhaps he had suffered *yissurim* during his lifetime? Immediately a giant chariot appeared, filled with all the angels created by all of his suffering, which has the power to cleanse a person of sin. The man watched as each angel created by his suffering removed one of the black angels of created by his sins.

The man began to feel reassured, seeing that the side of the scale holding his sins was becoming lighter. But after all his sufferings had been weighed, he saw that the side of the scale holding his evil deeds was still heavier than the other side, the one holding his mitzvos. He began to tremble, realizing the serious situation he was in. Soon a verdict would be given — and here the scales were weighted against him! In his anguish, he shouted in protest: "Please, add just a little more suffering!"

His own shouts woke him from his dream. The people around him, startled by his cry, asked what had happened. He realized then that everything he had seen had all been a dream. He rose to leave. The Rabbi's wife called after him, "Weren't you waiting to speak to the Rav?"

"It is no longer necessary," he replied. "I have received my answer from Above." (Told by R. Shabsai Yudelevitz זצ"ל, well known Yerushalmi *maggid*.)

≈ Don't Shorten My Suffering

R. Yaakov Galinsky שליט"א, a renowned lecturer, inspires Israeli audiences with the following true story:

A terminally ill person was attached to an artificial respirator and lay suffering terribly. His doctor, thinking to spare him more suffering, disconnected his life-support system and the man died soon afterwards.

A few days later, the deceased man appeared to the doctor in a dream and said as follows:

"I had four days left in which to live, in order to suffer terrible *yissurim*, after which I would have gone directly to Gan Eden, cleansed of all my sins. Because you caused me to die four days early, I lack that measure of suffering. Now I do not know how long I will have to suffer here in Gehinnom to be purified" (because suffering in the physical world atones much more than suffering in Gehinnom).

The doctor woke up from his dream completely shaken and became a *ba'al teshuva* due to his fear of the Final Judgment (*L'Shichno Sidreshu*, vol. I, p. 311).

❧ We Are Cogs in the Machine of Creation

The following story by R. Yom Tov Ehrlich is based on the writings of R. Chaim Vital:

Newly married Chaim walked his younger brother David home from *shul* one Shabbos evening to wish his mother a good Shabbos.

The house glowed with warmth and peace. Candles burned brightly, announcing the arrival of the holy Shabbos. The only thing disturbing the restful atmosphere was the empty chair at the head of the table, the chair that had once been their father's. Since he had gone to his eternal rest two years earlier, longing and anguish filled their hearts.

Their mother sat in her usual place, reading.

"Good Shabbos," her sons greeted her joyfully.

"Good Shabbos," she answered them, trying to hide her tears with a smile.

"Mother! You're crying again," Chaim exclaimed in distress. "Please. Today is Shabbos — crying is forbidden."

"But you know as well as I do," the widow sobbed, "that exactly two years ago today your father left this world! How can I not cry?"

"Yes, Mother," Chaim said kindly, "it is true — today you have a reason. But what about yesterday and the day before? Two years have already passed, and still you are not comforted. You continue to cry and mourn, but do you think this makes Abba happy in Gan Eden? As for our Creator — it is certainly against His Will. The *Shulchan Aruch* tells us when to mourn and when not to mourn. If you behave differently, you are disobeying Hashem's Will. Forgive me, Mother, for speaking to you this way," Chaim pleaded.

His mother stood up and wiped away her tears. "You are right, Chaim. But, even though I wish with all my heart to forget, I am not able to." She began to sob.

Little Shoshanna begged her, "Mommy, Mommy, we want you to be happy all the time."

"I also want to be happy," her mother whispered. "I promise I will try my best."

Chaim wished his mother "Good Shabbos" and left for his own home. His younger brother, David, made Kiddush over the wine, and the whole family sat down to a wonderful Shabbos meal. A feeling of well-being enveloped the table and everyone felt the true peace of Shabbos. Their mother even laughed. The children told stories from the weekly *parasha*, and their mother felt so much *nachas*.

By the time everyone was ready for sleep, it was much later than usual. The widow felt a sense of quiet such as she had not felt since the day her husband left her. She began to think about her fate. She realized, perhaps for the first time, that she was not the only person in her situation. But she also realized that many other young widows had found happiness again, because, unlike her, they had accepted their bitter lot. Her thoughts drifted to the *shidduch* that had recently been proposed to her. How could she betray her beloved husband's memory! Sleep overcame her, and she dreamt a beautiful dream.

In her dream she saw people running, so she ran too. They all ran out of the city until they came to a thick forest. Even though it was dark, they continued to run. Suddenly, there was a burst of light, and the forest ended.

The sun shone brightly and she saw before her a large garden filled with beautiful flowers which filled the air with a wonderful fragrance. The garden was filled with streams of sparkling blue water. Suddenly, a white-bearded Jew dressed in a long white garment appeared before her eyes. He asked her if she would like to see her husband. Heart pounding, she followed him. The sage stopped near a large tree laden with beautiful ripe fruit. From afar she saw a spacious clearing, surrounded by a golden fence. She saw colorfully dressed Jews sitting in rows learning Torah. In their midst a young man stood teaching them.

"Please wait a moment," said the elderly Jew. "Soon they will conclude the lesson and you will have a clearer look."

She could not believe the dazzling sights her eyes beheld. When the lesson ended, the teacher began walking towards her. She almost fainted when she saw it was her husband.

"Avraham!" she cried, and swooned against a nearby tree.

"Yes, it is I," her husband replied. "Be calm."

For a long time, she remained where she was with her eyes closed. When she recovered, she opened her eyes and asked, "Why did you leave me at such a young age?"

"Please understand," he answered serenely, "that the world in which you live is like a land of exile. People are sent there to complete specified tasks, or to suffer for earlier transgressions. The true world is here. Before you ever knew me, I once inhabited the world below. I was a Torah genius and perfectly righteous. My only fault was that I was unwilling to marry and bring children into the world because I wanted to remain undisturbed in my learning.

"When I departed from that world, I was made head of a yeshiva in Gan Eden, where I began to ascend to ever-higher levels. But when they found out that I had never married and had never had children, I was sent back to the lower world in order to marry and bring children into the world.

"So, I married you and, *baruch Hashem*, we were blessed with children. When our seventh child was born, I was called again to return to my yeshiva in Gan Eden, where everyone awaited me. Great is your merit that I am your husband, for I have a good name here. When the right time will come, we will again live together in this world in delight."

"But," his widow protested, "I did not know you were such a great scholar. You never had much time to learn."

Her husband replied, "I too did not know, since I came to the lower world only to correct what I lacked — that is, to marry and have children, and to provide for them. When I departed from that world, my mind was immediately filled with endless Torah knowledge."

His wife continued her questions. "Why doesn't our Chaim prosper in his affairs?"

Her husband responded, "You surely remember the *din Torah* Chaim had with a certain Jew. Although Chaim won legally, he was judged guilty of causing great pain to the other Jew, and faced a harsh sentence. I prayed on his behalf and asked that he be given only four difficult years. In just one more year, the period of his penalty will be complete and he will begin to prosper."

"And what about our David? Not a single *shidduch* has been offered him. I don't even have the money to make a wedding."

Her husband smiled and explained: "The reason for that situation is that David's mate was late in coming into the world. She is now only thirteen years old and lives in a distant land. In another five years she will come to your city. She will then become engaged to David and her family will pay for the entire wedding."

His widow began to tremble as a painful memory arose within her. In a soft voice, she asked her husband, "Why was our three-year-old son killed by a drunk?"

Her husband smiled and said, "Follow me!"

She began to walk towards a light-filled garden. Small trees lined her path. Radiant beams of multicolored light shone from above, while beautiful songbirds flew from tree to tree. She found herself able to understand their songs. Some were singing, "Light is planted for the righteous, and joy for the upright in heart." Others were singing, "To sing to Your glory...." She heard: "Peace, peace to the distant and the near...." Small deer leaped back and forth, singing, "I will sing of Your might; I will laud Your kindness daily." Even the grass was singing: "May Hashem's glory be forever!" The trees too joined in with: "All the trees of the forest will sing."

Suddenly, she saw leaping circles of fire in many colors. They positioned themselves near her in column-like formations, followed by small angels who also settled down near her. A wonderful melody played by musical instruments was heard from all sides, and she felt her soul slipping away. Her husband rushed to place a flower from the garden close to her. Her strength returned, and a *chuppa* canopy made of sparkling precious stones appeared before her. Under the canopy facing her stood a small angelic form. She recognized her murdered son, who was now laughing with great joy. Again she felt faint, and again her husband gave her the flower to smell. She opened her eyes, and saw that she was not mistaken — it really was her son.

"Why did you leave me when you were so young?" she asked.

"Everything is in accordance with the plans of the Creator," he answered. "I had already been in the world once before, as a member of a prominent family. There had been wild attacks on the Jews in our town, and the gentiles murdered everyone. I was the only survivor. I was then about six months old and a gentile woman took me in to her house and raised me, until I was redeemed by Jews. They taught me Torah and I studied until I became a great Torah scholar. I lived the rest of my life in comfort and peace. When I left that world, I was received in the True World with joy. I rose higher and higher, until I reached a point where I could rise no higher because I had nursed from a non-Jewish woman. It was decreed that I be born again to a Jewish mother, and live those early years in purity. That way, I would be able to continue to rise in the upper world.

"I was then born to you, Mother. It was a great merit for you. After three years I was taken back to my place, for there was nothing left for me to do in that lowly world."

"But why were you taken in such a horrible way?" his mother asked.

"When I was about to depart from the world," explained her son, "a terrible decree was issued against the Jews of our town — everyone would have died, including you and Abba. I was given the honor to be the sacrifice for the entire town. I was killed for their sake and thus the town was spared. For that reason I receive all this honor now. Nobody in Gan Eden is allowed to approach me except for Abba, who can see me whenever he wishes." The child laughed softly, and wandered away until he disappeared from view.

"So you see now — there is an answer to all your questions," the Torah scholar told his wife. "Our Creator does no evil.

"I must return now to my students," he concluded. He escorted her to the place where she had first opened her eyes, near the great tree, where he said to her: "It is very good here, but I cannot bear to see your suffering. You will do me a great favor if you now begin to live happily. You have been offered a *shidduch* — please accept it."

He vanished, and once again the old man appeared and led her back to the forest.

She awoke from her dream a changed person. For a long time she lay in her bed with a smile on her face, as the images of her content husband and smiling son lingered in her mind. A great stone had been lifted from her heart, and she was consoled.

She remarried, and lived a life of happiness and contentment.

*   *   *

The Ari *z"l* taught deep secrets of the Torah and, in particular, the subject of *gilgulim*, transmigration of souls. He taught that all creatures are like cogs in the great machine called Creation. *HaKadosh Baruch Hu* places each cog in the world and adjusts it to suit the operating needs of the mechanism. He brings into the world souls that have a function in this world, and removes the souls that are needed Above, for this world and the Next World are both part of the same machine.

Here below, the machine operates with souls plus bodies, while Above, it works with souls alone. If we would know how it all works, we would never become upset, for in the very near future, all the souls will return to this lower world. Here, they will serve Hashem with body and soul combined, until all the physical bodies will become purified and soul-like. This last stage will take place towards the end of the sixth millennium, which will be followed by the "Great Shabbos" (R. Chaim Vital, who heard it from his great teacher the Ari *z"l*).

❧ It Is the Will of Hashem

When the son of a great *talmid chacham* was killed in a bomb blast in Yerushalayim, R. Nota Tzeinwirt ל"צז, one of the special *tzadikkim* with whom Yerushalayim was blessed, came to console the grieving family. He posed the following question: "If Avraham had in fact slaughtered Yitzchak in the *Akeida*, would he have sat *shiva*?"

The mourning father answered that presumably he would have been required to.

"Why?" asked R. Nota.

"Because if he wouldn't have mourned, it would have implied that when a person dies as a result of Hashem's command, mourning is unnecessary. It would follow then," the father continued, "that when one sits *shiva* for a relative, he does so because Hashem did *not* want that person to die. But that is certainly not true! In my case, was it not Hashem Who decreed my son's death? If Hashem had not decreed it so, the boy would not have died!"

That is exactly the point R. Nota wanted to make. When someone dies, it is only because Hashem wanted it so. A relative then cries and mourns his loss *because that is also the Will of Hashem*. But mourning and crying beyond that prescribed by halacha is going against Hashem's Will.

In this manner, R. Nota consoled the mourners, who were now able to accept their loss as a manifestation of Divine Will.

❧ Tatteh's Last Will and Testament

One Thursday afternoon in the summer of 1960 I came home from work to find Tatteh waiting for me in the courtyard. I greeted him as I always did with a kiss on the hand.

"Basyaleh," he said to me in a soft voice, "how would you like to go rowing with me on the river? I want to talk with you somewhere where it's quiet. My mind is in such turmoil to-day — I was thinking that the sound of the flowing water might help to put me at ease."

Enveloped in a deep silence, we walked toward the Dnieper (which runs through the middle of Kiev). We rented a boat at a small dock and we rowed downstream, out of the city and past the farmers' fields. Tatteh began to speak to me, in a quite, intense voice.

I listened in silence as Tatteh talked about how human life is only a passing thing. Yet, although his life is transitory, man holds within him an eternal core, his soul, that grows or withers according to man's deeds. After a while I began to be disturbed. It had dawned on me that no one but a man making his final reckoning would speak this way.

When he paused for a moment, I got up my courage and protested, "Tatteh, what has gotten into you? Have you had a bad dream or something? *Baruch Hashem*, you are so strong, so healthy! Everything is all right; why talk about such a depressing subject? Look around at G-d's beautiful world, listen to the music of the river, listen to the birds singing! It's not every day we get to have such a lovely outing together — why spoil it?"

Tatteh gave me a forgiving look and said, "My dear, talking about death doesn't kill anyone, and it doesn't have to spoil the outing for you, either. A person must live with a clear realization of what King Solomon said: 'The day of death is better than the day of birth.' The Gemara points out that the words could also read *'from* the day of birth,' and there is another lesson for us: from the day a man is born, he is drawing ever closer to his death. Of course it's a slow, gradual process, but no human being has ever managed to escape it. So when a person feels the need to talk about death, why put it off? After all, no one knows when his **time** will come.

"As you know, Basyaleh, I once had sons, fine, talented sons. I sacrificed myself to teach them Torah and to bring them up believing in G-d — and you know what it cost me just to live a Torah life myself. But it was decreed in Heaven that my sons would not live, and that I would depart from this world without even leaving someone to say Kaddish for me. So, Basyaleh, I want you to be my Kaddish! I want you to be my *matzevah* (tombstone)! That is my last wish, all that is left of the hopes and ambitions I once had."

There was a deep silence.

"Of course, Tatteh," I said softly. "I can say Kaddish for you, as there are no sons. But what do you mean when you say that I should be your *matzevah*?

"You didn't understand me, Basyaleh. A *matzevah* isn't just a row of stones or a marble slab. That's just a marker for a grave. No — a man's *matzevah*, his monument, is the sum of all the good deeds he did from his birth until his death. And the good deeds that his children do after him — they too are part of his eternal *matzevah*.

"I don't need to write a will just to tell you to keep Shabbos or to eat kosher. *HaKadosh Baruch Hu* already told you that on Mount Sinai. I know that the Torah is deeply rooted within you, and I am not worried about whether you will remain true to the Torah after I am gone.

"No; I am thinking of more than the basics. This is what I want to ask of you: try always to behave with such holiness that, wherever you go and whomever you meet, everyone will point to you and say, 'There is Reb Yehuda Leib Meislik's daughter.' Your every move will be my everlasting memorial, so that my name is remembered. That will be my Kaddish and my *matzevah*!"

Tatteh paused a moment to let this sink in. Then he went on: "I want you to understand what our Sages said: If children leave the ways of the Torah, then their father's merit cannot save them, even if he is a *tzaddik*. But on the other hand, if the child is a *tzaddik*, his merit can save his father from Gehinnom, even if his father is a *rasha* (evil-doer). I am sure that the mitzvos you do will save me from Gehinnom and help me to get into Gan Eden. So I am asking you for my sake, Basyaleh, to do mitzvos with all your might, and not to do anything that might take me out of Gan Eden. The harder you try to behave like a true daughter of Israel, and like the daughter of Leib Meislik, the higher my soul will rise in Heaven and the closer I will get to the Divine Presence. If the *yetzer hara* (evil inclination) should try to tempt you, don't listen to him, because if, G-d forbid, you should fall into his trap, the labor of a lifetime will go down the drain.

"What do I mean, the labor of a lifetime? Let's take that bridge over there for an example. Hundreds of people worked on it. Every one of them put great effort into the construction until finally the bridge was completed. And then, of course, the contractor presented his bill to the government.

"But before the government authorizes payment, they have to test the bridge to make sure it has really been made as strong as they specified and will bear the weight of all the traffic that will be crossing it. How will they test it? They'll take a train of forty loaded freight cars and run them across the bridge, and if it stands the test, all the workers will receive their payment and go home full of pride.

"So the test begins. One after the other the freight cars roll across the bridge. The contractor and all his employees stand and watch. Their hearts are thumping, because it isn't only the money that's at stake. If the bridge holds up, they will be honored; their reputations will be made. If it doesn't, they are ruined.

"The freight cars cross one by one, and with each one that makes it to the other side, the men watching feel prouder, and the suspense builds.

"Thirty cars have already crossed — thirty-one — now the

fortieth car is on the bridge, the last one. The men watching hold their breath — and when the car reaches the middle, the bridge buckles under the load and collapses. The car plunges into the depths, drawing all the others with it. All the toil of the engineers, the technicians, and the laborers was in vain. In one moment they have lost their wages and their glory; instead of going off crowned with laurels, they must hide their faces in shame.

"It is the same with the bridge of the generations, starting with our father Avraham down to our generation. Our fathers and our fathers' fathers crossed the bridge of Life; they stood all the tests and the hardships that were given them to bear. And they passed the ultimate test of clinging to their belief and trust in G-d. When I get to the next world, I will meet them all there, all the ancestors of the Meislik family. If, G-d forbid, the last generation before the *Mashiach* should fail the test, all the toil of the previous generations would be ruined.

"So please remember, Basyaleh, that the eyes of all our fathers and mothers are on you, anxiously hoping that you will be a credit to them. Perhaps the *yetzer hara* will tempt you to leave the true and holy path, and say to you, 'Look, Basya, everybody is doing it. G-d has forgotten His world for now; later on, when *Mashiach* comes, you can get back to keeping the mitzvos.' Answer him like this: 'My father, my grandfather, and all the generations before them kept the mitzvos. I am the only one of my family left. Am I going to leave the path that was walked by every generation of the Meislik family, going all the way back to the first Jew? Am I going to put all my ancestors to shame?' If you always think this way, with G-d's help you will escape the traps of the *yetzer hara*.

"Remember: a momentary lapse on your part, however slight, might disturb my rest in Gan Eden, and every moment that you resist temptation, my rest will grow sweeter."

That night Tatteh suffered a stroke. Four days later he returned his pure soul to his Maker.

(Reprinted with permission from Voices in the Silence,
by Basya Barg, pp. 232-237)